C O L O N I A L
N E W   H A M P S H I R E

A HISTORY

A HISTORY OF THE AMERICAN COLONIES
IN THIRTEEN VOLUMES

GENERAL EDITORS:
MILTON M. KLEIN & JACOB E. COOKE

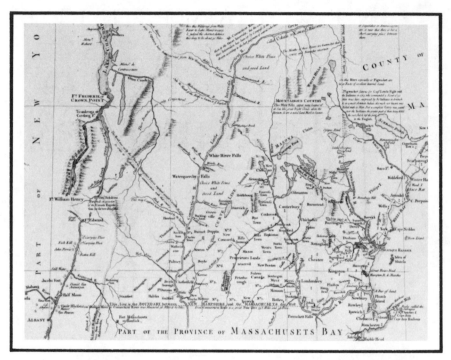

Detail from "An Accurate Map of His Majesty's Province of New Hampshire in New England" published in 1761 by Colonel Joseph Blanchard and the Reverend Samuel Langdon. In 1761 New Hampshire claimed jurisdiction over what is now Vermont. *Courtesy of the New Hampshire Historical Society.*

JERE R. DANIELL

COLONIAL
NEW HAMPSHIRE

A HISTORY

kto press

A DIVISION OF KRAUS-THOMSON ORGANIZATION LIMITED
MILLWOOD, NEW YORK

First printing 1981

Printed in the United States of America

Library of Congress Cataloging in Publication Data

Daniell, Jere R.
  Colonial New Hampshire.

  (A History of the American Colonies)
  Bibliography: p.
  Includes index.
  1. New Hampshire—History—Colonial period, ca. 1600–
1775.   2. New Hampshire—History—Revolution, 1775–1783.
I.   Title. II.   Series: History of the American colonies.
F37.D25   974.2'02   81-6046
ISBN 0-527-18715-1   AACR2

TO MY PARENTS
MARY HOLWAY DANIELL
AND
WARREN FISHER DANIELL

CONTENTS

ILLUSTRATIONS

EDITORS' INTRODUCTION

The history of what one contemporary official labelled "little New Hampshire" has been overshadowed by that of its better-known neighbors, particularly the more populous and politically more important colony of Massachusetts Bay. The present comprehensive survey of colonial New Hampshire—from its origins to the American Revolution—not only makes amends for that situation but also fills a scholarly vacuum that has frequently been deplored by historians of the colonial era. Until recently, they were obliged to rely on Jeremy Belknap's three-volume *History of New Hampshire,* published in the late eighteenth century, a commendable work for its day but long since outmoded. Then, during the decade of the 1970s three excellent books on selected periods and aspects of New Hampshire's formative centuries appeared (one of them by Professor Daniell) that partially atoned for two centuries of neglect. But there still remained the need for a synthesis of fresh scholarship in a work encompassing the entire sweep of New Hampshire's colonial history. This challenging assignment has now been met by Jere Daniell who, compressing the complexities of his subject into a single short volume, recounts with succinctness, clarity, and synthetic facility the story of the transformation of this small colony into an independent state.

The central theme of New Hampshire's history, particularly in the seventeenth century, was "the giant strides made toward the formation of civilized communities in the frontier wilderness." The area that became New Hampshire was first granted to enterprising settlers by the Council of New England, then joined for a short period of time to Massachusetts, and in 1679 became a separate royal colony. By that date, the small colony could boast of four flourishing towns (Portsmouth, Dover, Exeter, and Hampton) and a population of more than two thousand settlers, drawn in large part from Massachusetts in search of economic opportunity and in some instances relief from the latter's unswerving orthodoxy. More arresting yet, New Hampshire in 1679 already exemplified a stable social life modelled on Massachusetts and based on a framework of closely knit family life, firm community regulations, and remarkable religious unity and church discipline. The combination was to characterize this essentially Puritan colony throughout its colonial history. Society, government, and religion in colonial New Hampshire were, in sum, distinguished less by tolerance and diversity than by uniformity and stability.

Contrary to the familiar stereotyped view of the colonies as seedbeds of American democracy, New Hampshire politics and government (at least for almost six decades of the eighteenth century) may be subsumed in three words: "the Wentworth oligarchy." The Wentworth family and faction, in Daniell's words, "completely dominated provincial politics." (One of the members of this family, Benning Wentworth, served as governor for no less than twenty-five years, the longest tenure of any governor in British North America.) Why was this allowed by New Hampshiremen? The answer is that the Wentworths succeeded in convincing most voters and their elected representatives that what one contemporary aptly described as "family government" served New Hampshire well. And so it did. During the decades of oligarchic rule the "internal politics" of New Hampshire were "relatively harmonious and stable" and the colony "grew in size and population, prospered economically and matured socially."

The popularity of the Wentworths was, however, more superficial than substantive, and the tenuous basis of their political power was never more dramatically revealed than during the period of domestic turmoil and imperial crisis that immediately preceded the Revolution. New Hampshiremen energetically embraced the protests against what American patriots construed as England's arbitrary and unconscionable assaults on the colonists' traditional liberties. The benevolent family oligarchy embraced the cause of the Crown and was jettisoned in the wake of the surging tide of New Hampshire whiggism. In 1775, royal government collapsed and its representative, Governor John Wentworth, was driven out of the province.

The transition from royal to revolutionary status was remarkably smooth. The structure of New Hampshire's government had always been rooted in local rather than provincial institutions. Town administration, the militia, and the county judiciary continued to function under republican authority as easily as they had earlier under the command of the King. The social and economic underpinnings of New Hampshire life were not convulsed by the separation from Great Britain. In the Granite State, the Revolution—whatever it was elsewhere—was a political movement, essentially designed to preserve and defend long-established and deeply cherished constitutional rights. New Hampshire patriots, toward this end, created a new government in January 1776 (the first of the colonies to do so) and joined their fellow Americans on the hard and hazardous journey to independence. The colonial history of New Hampshire, viewed in conjunction with the history of the other twelve colonies, helps to clarify further the meaning of a revolution whose inception, however fortuitous, produced consequences so momentous that they live with us still.

MILTON M. KLEIN
JACOB E. COOKE

PREFACE

Friendship, circumstance, and inclination all played important roles in my decision to write a history of colonial New Hampshire. A graduate school friend, Thomas J. Davis, asked me to write the New Hampshire volume for a series on the thirteen original states he helped plan as the historical editor at Charles Scribner and Sons. At the time— twelve years ago—I was just finishing a manuscript on late eighteenth century New Hampshire and beginning to think about future writing. Davis's offer intrigued me. My family had roots in New Hampshire's past, I had every intention of remaining a resident of the state for some time, my curiosity about the origins of New Hampshire had been whetted by investigation of the revolutionary period, and the existing literature on the colonial period appeared thin. In fact, the three volume *History of New Hampshire* written by Jeremy Belknap nearly two centuries ago remained the single most frequently cited source of information. Much as I respected Belknap, his work needed redoing.

Since then the state of the literature has improved considerably. In 1970 Charles Clark published *The Eastern Frontier*, a history of early Maine and New Hampshire especially rich on expansion of settlement in eighteenth century northern New England. My own *Experiment in Republicanism*, which includes chapters on late colonial politics, came out the same year. David Van Deventer's impressive *The Emergence of Provincial New Hampshire, 1623–1741* appeared in 1976. It emphasizes economic development, gives a thorough description and explanation of maritime trade, and includes a wealth of statistical information. Several useful articles on colonial New Hampshire have also been published since I began gathering material for this volume.

Although *Colonial New Hampshire: A History* owes much to this recent literature—parts of chapters seven and eight rest heavily on the work of Clark and Van Deventer, and chapters nine, ten, and the epilogue summarize developments covered more completely in *Experiment in Republicanism*—most of the volume is reasonably fresh. The first six chapters cover subjects treated either skimpily or inaccurately in existing literature. I have tried to deal with social and religious change in conceptual terms utilized by modern historians who have written about other New England colonies, but never about New Hampshire. My discussion of local developments emphasizes the abstract as much as the concrete: it should help town historians place their work on individual communities in a broader context. The main purpose of the volume remains unaltered. No comprehensive history of colonial New Hampshire has been written since Belknap's time. Readers may judge for themselves how successfully I have filled the gap.

My debts are many. The bibliographical essay credits past writers whose labors made my task easier. Manuscript librarians in the New Hampshire Historical Society and many other repositories gave me much needed assistance. James Axtell criticized chapter one and Charles Clark criticized the entire manuscript; the general editors of the whole series—Jacob Cooke and Milton Klein—made countless suggestions for improvement, most of which I accepted. Mark Sonnenfeld drew the maps from rough sketches which I prepared. James Garvin, curator of the New Hampshire Historical Society, helped locate and identify illustrative material. Scribner's and Dartmouth College helped finance the research. The bulk of my writing was done during sabbatical leaves from Dartmouth. Gail Patten proved an exceptionally accurate, speedy, and efficient typist. I, of course, assume full responsibility for whatever mistakes have remained undetected in the manuscript.

Hanover, N.H.   Jere Daniell
September, 1980

COLONIAL
NEW HAMPSHIRE

A HISTORY

1

THE ALGONKIANS

Sometime in the mid-1680s a small group of Pennacooks left their homeland in the upper Merrimack valley to join with fellow Indians to the northeast. They were accustomed to travel and had left their village many times before, but this departure meant more than the others: they had little expectation of returning. Their troubles were almost too vast to comprehend. The oldest among the migrants could remember the days when their sagamore Passaconaway commanded respect from perhaps a dozen bands and tribes in the valley area. Over five hundred strong, they had been able to protect themselves against their traditional enemies to the west, the Mohawks, and to maintain peace with the "English" strangers who had first arrived during their childhood. Now everything had changed. Disease, warfare, and defection had reduced their numbers to fewer than one hundred. The fish and game on which they depended for much of their sustenance had become scarcer each year, and many fields, where they grew maize and other foods, had been ruined. Indeed, they were threatened with immediate death. Kancamagus, Passaconaway's grandson and their present leader, had learned of negotiations between the English and Mohawks which might lead the latter to launch an eastward invasion. If such an attack came, the Pennacooks would be too weak for effective resistance. There seemed no possible course of action but to abandon the land and villages they knew so well.

The Pennacooks were not the only group of Native Americans resident in what is modern New Hampshire when European settlement began, but they were the largest, and their fate symbolized that of the entire pre-colonial population. At the beginning of the seventeenth century the area contained about three thousand Algonkian Indians, many of them settled in villages which had changed little in the past several generations. The arrival of the English, however, disrupted the Algonkians' pattern of living and triggered a series of developments which quickly destroyed their society. Before the end of the century it was clear that the future lay with the white man.*

The Indians of New Hampshire were members of the complex but linguistically unified Algonkian culture which dominated New England and most of eastern Canada in the centuries before European settlement. The "tribe" provided the largest unit of communal organization among the Algonkians. These groups ranged in size from perhaps two hundred to a thousand, with the average size about five hundred. They practiced both hunting and agriculture, with the latter more important in the south, the former in the north. The pattern of living within each tribe reflected its economic needs. In most of New England there was a central village—located near a body of water— which tribal members occupied in the spring and fall for planting and harvesting. Each tribe had its summer fishing grounds, usually on a lake or the ocean where cooling winds offered relief from the ever present insect hordes. Surrounding the village were lands where in the fall and winter smaller family-oriented groups or "bands" hunted in a manner designed to conserve the available game. Each band worked an area of perhaps twenty square miles and sometimes maintained a small village of its own. The greater the dependence on hunting, the

---

*First, a disclaimer. Anyone attempting to study the history of New Hampshire's native inhabitants quickly learns that he must live with indefiniteness. The Indians themselves were non-literate and left no written records of their institutions, behavior, or beliefs. Little formal anthropological or archeological research has been undertaken either, mainly because scholars interested in northeastern Indians have found cultural artifacts more numerous and easier to locate elsewhere. The result is an almost total dependence on European reports and these are scarce and notoriously undependable. Preoccupied with the problems of survival and limited by their own religious and social preconceptions, the English settlers of New Hampshire and Massachusetts simply did not record much which would enable us to gain an understanding of the native American culture they encountered. French settlers among the Algonkians, especially the Jesuit missionaries, were much more interested and observant, but they rarely came as far south as New Hampshire. Their reports are more helpful in a general rather than a specific manner. What follows, then, is not the product of research which produces certainty, but an attempt to piece together a study from decidedly scanty materials.

more independent the band was from tribal identification. Tribes themselves sometimes joined in loosely defined patterns of allegiance, most
frequently for military purposes.

It is impossible to be precise about the identification of New Hampshire's native inhabitants, but the general picture is clear enough.
North of the White Mountains roamed bands of Sokokis (some anthropologists consider the Sokokis a subgroup of the Abenakis) whose
domain stretched from Lake Memphramegog on the west to Lake
Umbagog on the east. Predominantly hunters, their villages were small
and easily moved. They had little contact with Englishmen until the
late eighteenth century. Nearly as remote were western bands of Abenakis who maintained permanent villages near Bartlett, Conway, and
Ossipee Lake in the Saco River watershed. Europeans knew them collectively as the Pequackets or Pigwackets, the name also used to identify
a large village near Fryberg, Maine. The southwestern corner of New
Hampshire served as hunting ground for a third tribe, the Pocumtucks
who inhabited the Connecticut River valley in western Massachusetts.
One band or cluster of bands, the Ashuelots, had semi-permanent
residences along the river which bears their name. Undoubtedly some
bands of the Nipmuc tribe of central Massachusetts also had hunting
territory in the same general area.

By far the most numerous and potentially powerful group of Native
Americans in New Hampshire were the Pennacooks. The term itself
is confusing, for it was used by the English to identify both the tribe
which maintained a thriving village near Concord as well as a larger
entity, the tribe plus various semi-autonomous bands which at times
accorded allegiance to the Pennacook sachem Passaconaway. Many place
names used today reflect the attempts made by Englishmen to identify
either the bands themselves or, sometimes, the rivers and lakes near
their villages. The Pemigawassets lived to the north, occupying intervales along that river. The term Winnipesauke may have referred
to a Pennacook band as well as to the huge lake in the center of the
state. At its outlet was the village of Acquadoctan, where bands from
both the Saco and Merrimack watershed gathered for the spring fishing.
To the south were the Souhegans and Nashuas. Some historians suggest
that Pennacook influence extended as far east as the Piscataquas and
Squamscotts in the Great Bay area, and as far west as a band of Mascomas
in the upper Connecticut River valley. The linkage of these groups to
the Pennacooks, however, is doubtful.

The Algonkians of New Hampshire developed numerous skills in their struggle for survival. They knew how to construct bark canoes, to produce clay and stoneware pottery, to tan and dye leather as well as to manufacture clothing and snowshoes from the finished product, and to make rudimentary wooden and clamshell garden tools. All the tribes and bands south of the White Mountains farmed with success, using fish for fertilizer in their well cleared fields; beans, squash, pumpkins, cucumbers, and corn (or maize) were their main crops. Their hunting and fishing prowess was equally developed. Fields were seeded with grass to entice deer from the forest. The Algonkians employed bows and arrows, spears, and ground traps to capture and kill game. Bone hooks, pointed stocks, and perhaps simple circular weirs were used in fishing. The sufficiency of these methods to the life pattern of the Algonkians helps explain why they never learned to domesticate animals or to develop the weaving skills practiced by other North American natives.

Undoubtedly, social relationships among members of New Hampshire's tribes and bands followed prescribed and detailed rules, but what those rules were remains a mystery. Observations by Englishmen, however, make some things certain. The political organization of social groups did not conform to the European pattern of hierarchy and centralized authority. Christopher Levett, a perceptive English visitor to New Hampshire's first coastal settlement in the mid-1620s, wrote of the natives that "Their Sagamores are no Kings...for I can see no government or law amongst them but club law." They called anyone who happened to be in charge "sagamore," he added, and appeared to change leaders frequently. A century later the Portsmouth merchant Samuel Penhallow labeled Abenaki government "anarchical" and described their chiefs as having "little respect and honor shown them." Even Passaconaway, whom the leaders of Massachusetts Bay thought the most powerful sachem in northern New England, had little influence outside his own immediate tribe before the English began arriving in numbers. What influence he did have stemmed not so much from firm control of a governmental apparatus, but from his reputation— the terms are Puritan—as an extraordinary "magician" or "sorcerer."

Kinship patterns and sex roles also differed in significant ways from those familiar to Europeans. Extensive tabus limited marriage possibilities among Indians of seemingly equal social and economic status.

Families, as in Europe, were dominated by men, but tradition dictated that women should be responsible for such fundamental activities as the production of agricultural goods. The Indians also practiced polygamy. The more wives a man had, the higher his social status; his economic status and that of his family also benefitted, for more wives meant larger crops and more hands to tan leather and make clothing. Christopher Levett recorded the response of one native who learned that King James's only wife had died. The Indian "wondered, and asked me then who did all the king's work. You may imagine," Levett noted with more sensitivity than most Englishmen mustered when confronted with Algonkian culture, "he thought their fashion was universal and that no king had any work for them but their wives."

The Algonkian "mind" appeared even stranger and more mysterious to Europeans than did their social organization. Native perceptions did not distinguish between "natural" and "supernatural" phenomena. Every object was possessed with qualities not only of shape, weight, and size, but also of spirit, and manipulation of the latter could alter the former. The Indians who reported that Passaconaway could make water burn, rocks move, trees dance, and could transform himself into a flaming man never questioned the truth of their statements; such powers were always potentially available to a highly skilled and gifted man. Furthermore, personal fate was a function of spirit. Levett wrote that the Indians ascribed all their good fortune to Squanto, their bad fortune to Tanto, and seemed baffled at the idea that an ordinary individual might have any control over these entities. Spirits appeared mainly in dreams, which foretold the future. Every sagamore, according to Levett, was accompanied by an interpreter of spiritual manifestations called a powwow, and paid close attention to his advice. Passaconaway, it can be assumed, gained influence from his dual role as sagamore and powwow. The Puritans thought of powwows as witches in consort with Satan and native belief in numerous spirits was to them dangerously heretical. To the Pennacooks and their neighbors both powwows and spirits played normal and essential roles in everyday existence.

New Hampshire's Indians had been weakened by a series of disasters before the English began settling. In the late sixteenth century bands of Mohawks—a tribe belonging to the linguistically distinct Iroquois culture—moved eastward from the Hudson River valley. The migration triggered a massive redistribution of territory among western Algon-kians. Some natives who had occupied land in Vermont moved both south and east. Mohawk warriors crossed the Connecticut River into lands long occupied by the Pennacooks and launched a successful attack on the tribal village near Concord. Although the invaders left soon, the Pennacooks, at least according to legends, never fully recovered from the attack. Even more serious was the epidemic which struck New England between 1615 and 1620. Neither the cause nor the nature of the disease is known for certain, but the results were un-mistakable. Perhaps a third of all coastal Algonkians between Narra-ganset Bay and Penobscot Bay died, as did fewer but still large numbers in the interior. The Piscataquas and Squamscotts suffered irremediable losses; many of their surviving members moved inland and joined bands and tribes in the lower Merrimack valley.

Recent experience undoubtedly affected the Indian response to ex-plorers, fishermen, and traders who appeared with increasing frequency during the first quarter of the seventeenth century. There was little reason to fear the newcomers—they were too few in number for that—but trade with Europeans offered enticing possibilities. A few guns, which clearly possessed more spirit and power than their own weapons, would enable them to resist further encroachment from the dreaded Mohawks and make hunting much easier. Metal hooks and woven nets would be useful for fishing. Iron kettles were superior to their own greenwood products, as were the knives and metallic garden tools possessed by the English. Blankets would reduce their dependence on animal hides for clothing. The strangers, thought some natives, might help them combat the evil spirits which in recent years had so decimated their communities. Even if that were not true, their strong water provided quicker and more certain access to spiritual experience than did native stimulants. Much could be gained, then, by providing Europeans with the furs and any other goods sought in exchange for their products.

The Piscataqua area served as the initial focal point for exchange. At various times trading posts existed at what are now Odiorne's Point, Portsmouth, Dover Point, and the mouth of Salmon Falls River. It is not clear which tribal groups had direct contact with English vendors, but most likely the Pigwackets and remaining Piscataquas were deeply involved. They, in turn, probably served as middlemen, purchasing furs from Sokoki bands in the north country and various hunting parties from as far west as central Vermont. By mid-century, however, the center had shifted to the Merrimack valley as settlement by the English, new epidemics among coastal natives, the gradual destruction of fur bearing animals in the seaboard region, and development of trade routes down the Saco and Androscoggin Rivers undermined Piscataqua business. The Pennacooks played the dominant role in managing this new trade, much of which took place at a large "truck house" or trading station established near their village at Concord. As a result, Pennacook influence among tribal groups in central New Hampshire increased.

Trade with the English proved a mixed blessing. To be sure, metal cutting tools were sharper and more durable than wooden, bone, and clamshell instruments, but the anticipated overall improvement in standard of living and community stability did not materialize. It took many furs to purchase a gun and the few acquired did nothing to redress the military superiority of the Mohawks, who obtained many more. In fact, one abortive mid-century attack on that tribe cost the Pennacooks many more warriors than they could afford. Tribal members had to travel greater and greater distances to obtain furs which not only disrupted family life but produced more frequent encounters with competitors in the trade. Not infrequently hunting parties failed to return, thus further reducing an already declining male population. Dependence on the European goods that could be acquired also created problems. Ownership of guns, knives, and blankets, for example, gave an individual or family new status and disrupted the existing social order. Liquor caused serious trouble, mainly because Indians equated drunkenness with possession by an evil spirit, and felt that their behavior while drunk was something for which they were not personally responsible. Arrival of a keg often meant fights, destruction of property, and occasionally murder. One Pennacook sagamore noted in the 1670s that rum "would make the Indians all one Devil."

As trade increased an even more serious threat to native American culture arose. In the 1630s the strangers began arriving in large enough numbers to establish permanent communities along the coast; by the end of the decade English population in all New England had surpassed that of the Algonkians. Settlement brought few advantages—more trading opportunity was the most significant—and many disadvantages. Domesticated animals left by the English to forage often ruined fields planted for fall harvest. Englishmen refused to acknowledge the traditional right of individuals and families to key fishing locations during the spring run, and hunted on lands long controlled by the Indians. Increased contact with the English, many natives soon learned, meant more and more sickness. Sometimes they blamed the epidemics on native gods angered by the weakening of traditional mores, sometimes on the superior power of the Europeans, but whatever the explanation, they saw their numbers dwindle.

Despite the seriousness of these developments, most Algonkians of southern New Hampshire gave little consideration to concerted military action against the English intruders. The Pennacooks considered the Mohawks their most dangerous enemy until late in the seventeenth century. Loss of the Piscataqua region to the English, they felt, still left them dominant in the interior, and Massachusetts Bay inhabitants seemed too far away to be a threat. In any case, they were not a people accustomed to fighting, especially against a superior enemy. The only evidence of aggressive intentions is a farewell speech given by Passaconaway to a gathering of tribal bands in 1660. Some of the men present apparently had blamed the tribe's declining fortunes on Passaconaway's friendliness toward the settlers. He defended himself, according to one witness, by claiming that he had been "as much an enemy to the English on their first coming into these parts as anyone whatsoever" and that he had tried "all ways and means possible to have destroyed them," or "at least to have prevented their sitting down here." But Passaconaway limited his aggressiveness to the "incantations" and "sorceries" on which his reputation had been built, and they proved ineffective. No other sagamore could possibly have organized an effective attack on the coastal area after the 1620s.

The policy, instead, was to seek survival through accommodation. Accommodation meant, in the first place, avoiding involvement in the warfare which periodically broke out between settlers and natives in southern New England. New Hampshire Indians took no part in the Pequot War during 1637 and may well have sympathized with the English. Passaconaway's leadership in the middle part of the century guaranteed maintenance of the general peace. He believed, as he reminded his followers in the same farewell speech, that although natives might do "much mischief" to the English if the two races began fighting, the inevitable result of such conflict would be total tribal destruction; his people, therefore, never should "contend with the English, nor make war with them." His successors followed the advice, at least for the next quarter century. When King Philip's war broke out in 1675, Passaconaway's son Wonalancet gathered remnants of the Merrimack valley tribes about him and moved north to the Coos region to avoid trouble. This group of about one hundred witnessed the destruction of wigwams and food stores at Pennacook, yet took no retaliatory measures. Soon after the war ended and native sagamores signed a formal peace treaty, an episode occurred which taxed their capacity for self-restraint even more. They had returned to Pennacook and been joined by bands of refugee Nipmuc Indians, some of whom had fought for King Philip. Invited in the summer of 1676 to visit Major Richard Waldron at Dover in what they interpreted as a peaceful gesture, the two tribes joined in games with the Englishmen present. One was to be a sham battle, but at a moment when the Indians were unprepared, the English surrounded them, separated out the Nipmuc, then quickly sent the males in tethers to Boston; the leaders of Massachusetts Bay hanged some and shipped the rest to the West Indies where they were sold into slavery. The Pennacooks must have been shocked and ashamed, for Waldron had violated what all Algonkians thought of as fundamental obligations to invited guests. Still, Wonalancet and his followers, mindful of the war just ended, made no immediate attempt to seek revenge.

In fact, some natives provided positive wartime assistance to the English. Wonalancet, according to at least one account, helped discourage the Nipmucs and Pocumtucks, who also were allied with King Philip, from attacking northern settlements under Massachusetts Bay jurisdiction. His actions may help explain why Chelmsford and the communities of Exeter, Hampton, and Dover in what soon became the separate jurisdiction of New Hampshire, never came under attack. Equally important was the middleman role the Pennacooks played in the return of settlers captured by the Indians. Mary Rowlandson,— the wife of the minister in Lancaster, Massachusetts—her son and her nephew all were taken by warriors to Pocumtuck villages in the Connecticut River valley, perhaps as far north as Charlestown. There they were separated, and although she eventually was redeemed by Massachusetts Indians, the two children turned up in a group of six captives delivered by Wonalancet to Major Waldron at Dover. The citizens of

Portsmouth willingly paid the ransom and thanked the friendly sagamore for his role in the affair.

Accommodation also meant avoiding trouble with the settlers when
the two races were not engaged in open conflict. Many native groups
found removal or separation the most effective method of accomplishing
this goal. Algonkians near the coast who survived the early seventeenth
century epidemics moved into the interior, some to Acquadoctan,
others to the Merrimack valley, still others to villages in Maine. Passaconaway seems to have pursued a conscious policy, at least initially,
of keeping his people away from English population centers. Bands to
the north and west, of course, had little direct contact with white men
and undoubtedly considered themselves fortunately situated.

Inasmuch as contact proved unavoidable, Indian leaders did everything in their power to impress the English with their desire to remain
on amiable terms. The task was not an easy one, for settlers assumed
from the beginning that not one of their pagan neighbors could be
trusted and the behavior of the Pequots and King Philip's followers
reinforced that assumption. Even peaceful gestures frequently led Englishmen to suspect a plot designed to lull them into a state of un-
preparedness. For example, in 1642 rumors circulated in some Massachusetts towns of a conspiracy organized by Pennacook sagamores.
An expedition to disarm the supposed troublemakers travelled up the
Merrimack, and although its leaders could uncover no evidence to
substantiate their suspicions, three hostages, including one of Passaconaway's sons, were taken back to the Bay Colony. The Pennacooks,
however, did not retaliate. Passaconaway convinced his fellow tribes-
men to stay put, negotiated successfully for return of the hostages, and
then, Governor John Winthrop recorded happily, "delivered up his
guns." Two years later Passaconaway and several other sachems in New
Hampshire formally "submitted" to English jurisdiction by agreeing
to enforce pertinent colonial laws within their respective tribes and
bands.

From this point on the Indians appear to have accepted a good deal
of English involvement in their affairs. When the sagamore of the
Nashuas died in 1654, Massachusetts dispatched two men to ensure
that a sachem known to be friendly would become the new sagamore.
No report of their success or failure survives, but the Nashuas caused

no future trouble and many band members soon joined the community of christianized or "praying" Indians at Wamesit, near Pawtucket Falls on the lower Merrimack. Permitting the English to establish a trading center in the upper part of the same river valley meant continuous contact between the races and some loss of control over decisions affecting tribal members. Hunters now focused attention on the acquisition of furs sought by the traders, not on food as they had in pre-contact days. The constant presence of Englishmen limited the freedom of the Pennacooks to engage in any activity that might arouse suspicion. Inevitably, animosities arose between individual natives and the men who controlled the supply of European goods. An event occurred in 1668 which made clear just how much had been compromised. Although the sale of liquor to Indians had been outlawed by Massachusetts, the law proved impossible to enforce. One night a man possessed by the evil spirit of rum murdered a trader he suspected of cheating him. Shocked sachems at Pennacook gathered to discuss their alternatives. Native concepts of justice would not have held the man responsible for his act, but English law, dependence on trade, and the commitment to maintain racial harmony all dictated immediate punishment. The man was executed and profuse apologies were made for his behavior.

Acceptance of English authority did not always work to the disadvantage of native interests. Passaconaway, fascinated by the technological skills of the English, convinced them at one point to help build a fort near Ossipee Lake for Indian use should the Mohawks attack. Some Algonkians also learned how to take advantage of the legal institutions of the foreign intruders. They were happy to "sell" land in exchange for tools, blankets, and liquor, especially in the coastal areas where they knew settlers would take what they wanted anyway. As early as 1641 one Indian sued successfully in the local court at Exeter for the destruction of his corn crop. The court at Piscataqua ordered restitution for a fishing net stolen from a native residing in its jurisdiction. Passaconaway, soon after his retirement, petitioned the Massachusetts General Court for land on which to live out his remaining years, and received a grant of several square miles along the Merrimack below Amoskeag Falls. Even acceptance of authority which in some ways compromised native autonomy had its advantages. It is probable, for example, that the sagamores at Pennacook were not entirely unhappy to rid themselves of a man whom the spirit of strong water made so violent.

A similar pattern of accommodation characterized the response of New Hampshire's native inhabitants to the religion of the newcomers. All Algonkians were polytheistic, at least in the sense that they thought the world was controlled by a number of autonomous spirits each possessing differing degrees and kinds of power. Members of individual tribes had constant involvement with their own spirits, and they knew from past experience that other tribes and cultures had different spirits. They feared the Mohawks, for example, because of their influence with whatever powers made men effective in war. Contact with Europeans quickly convinced them that the spirits of the newcomers must be powerful indeed: how else could the size of their ships, the plenitude of their ironware, and the ability of their cannon and guns to kill at a distance be explained. Perhaps these spirits could be harnessed for their own benefit; at the very least they must find out as much as they could about them.

The Sokokis and perhaps Pigwackets encountered Frenchmen first and therefore were introduced to Roman Catholic concepts of Christianity. No record of their early response survives, although it is known that in the eighteenth century, Sokokis joined the community at St. Francis where Jesuit priests gained many converts. Algonkians in southern New Hampshire, on the other hand, were exposed to the Protestantism of Englishmen, many of them Puritan dissenters whose religious perceptions included a particular emphasis on the eternal struggle of two supernatural entities, God and Satan (or the Devil), for control of man's destiny. The Piscataquas, Pennacooks, Pocumtucks, and others found the idea of just two basic spirits strange, but were intrigued by what they and the strangers seemed to believe in common. It is likely, for example, that the native who told Christopher Levett that his people ascribed all good fortune to Squanto and all bad fortune to Tanto were responding to Levett's explanation of the relationship between God and the Devil. Indian observers also noted the presence of English powwows, or ministers, who interpreted God's will and warned against succumbing to the evil powers of Satan. The structural similarity between the two patterns of religious belief and practice reinforced the native curiosity triggered by the apparent power of the Christian deity.

The curiosity was reflected most clearly in the Pennacook response to the missionary activity of the Massachusetts Bay minister John Eliot. By the middle of the 1640s Eliot had gained a number of converts in the Boston area. As settlements spread north and west, so did the center of his efforts. Eliot, who had learned to speak an Algonkian dialect understood by the Pennacooks, met Passaconaway sometime in 1647 and tried to convince the powerful sachem and his people to join the swelling ranks of "Praying Indians." Passaconaway, Eliot reported, responded in the following manner: "You tell us of praying to God... and we like it well at first sight," but "we know not what is within. It may be excellent or it may be nothing; we cannot tell.... If you would come unto us, and open it unto us, and show us what it is within, then we should believe that it is so excellent as you say...." Eliot did just that, with mixed results. Passaconaway himself had a change of heart and fled into the woods to avoid listening, but other Pennacooks provided an attentive audience. Indeed, several asked sensitive questions about the social implications of Christian beliefs. "Suppose a man before he knew God," went one such query, "hath had two wives, the first barren and childless, the second fruitful and bearing him many sweet children.... Which of these two wives should be put away?" Eliot understood that in such a circumstance Christian and Algonkian morality would be in conflict, so avoided the problem by refusing to answer until he consulted other Puritan clergymen.

Just how many New Hampshire natives succumbed to proselytizing is not clear. Although Eliot never returned to the village at Pennacook, Passaconaway remained curious enough to extend a second invitation and in his declining years may have become a convert: Wonalancet's testimony that his dying father advised him "to love the English and love their God also, because the God of the English was the true God and greater then the Indian Gods" at least suggests the possibility. Wonalancet himself was baptised in the early 1670s soon after he and several other Pennacooks moved south to settle near the community of praying Indians at Wamesit. Some surviving members of the Nashuas and bands in the Great Bay area also submitted to the gospel either at Wamesit or in the churches of coastal towns where they resided.

The total number of converts, however, must have been small. Wonalancet's move cost him the support of many Pennacooks, who returned
to their homeland under new leaders decidedly antagonistic to the
English and their religion. King Philip's War brought an abrupt end
to missionary efforts outside Wamesit itself, and Waldron's deception
in the sham battle so infuriated the natives that they avoided further
contact with all Englishmen.

By the 1680s the Algonkians of southern New Hampshire understood
that continued accommodation would not guarantee their cultural survival. The English were arriving in ever greater numbers, and building
homes closer and closer to the areas where they fished, hunted, and
planted their crops. Remnants of the tribes and bands gathered in
village councils to assess their respective situations, and to decide how
best to proceed. Inevitably, disagreements arose. Some individuals
assumed a fatalistic attitude: the gods were angry and had already
decided their fate: nothing could be done except to forego the benefits
of traditional community living, make peace with the powerful intruders, and live out their days on the fringe of settlement. Others felt
differently. Much could be regained, they argued, if a complete break
with the English and their ways were made. The gods would no longer
be angry, population then would increase, and sometime in the future
the English might even be forced to leave. As for the present, only one
course of action seemed possible: the survivors of the Pocumtucks,
Pennacooks, and other tribes and bands must move to the relatively
undisturbed villages of other Algonkians to the north and east.

From the advocates of migration emerged new leaders. They gathered
their followers about them and left. Kancamagus led only the largest
of the resulting groups. In their new and safer surroundings the embittered sachems not only brooded on tragic events of the past half
century, but sought ways to repay those responsible for the fate of their
peoples. The opportunity soon arose.

2

ADVENTURERS, PLANTERS, ÉMIGRÉS

Interactions among three distinct groups of individuals other than Algonkians shaped the pattern of settlement in early New Hampshire. Merchants and gentry from English seaports, especially those in the west country, provided capital for both exploration and the establishment of fishing and trading enterprises from which they hoped to gain a profit. These "adventurers," the most important of whom were Sir Ferdinando Gorges and Captain John Mason, dominated the Council for New England, a body which in the years between 1622 and 1635 made over a half dozen land grants in the territory surrounding the Piscataqua and Merrimack watersheds. Men and women hired by the adventurers to "plant" themselves in the New World comprised the second group. They faced the difficult dual task of satisfying the economic expectations of their employers and establishing secure outposts of European civilization in inhospitable and unfamiliar wilderness surroundings. In the 1630s émigrés from Puritan settlements in Massachusetts joined the settlers sent directly from England. Some of these émigrés moved north because they found themselves unwilling or unable to accept the demands of life in the Bay Colony. Others migrated with the full support of Massachusetts magistrates eager to extend Puritan authority throughout New England.

Conflicts of interest among adventurers, planters and émigrés dominated the first twenty years of settlement history. Gorges, Mason, and their associates not only faulted their employees for failure to produce a profit, but condemned Massachusetts men for interfering with their trans-Atlantic enterprises. The first planters fought both their employers, who provided insufficient supplies and too much criticism, and émigrés intent upon extending Puritan influence to the Piscataqua.

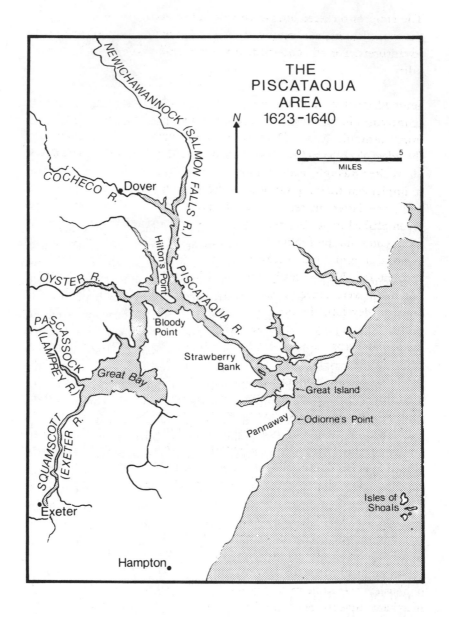

THE
PISCATAQUA
AREA
1623-1640

N

0   5
MILES

NEWICHAWANNOCK (SALMON FALLS R.)

COCHECO R.

Dover

PISCATAQUA R.

Hilton's Point

OYSTER R.

Bloody
Point

PASCASSOCK
(LAMPREY R.)

Strawberry
Bank

Great Bay

Great Island

Odiorne's Point

SQUAMSCOTT
(EXETER R.)

Pannaway

Exeter

Isles of
Shoals

Hampton

The émigrés bickered among themselves, exacerbated tensions among the first planters, and exhibited total indifference to complaints of the adventurers. For all concerned, it was a period of confusion and instability.

Several factors account for the early seventeenth century interest of west countrymen in the New World. For the past quarter century gentlemen from Cornwall, Dorset, Devonshire, and Somerset had been promoting the idea of colonization, and two of them, Humphrey Gilbert and Sir Walter Raleigh, had expended huge sums of money in an attempt to implement their aspirations; the former concentrated on Newfoundland, the latter on settlements further south. Raleigh's efforts had accomplished little, but the plantation in Newfoundland served as the focal point for profitable fishing enterprises and the fishermen had engaged in minor but successful trade with "savages" they occasionally encountered. No one really knew how large that trade might become, but many were eager to explore the possibilities. If significant trade failed to develop, the New World still offered immense potential for profit. The supply of fish seemed inexhaustible, and timber, furs, medicinal herbs, and exotic foods—all of which could command a ready market—reportedly were plentiful. Even gold or other metals might be found. Exploration, furthermore, might lead to discovery of a northwest passage to Asia and the East Indies, thus opening a trade route which would make the English more competitive with Portuguese and other southern European merchants. Finally, diplomatic considerations favored trans-Atlantic enterprise. Defeat of the Armada had eroded Spanish domination of the high seas. The crown, indeed all of England, now shared the west countrymen's fascination with North America.

The "discovery" of territory included in modern New Hampshire was one product of west country economic ambitions. Probably the first Europeans to set foot on New Hampshire soil were fishermen from Newfoundland attracted by cod and mackerel in waters off the Isles of Shoals; these same men may also have visited the mainland. In 1603 merchant adventurers from Bristol, in Somerset County, financed a voyage which resulted in the first recorded observations of the Piscataqua area. They hoped both to make a profit—the previous year Bartholomew Gosnold had returned from a trip along the New England coast with a load of sassafras which more than paid for the expedition—

and to learn as much as possible about New World rivers which might serve as avenues for future trade. Martin Pring, a twenty-three year old seaman who later became commander of the entire East India squadron, was put in charge of the expedition. Accompanied by several veterans of Gosnold's voyage, Pring not only looked for sassafras but explored several inlets including Piscataqua. He labeled it in his journal "the best" of those investigated and mentioned having "rowed up" the river "ten or twelve miles." Pring found little sassafras, however, and the commercial failure of the project in conjunction with that of a subsequent voyage under George Waymouth discouraged further explorations in the area. The unsuccessful attempt by west country adventurers to establish a settlement up the coast at Sagadahoc in 1607 so accentuated discouragement that no major additional enterprises were undertaken for more than a decade.

Three developments helped revive west country enthusiasm by the 1620s. One was the survival of the Jamestown colony, financed by London merchants under authority of the Virginia Company, a corporate entity chartered by the crown. Published reports by Captain John Smith provided a second stimulant. Smith, who considered himself the savior of the Jamestown enterprise and whose capacity for self-advertisement had made him a recognized expert on colonization, visited both the Isles of Shoals and Piscataqua in 1614. He gave the former his name (which for years were known as Smith's Isles), cited the latter for its excellent harbor, and in general promoted the idea of settlement on New England shores. The growing personal commitment to colonization by the wealthy and energetic west countryman Sir Ferdinando Gorges served as the final catalyst.

Gorges's interest in America stemmed from his position as military commander of the government fort at Plymouth, the largest seaport on the south shore of the Cornwall Peninsula, and the close association among his family and the Raleigh and Gilbert families. Intrigued by reports from the New World, he had been a chief supporter of the abortive Sagadahoc expedition. Three Indians brought to England by George Waymouth had lived in his household. Eager to return to their homeland, they undoubtedly described it in terms which whetted their host's appetite for further adventure. By 1615 Gorges had gained the support of other west countrymen and was prepared to launch a major colonization effort.

His initial move was to convince royal officials that the Virginia Company should not have exclusive control over New World settlements. Success came in 1620 when the crown created the Council for New England with authority to grant land, control trade, and administer all colonies in North America between the fortieth and forty-eighth parallel. Gorges not only influenced the selection of original Council members but arranged for his own appointment as president. Next Gorges sought to exercise his new authority. He quickly issued the so-called Pierce patent to the Pilgrims when he learned that they, by accident, had settled in territory under Council jurisdiction. Two years later, his personal fortune enhanced by a recent remarriage, Gorges put the Council in full operation. More than a dozen formal patents to a variety of potential adventurers, all either merchants or members of the English aristocracy, were issued between March 1622 and June 1623. Among the grantees were David Thomson, Gorges himself, and Captain John Mason, the three men most responsible for sponsoring early English settlements in New Hampshire.

Thomson had known Gorges for some time. A resident of Plymouth with experience both in overseas trade and the marketing of fish, he sought and gained part-time employment as a messenger and clerk for the Council for New England. Payment for his services included a grant of 6000 acres and an island of undetermined size somewhere in the territory administered by the Council. In 1623 he and three other Plymouth merchants formed a small company to establish a trading center in New England. Thomson set sail on the *Jonathan of Plymouth* that spring, selected a site which he called Pannaway (now Odiorne's Point) at the mouth of the Piscataqua, and thus became a planter as well as an adventurer. In neither role was he particularly successful. Four years later Thomson moved to an island in Boston harbor, where he soon contracted an illness and died. The trading company apparently lost money for everyone involved.

Gorges had far greater ambitions than Thomson. In 1622 the Council issued a patent for the province of Maine—defined to include all the land between the Merrimack River and Sagadahoc—to Gorges and Mason, who had recently completed six years of service as the Governor of Newfoundland. Sir Ferdinando's long range plans included the planting of a colony somewhere in Maine under his personal leadership, but first he felt it necessary to establish the governing authority of the

Council over present settlements in New England. To accomplish this he had his son Robert appointed "Governor-General" and sent him on an expedition which arrived at the Pilgrim colony of Plymouth in September 1623. Robert Gorges and the planters who accompanied him occupied a group of abandoned buildings north of Plymouth at Wessaguset. The following spring the governor-general sailed north to consult with Thomson and a third Council associate, Christopher Levett, on how best to proceed. At Pannaway, however, he found letters from his father announcing that financial considerations necessitated postponement of further activities. A few of the Wessaguset planters may later have joined Thomson, but that was the only direct impact Gorges's New England project had on the Piscataqua. For the next four years Sir Ferdinando fought in the wars conducted by the Duke of Buckingham against Spain and France, and paid little attention to the New World. Gorges played a subordinate role to his long time friend Captain John Mason in subsequent ventures affecting New Hampshire.

Mason's fascination with New England grew out of his experiences in Newfoundland. There is no evidence he actually visited the area, but he talked at length with fishermen who had and he was convinced by their reports that the mainland rivers could become avenues for major trade with the natives in the interior. Influence with Gorges gained Mason the second patent issued by the Council for New England, the grant of Mariana which included the coastal region south of the Merrimack. Legal technicalities and limited finances prevented Mason from taking up the Mariana patent, so he joined forces with Gorges in the Maine patent and cooperated with Council members sponsoring the expedition led by Robert Gorges. The abandonment of that project did not discourage him. After service in the wars (Mason's appointment as paymaster for the English armies helped enhance his personal fortune) he made an arrangement with Sir Ferdinando to split Maine into two parts. Mason's portion, confirmed by formal grant from the Council on November 7, 1629, included the territory between the Merrimack and the Piscataqua. He named it New Hampshire, after the English county of Hampshire where, in the city of Portsmouth, the family estate was located. Thereafter Mason spent much of his money, energy, and time attempting to exploit the resources of his New World domain.

His first major effort involved still another patent from the always

Gorges and Mason naming their provinces.

Modern cartoon depicting the naming of New Hampshire. Source unknown.
Courtesy of the New Hampshire Historical Society.

obliging Council for New England. Ten days after granting New Hampshire, the Council gave Mason and Gorges a charter for the Laconia Company, an enterprise designed to capture fur trade from French and Dutch entrepreneurs by discovering and controlling what was described as the "Lake of the Iroquois." In fact, no such lake existed, but Mason thought it did. The French explorer Samuel de Champlain had reported its existence and New World natives, referring probably to both Lake Winnipesauke and Lake Champlain, had seemingly confirmed his reports. All major rivers in New England as well as the St. Lawrence and Hudson supposedly had their origins in the lake territory, where endless swamps and streams harbored a limitless supply of beaver and other fur bearing animals. Mason and Gorges provided funds enough to outfit an expedition under the leadership of Walter Neale, a military associate looking for employment. Neale and the planters who accompanied him managed to establish three different settlements along the Piscataqua but failed to develop a profitable fur trade. Attempts to make money by switching from trade to fishing, and to beef up capital resources by bringing in merchant adventurers, which involved a second Council patent, did little to help the Laconia Company. Sometime before 1634 it became bankrupt and went out of business.

Mason, however, persisted. He still had the patent for New Hampshire and had gained some additional land on the east side of the Piscataqua in the distribution of Laconia Company assets which had accompanied its dissolution. Now he simply assumed responsibility on a personal basis for what previously had been a corporate enterprise. He provided additional support to existing settlements and financed at least one new project. Mason also took steps to maintain his influence with those in England who controlled colonization. In 1632 he gained appointment as a full member of the Council for New England and soon became its vice president. When royal officials decided to dissolve the Council and assume direct control of New World settlement, he managed to have his patents reconfirmed and then campaigned to obtain a commission as Vice-Admiral for New England. He also joined with Gorges in seeking abrogation of the Massachusetts Bay charter, which included territory covered by his patents. Moreover, Mason kept alive his dream of making a profit from adventuring. In one of his last letters to New Hampshire he wrote: "I have disbursed a great deal of money in the plantation, and never received one penny; but hope, if there were once a discovery of the lakes, that I should, in some reasonable time, be reimbursed again." Mason died suddenly in December 1635, at the age of forty-nine. His death, the failure of the Laconia Company, the dissolution of the Council for New England, and the political upheavals which disrupted England for the next quarter century brought adventuring in New Hampshire to an abrupt end.

The New World appeared quite different to those who actually planted there than to adventurers, most of whom remained in England. Gorges, Mason, and their associates could read the exploration and promotional literature and envision a land of plenty in which the availability of food made survival easy, in which a native population eager to share in the material benefits of European civilization offered the potential for profitable trade, and in which vast untapped natural resources awaited exploitation. Settlers, however, quickly learned that nothing would be quite as simple as they had been led to expect. To be sure, the resources were there, but catching fish required hard work, precious metals proved difficult or impossible to locate, and the natives seemed incapable of delivering enough furs to make trade profitable. In fact, obtaining enough food to survive required an immense amount of energy. "I will not tell you," Christopher Levett reported for the benefit of friends in England after his visit to the eastern shores, "that you may smell the corn fields before you see the land, neither must men think that corn doth grow naturally (or on trees), nor will the deer come when they are called or stand still and look on a man until he shoots him . . . nor the fish leap into the kettle, nor on the dry land, neither are they so plentiful that you may dip them up in baskets, nor take cod in nets to make a voyage, which is no truer than that the fowles will present themselves to you with spits through them. . . . But certainly," he concluded on a sober yet optimistic note, "there is fowl, deer, and fish enough for the taking if men be diligent."

Levett's observations stemmed in part from a month spent in 1624 as a guest of David Thomson at the first English settlement on the Piscataqua. Thomson had arrived the year before with about ten others, including his wife. The group members went about their task intelligently. They selected an easily defensible site near a good supply of fresh water. They built a large stone house so sturdy that it remained standing at least sixty years; a second building may have been constructed up the Piscataqua near the mouth of the Cocheco River. No records survive to indicate the extent of their fishing and trading, but they did engage in both. The men used fishing stages already on the Isles of Shoals and constructed others north of the main plantation. In 1626 Thomson, in conjunction with leaders of the Plymouth colony, bought out the stock of a trading post on Monhegan Island. He also cooperated with the Pilgrims in getting rid of the troublesome Thomas Morton of Merrymount, footing part of the expenses incurred in sending Morton back to England. But the plantation ultimately failed, despite the diligence of its members. It is not clear precisely what motivated Thomson to move south. Probably he had given up hope of profiting from his present activities and felt that farming would be much easier on the island in Massachusetts Bay which he had selected for his new site. The Bay area also afforded him the company of several other English planters who had settled there.

The second New Hampshire plantation was an indirect offshoot of the first. Sometime in the mid-1620s Edward Hilton, a London fish-monger whose brother William had been living at Plymouth, joined Thomson at Pannaway. William then moved north, and the two broth-ers set up fishing stages, probably near the "Great Island" on which Newcastle is presently located. When Thomson left for the more civ-ilized environment of Massachusetts Bay, the Hiltons took the bold step of moving in the opposite direction. They abandoned their fish drying operation, where the Isles of Shoals continued to serve as the center for that activity, and joined with other planters from Pannaway to establish a colony seven miles up the river at what soon became known as Hilton's Point. There they constructed several houses, planted cornfields, and engaged in trade with native bands residing in the Piscataqua watershed. The Hiltons began without formal title to the land, but the arrival of Laconia Company employees nearby and settlers further south under a Massachusetts Bay Company charter, made them anxious about their squatter status. Edward immediately left for En-gland where in 1631 he and a group of Bristol merchants obtained from the Council a patent to about twenty-five square miles of land stretching from the mouth of the Oyster River up the west side of the Newichawannock. The patent and the added financial support enabled Hilton to attract still more planters. Soon, however, he learned that Massachusetts leaders, who as early as 1632 had designs on the entire Piscataqua area, might challenge the legality of the title. To avoid conflict, the Bristol associates sold the patent to a group of English Puritans from Shrewsbury, although Hilton himself kept title to the land surrounding his plantation on the point. The price of £2150 helped Hilton's group turn a neat profit on their investment, the only adventurers in early New Hampshire to do so.

Meanwhile Walter Neale and other Laconia employees had been engaged in a variety of enterprises. A total of sixty-six men and twenty-two women were sent out to the colony in the first two years of company operations. They arrived with equipment for fishing, lumbering, and a salt works, a large stock of blankets, cloth, kettles, liquor, tools for trade, and seeds for planting both grain and grape vines. Neale set up operations at Thomson's stone house, which the company had leased. His main assigned tasks were to govern the entire operation and to engage in explorations until he discovered the Lake of the Iroquois. Ambrose Gibbins served as factor for the company, responsible for all trading activities. He established a small colony and trading post at the falls of the Newichawannock where Indians frequently gathered for spring fishing. A third plantation in which Thomas Warnerton, another ex-soldier and the son of a Council member, played the key role was begun under company auspices at Strawberry Bank. There a "great house," which later became known as Mason Hall, was constructed. A deep ditch and strong palisade with eight small cannons protected the house from uninvited intruders.

From the beginning the colony floundered. Neale fulfilled neither of his responsibilities. The scattered nature of settlement made effective governing difficult at best, and the behavior of Gibbins and Warnerton, who often challenged his authority, complicated matters. Exploration proved much easier to plan than execute. Neale set out several times, but never even reached Winnipesauke, much less lakes further in the interior. Gibbins tried harder but fared little better. The natives, as many as a hundred at a time, showed up at Newichawannock, but they proved hard bargainers and in any case could not deliver sufficient furs to satisfy investors in England. To pay for recurring expenses Gibbins shifted the focus of company activities. He put some of the few available men to work manufacturing clapboards and pipestaves, others building salt pans, and still others constructing additional fishing facilities at Pannaway and the Isles of Shoals. In 1632, after the company gained legal title to the Isles, the Newichawannock operation was reduced in size and the offshore trading "magazine" expanded, but that too failed to produce a profit. The badgering of disappointed adventurers only accentuated Gibbins's frustrations: "A plantation must be furnished with cattle and good hired hands and necessaries for them," he wrote bitterly in 1633, "and not think the great looks of men [he undoubtedly referred to Neale and Warnerton] and many words will be a means to raise a plantation." Social tensions exacerbated difficulties within the company. Feuding among Neale, Gibbins, and Warnerton was only part of the problem. The absence of facilities for accustomed social activities and plentiful liquor led to unresolved personal conflicts. The three to one sex ratio produced so many complaints that at one point Gibbins asked that more women be sent. The company agent in England never complied with the request.

On top of all this, the company leaders had to meet several outside challenges to their legal authority. The first Laconia charter gave the company title only to the land surrounding the undiscovered lake or lakes. Mason and Gorges assumed that their patents to Mariana, New Hampshire, and Maine would legitimize settlements along the seacoast. Others, however, disagreed. The charter granted by the crown to the Massachusetts Bay Company not only included all of Mariana, but could be interpreted to include large sections of New Hampshire and Maine. The overlapping authorities resulted either from simple geographical confusion on the part of royal officials or their conscious attempt to limit the authority of the Council for New England. Furthermore, the Council itself took action which conflicted with Mason's New Hampshire patents when it issued the charter to Edward Hilton. Although these jurisdictional conflicts caused the greatest concern in England—the company's major response was to obtain a second patent from the Council for New England which gave it title to "Pascataway," defined to include both the Isles of Shoals and all the land in the Piscataqua area not granted to Hilton—it did affect company planters in America. Gibbins, charged by Mason with responsibility for taking up the Mariana patent, never did so for fear of alienating the Massachusetts leaders. He also had to delay making the Isles of Shoals the center of operation for trading activity until he received word that they did, indeed, belong to the company. Neale, as governor of the plantation, was frequently involved in territorial disputes. He and the Hiltons apparently had a number of arguments before Edward obtained his patent. When Mason and Gorges began maneuvering in England against the Massachusetts charter, Neale found himself a prime target for Bay leader suspicions. They opened his mail and sent spies to report on his activities. They helped engineer the sale of Hilton's patent, then employed the agent for the new owners, Thomas Wiggin, to enforce Massachusetts claims to land covered in the Pascataway patent. One result was a confrontation between Neale and Wiggin over rights to what henceforth became known as "Bloody Point." It is doubtful, however, if the two men exchanged anything more violent than harsh words.

Troubles in the plantation came to a head when letters were received from England announcing the refusal of company adventurers to pump additional money into their New World investment. Neale, ordered to dismiss his household and return to England, did so immediately, and may well have considered himself fortunate to be relieved of his responsibilities. Gibbins was left in charge of operations at Newichawannock, Edward Godfrey at the mouth of the Piscataqua, and Warnerton at Strawberry Bank, but all those men soon began to suspect the total collapse of Laconia operations. When their fears became reality, they, like other company employees, were left to fend for themselves.

The various Laconia settlements experienced different fates. Pannaway was all but abandoned within a few years although Gibbins settled his family nearby. Godfrey moved to Maine. The old trading establishment upstream on the Newichawannock fared somewhat better, mainly because Mason decided to finance the construction of mills there and sent the energetic Henry Josselyn to manage the operation. But after Mason's death that too floundered and Josselyn left to join Godfrey. The community on the Isles of Shoals, which Laconia operations had helped make the most active fishing center in the Gulf of Maine, kept on growing despite the company's bankruptcy. Employees there found other entrepreneurs eager to take advantage of their skills or became independent operators themselves. The vast majority of these offshore planters, however, lived on islands awarded to Gorges in the distribution of company assets (the distribution ultimately determined the southern portion of the present boundary between Maine and New Hampshire) and thus the Isles played a minimal role in subsequent New Hampshire history. Strawberry Bank also thrived. Warnerton stayed there and continued to exercise a good deal of influence over a constantly expanding population. Settlers drifted in from Pannaway, Hilton's Point, the Isles, and Newichawannock. Mason and later his widow used the "bank" and nearby Great Island along with Newichawannock as focal points for development under the New Hampshire patent, which resulted in some fresh migration from England. In addition, the Strawberry Bank area began to attract a few residents from Massachusetts Bay. After the mid-1630s the Bay colony became the single most important source of immigration to all of what nearly a half century later became the province of New Hampshire.

The Massachusetts men who moved north generally did so for one of two reasons. Some thought they had a better chance at Piscataqua— the term increasingly used to define the entire area surrounding the river—than at the Bay settlements to successfully exploit the New World's economic resources. They came to fish, trade, and engage in land development schemes. Most of those who emigrated for economic reasons maintained close contact with friends to the south and supported efforts by Massachusetts to include Piscataqua in its jurisdiction as long as they felt such inclusion would benefit them personally. Other émigrés, however, left Massachusetts because they found they could not accept the dictates of its government. Most departed voluntarily, but several came north under formal banishment by the Massachusetts General Court. The refugees included Anglican churchmen unwilling to worship under dissenting ministers, political enemies of the entire Massachusetts Bay enterprise, idealistic Puritans at odds with Governor John Winthrop's ruling clique, criminals seeking escape from Puritan justice, and more than a few men and women attracted by Piscataqua's reputation for social permissiveness. By the fall of 1640 former residents of Massachusetts accounted for more than half of the population of nearly a thousand Englishmen residing between the Piscataqua River and the northern boundary of the Bay Colony. The migration had had a profound effect on the plantations established under the Laconia and Hilton patents, and had resulted in the founding of two additional communities, Exeter and Hampton.

Both outcasts and opportunists (the terms are not mutually exclusive) came to Strawberry Bank and Great Island. A Massachusetts magistrate reported that as early as 1630 some "desperately wicked" settlers "hearing of men of their own disposition which were planted at Piscataway, went from us to them, whereby though our numbers were lessened, yet we accounted ourselves nothing weakened by their removal." A year later Thomas Walford, banished from the Bay Colony, decided to move north rather than return to England. Walford initially gained employment with the Laconia Company, remained after its dissolution, and became a permanent Piscataqua resident. The flow of refugees from Puritan authority continued for some time after that. When a man fled from Plymouth to avoid trial for murdering an Indian he was protected from seizure by Piscataqua residents: "It was their usual manner," complained a Massachusetts observer, "to countenance . . . all such lewd persons as fled from us to them." Not all the migrants, however, left because they had to. A few men came to work for the Laconia Company and several for Mason and his widow Anne. By far the most successful of the latter was Francis Norton, a Charlestown inhabitant hired by Anne to join Warnerton in managing the family enterprise at Strawberry Bank. Norton took up residence at Mason Hall where he presided over a household engaged in cattle raising, farming, and trading both with natives and with English immigrants. In the early 1640s he absconded with the cattle (Warnerton at the same time seems to have taken the stock in trade), sold them in Massachusetts, and retired in relative affluence.

One product of the migration was the accentuation of animosities between Piscataqua residents and their fellow New World settlers to the south. The animosities existed on two levels. Many of the new-comers received title to land either from managers of the Laconia operations, or from agents of the Mason family acting under authority of Captain John's various patents. Massachusetts claims to much of the same land inevitably produced anxieties which increased as the Bay Colony became increasingly powerful and autonomous. The émigrés also worried lest Massachusetts attempt to eradicate what its magistrates considered a serious threat to social discipline in New England, just as Plymouth magistrates earlier had gotten rid of Thomas Morton's community at Merrymount. Those magistrates clearly did think ill of Piscataqua. Winthrop, for example, once wrote that Warnerton "lived very wickedly in whoredom, drunkenness and quarrelling, so as he . . . kept the Pascataquack men under awe of him divers years," and his associates frequently cited the need for maintaining social order as justification for Massachusetts territorial ambitions. It is just as certain that most Strawberry Bank residents, whether awed by Warnerton or not, liked their freedoms. Warnerton himself took pride in living up to his reputation—Henry Josselyn's brother reported his having "drank to me a pint of kill-devel, alias rum, as a draught"—and once labeled all Massachusetts men "rogues" before expressing a wish "to see all their throats cut." He, other original company planters, and their émigré friends eventually came into armed conflict with supporters of Massachusetts, but at Hilton's Point not the Bank.

The plantation variously known as Hilton's Point, Dover, or Cocheco had been dramatically affected by the sale of its patent to Puritan investors in Shrewsbury. The sale had been arranged by Thomas Wiggin, a close associate of Governor Winthrop sent to England to defend the Bay Colony against its numerous enemies. Wiggin returned with authority to act as governor of the plantation and immediately launched a campaign to develop the land under the protection of Massachusetts Bay. For a time he succeeded. Sympathetic settlers, including Ambrose Gibbins and his family, moved over from Piscataqua while others came up from Boston and the surrounding towns. Wiggin arranged for construction of a meeting house and then hired a Puritan minister named William Leveridge to conduct services. When he asked Winthrop whether the Massachusetts General Court would assume jurisdiction over criminal cases involving plantation residents, he received an encouraging reply. Wiggin may also have persuaded some Massachusetts magistrates to support an interpretation of the Hilton patent which would extend its boundaries to include land south and east of Great Bay, where squatters had begun to build homes.

About mid-decade, however, Wiggin's plans began to go awry. In part his trouble lay in the not unjustified fear of older settlers, most of whom were Anglicans, that the extension of Puritan authority would be to their disadvantage. These churchmen refused to worship under Leveridge, who packed his bags and returned to Boston, and made clear their opposition to the idea of having Massachusetts courts handle criminal cases, or more important, decide disputes over land ownership. In addition, Wiggin found Bay Colony magistrates increasingly reluctant to extend their cooperation. Gorges, Mason, and other Anglican adventurers in England had joined forces with Archbishop Laud in an assault on the Massachusetts Bay Company, accusing its leaders, among

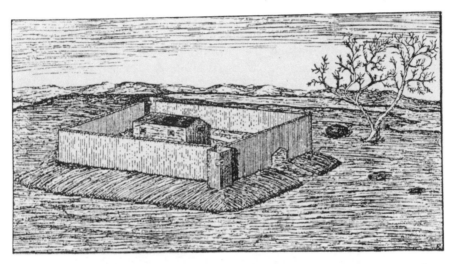

Unknown artist's rendering of the first meeting house in Dover. *Courtesy of the New Hampshire Historical Society.*

other things, of arbitrarily extending jurisdiction to land not included in the company charter. Winthrop and his assistants had no intention of providing additional ammunition to their enemies, which explains their denial in 1635 of Wiggin's request to try two men caught engaged in the act of sodomy. The moralistic Wiggin found the refusal particularly disappointing because the crime had been committed on Sunday. To make matters still worse, Wiggin found the region he supposedly governed suddenly invaded by a number of wealthy and influential refugees from Massachusetts authority. The new immigrants combined forces with the old settlers to drive Wiggin from power and keep the plantation in turmoil for the rest of the decade.

George Burdett was the first and in some ways the most dangerous of the Bay Colony fugitives. A minister by profession, Burdett had been shocked by what he considered the excesses of religious practice in the Boston area and moved north to replace Leveridge. The residents found both his preaching and his personality so pleasing that in 1637 they formed a "combination" and made him governor of the plantation, thus leaving Wiggin without authority except as agent for the Shrewsbury adventurers. Furthermore, Burdett began a correspondence with Archbishop Laud—the two may have become acquainted in England—in which he suggested that the best way for the crown to undermine Puritan domination of New England would be to fortify the Piscataqua area and use it as a base of operations under his leadership or that of the newly appointed governor of the region, Sir Ferdinando Gorges. Unfortunately for Burdett, Massachusetts leaders became suspicious, hired a spy who broke into his study and stole copies of the correspondence, and used the information to convince plantation inhabitants that Burdett's activities might ultimately destroy their independence. Burdett then left for Maine. In the early 1640s he returned to England.

Meanwhile other émigrés arrived, including Captain John Underhill who had been disarmed by the General Court for his uncompromising support of Anne Hutchinson in the series of religious disputes known collectively as the Antinomian controversy. Underhill reputedly had such an unstable personality and fierce temper that opponents of Mrs. Hutchinson feared for their lives. Accompanying Underhill was an evangelical preacher named Hansard Knollys who had come to America to avoid arrest by church officials, and who managed to alienate both Archbishop Laud and the Bay Colony magistrates. The two men quickly launched a successful campaign to convince Hilton Point settlers that under their leadership the colony could be protected from both Massachusetts and the crown. Underhill replaced Burdett as governor while Knollys assumed responsibility for ministering to the religious needs of the planters. Among Puritan leaders Hilton's Point gained the reputation as a dangerous outpost of Antinomian sentiment. Underhill was said to have labeled Bostonians as religiously zealous "as the scribes and Pharisees."

The leadership of the Antinomians, however, proved temporary. As religious controversies in Massachusetts subsided, Winthrop, Wiggin, and members of the General Court began to regret having alienated as powerful a man as Captain Underhill. Underhill, in turn, decided that in the long run cooperation with established Puritan magistrates would prove beneficial. Accordingly, he commenced negotiations with them. Knollys experienced an identical change of heart, mainly because most of his intended congregation had chosen to worship under still another fugitive clergyman, Thomas Larkham, a wealthy Anglican who earlier had purchased land from one of the Shrewsbury adventurers. Underhill's negotiations along with friction between the two ministers and their congregations triggered open conflict. Knollys publicly accused Larkham of heresy and worldliness, then issued a formal bull of excommunication. Larkham responded by knocking off Knollys's hat, at which point Underhill raised a guard to attack the group of churchmen who had gathered in support of Larkham. In one of the great comic opera sequences in early New Hampshire history, the Antinomians marched forth led by someone waving a halberd with a Bible attached to its tip. Knollys followed with a drawn pistol. The Larkham men retreated and sent a messenger to Strawberry Bank for help. Within hours the governor at the Bank, Francis Williams (an old Laconia Company employee and friend of Warnerton), returned with an armed company which surrounded the house where Knollys and Underhill had retired to celebrate their accomplishments. The next day the Larkham men called a court which, with Mr. Williams sitting as judge, found the Puritans guilty of riot, fined them, and ordered Underhill and several others to return to Massachusetts. There matters rested until, at the urging of emissaries from Massachusetts, Knollys rescinded his excommunication and the Williams court withdrew its fines and banishment order. Knollys soon returned to England under censure for "dalliance" with his house maids. Larkham and Underhill also left.

The Antinomian controversy also led to the founding of Exeter, a new plantation located on the Squamscott River, the main southern tributary of the Piscataqua. In 1636 John Wheelwright, a Puritan minister whose wife was Anne Hutchinson's sister-in-law, arrived in Boston. Although Wheelwright did not agree entirely with Mrs. Hutchinson, he soon became a favorite of her followers and thus gained the enmity of Winthrop and a majority of the General Court. It is not clear how much he understood about the delicacy of his position, but it is clear that he was too stubborn a man to compromise with those who thought him a threat to community order. Refusal to compromise led to formal banishment by the Puritan establishment. By the end of 1637 Wheelwright, who ministered to a small congregation at Mount Wollaston (now Quincy), was looking for a new home.

Rhode Island would have been the obvious choice since the Hutchinsons and a number of other Antinomians planned to join the community established there earlier by Roger Williams, but Wheelwright had other ideas. He took a boat north, landed at Piscataqua, and spent the better part of the winter looking for a convenient place to found a Christian community of his own. Several considerations dictated his choice of the falls at Squamscott. The site was sufficiently distant from Strawberry Bank to prevent infection from the hard drinking and blasphemous group of men working with Warnerton and Williams. Nearby salt marshes would provide a ready source of food for cattle while the land itself offered limitless supplies of lumber as well as a few fields cleared earlier by the Indians. Perhaps most important, Wheelwright discovered that neither the Pascataway nor Hilton patents covered the area, even though it lay outside Massachusetts. The decision made, he went to work. To establish title to the land, Wheelwright negotiated a purchase from the remaining resident natives. He brought the few pioneer squatters into his plans, added a number of Massachusetts men including several from his Mount Wollaston congregation, drafted a set of community regulations, and sent for his wife, children, and mother-in-law whom he had left in Massachusetts. That summer the energetic Wheelwright—Oliver Cromwell, among others, had attested to his physical strength and prowess—not only built himself a dwelling, but supervised construction of a town meeting house.

For the rest of the decade Wheelwright kept busy clearing land, farming, preaching, managing town affairs, and parrying the thrusts of Massachusetts magistrates made anxious by the presence of still another community of dissidents to the north. The last two of these responsibilities proved the most difficult. Population pressures within the Bay Colony, the apparent success of the Squamscott plantation and the eagerness of Wheelwright's followers to enlarge their settlement produced a steady flow of fresh immigrants. Unfortunately, at least for Wheelwright, not all the newcomers accepted his leadership. Many, in fact, sought reconciliation with Massachusetts, a reconciliation possible only on terms which Wheelwright opposed. The Squamscott planters increasingly found themselves involved in internal disputes reflecting their acceptance or rejection of their minister's actions. Meanwhile Wheelwright and Bay magistrates continued to feud. In the fall of 1638 the General Court members formally charged Piscataqua residents who supported Wheelwright with "unneighborly conduct." The same year they granted approval to a group of Puritans eager to found a town at Winnacunnet (Hampton) which lay within the territory the natives had sold to Wheelwright. Wheelwright complained but could do nothing to prevent the settlement. He did however, manage to keep the upper hand inside his own plantation.

The emigrants to Winnacunnet differed in one key respect from those who migrated elsewhere to the territory included in modern New Hampshire: they came with the full blessing of authorities in Massachusetts Bay. Governor Winthrop and the General Court had attempted as early as 1636 to take possession of salt marshes at Winnacunnet even though the area lay beyond the limits of the company charter. Their initial effort resulted in construction of what became known as the "Bound" house, a sturdy building the exact location of which is not known. The General Court next granted several Newbury inhabitants permission to settle, but the conditions of the grant were not fulfilled within the specified time. Thus in 1638 the General Court felt free to regrant the same land to a group of associated petitioners under the leadership of Stephen Batchellor, a Puritan minister recently arrived from Hampton, England. Batchellor's group included other newcomers to Massachusetts as well as inhabitants of Newbury, Ipswich, and Watertown.

Settlement in Winnacunnet progressed rapidly after the second grant. House lots were apportioned by a committee appointed by the Massachusetts General Court. Within a year a sufficient number of settlers had arrived to warrant the convening of a formal town meeting, the basic instrument for community organization according to Massachusetts law. Meanwhile a church had been established under Batchellor's leadership. The presence of both civil and religious institutions in an area well suited to the raising of cattle and planting of crops attracted still more planters. Soon about sixty families were engaged in the task of building homes and clearing fields. Hampton—the name had been changed at the request of Batchellor—had become the fourth major plantation between the Merrimack and Piscataqua rivers.

In 1640 the term "New Hampshire" had little or no meaning for the inhabitants of the four plantations. Many probably knew that Captain John Mason had used the name to identify territory included in one of his many patents, but few cared about the legal status of that or other patents granted by the Council for New England. The Council no longer existed, Mason had died, and crown officials were so busy trying to resolve England's internal problems that imposition of effective royal authority in New England seemed unlikely. What did concern the settlers were the conditions which affected their own efforts to establish a satisfactory pattern of existence in the New World. Experience thus far had not been reassuring. They had crossed the Atlantic in pursuit of prosperity and social stability, yet encountered economic frustrations, new forms of religious conflict, and constant bickering in matters involving government jurisdiction and community control. Many, like Ambrose Gibbins and John Wheelwright, had already moved several times in search of a better life. What the future would bring they could not be certain.

3

COMMUNITY DEVELOPMENT, 1640–1680

Contemporary Americans like to think of their early colonial ancestors as rugged individualists willing to risk property and life to free themselves from the arbitrary restraints of European society. In some ways the image is accurate: planters in the New World did have to be rugged to survive, they risked a great deal by migrating, and the majority, at least in New England, sought freedom from what they considered the growing oppressiveness of Anglican Church authority. But in equally important ways the image distorts reality. Seventeenth century Englishmen did not think of themselves as individualists. Life for them had little meaning other than in the context of established order. Preoccupation with the maintenance of such order influenced every dimension of their personal relations, especially in America where they found themselves cut adrift from many familiar norms and institutions. Moreover, the first planters were decidedly unromantic about their relationship with nature. They felt surrounded by a "howling" wilderness of dark forests filled with pagan, warlike, and uncivilized savages. The only way to preserve "civilized" life was to create as quickly as possible forms which would promote the order they sought.

For New Hampshire's earliest European settlers, the town served as the basic unit of community organization beyond the family. In the decades after 1640 the newcomers first transformed their plantations into towns modeled on similar institutions in neighboring Massachusetts. They labored constantly to shape relationships within and among the towns to make living in a strange land less hazardous and burdensome. Their goals were effective governance, economic prosperity, and stable social and religious institutions. In some ways the settlers failed, but their efforts at community building proved successful enough to provide a basic foundation for the later development of colonial New Hampshire.

Effective governance was sought on two levels. The first concerned local institutions and involved the transition from unstable ad hoc communal "combinations," most of which had been controlled by special interest groups, to more permanent, formal, and broadly representative town governments. At the same time settlers had to come to terms with Massachusetts magistrates who had long been eager to extend their jurisdiction northward. It took more than a decade of maneuvering for mutually satisfactory arrangements to be made, but by the mid-fifties the task was complete. The resulting system of authority left townsmen in almost complete control of community affairs, yet free to seek Bay Colony assistance when circumstances warranted.

Several developments helped make possible the formation of orderly local government. The conflicts of the thirties had left everyone involved both exhausted and worried lest political factionalism erode their capacity to survive in the New World. Settlers in Dover, Exeter, and Strawberry Bank observed with envy the apparent harmony of Hampton as well as other towns to the south, and became increasingly attracted to the idea of obtaining formal town recognition from the Massachusetts General Court. External migration was important, too. Although a few additional Anglicans arrived from England, most immigrants came from Plymouth or the Bay Colony. The newcomers were devout Puritans with considerable experience in the exercise of town government. A new set of attitudes toward Piscataqua on the part of Massachusetts authorities also made change inevitable. In the late thirties Winthrop and his associates had been cautious, fearful that pursuit of their territorial and jurisdictional ambitions might enhance Archbishop Laud's campaign against the company. They also hesitated to support plantations controlled, at least in part, by anti-Puritan social renegades. By the early forties, however, Bay Colony magistrates felt less constrained. Preoccupied with internal problems, Laud and his allies in England had no time to bother with overseas plantations. Moreover, the influence of Puritan sympathizers at Piscataqua appeared to be increasing. The General Court members therefore felt free to assume whatever degree of authority over the Piscataqua plantations that wisdom dictated and local sentiment supported.

Settlers in the territory owned by the Shrewsbury investors moved first. An initial application to the General Court was made in 1639 by a committee representing the Underhill-Knollys faction in local politics, but the Court refused to act. The next year a competing group including Anglicans, a few Puritan émigrés, and for unexplained reasons Knollys himself, took matters into their own hands by organizing a formal "combination for government" and sending it to England for approval. Their action elicited an immediate response. Encouraged by Wiggin and others, the Shrewsbury patentees formally transferred their civil authority to the Bay Colony because, they wrote, inhabitants in the patent had complained repeatedly "of the want of some good government amongst them and desired some help in this particular from . . . the Massachusetts Bay, whereby they may be ruled and ordered according unto God in both church and commonwealth." The Court needed no further urging. Late in 1641 it accepted responsibility for government in all the territory west of Piscataqua with the exception of Exeter, and after negotiations with a new committee, erected the town of Dover (also called North-ham) defined to include both Hilton and Bloody Points. As part of the bargain, Massachusetts excluded Dover from regulations which limited freemanship (the right to vote and participate in governmental affairs) to members of the Puritan church. The exemption, together with the failure of the home government even to respond to the request for recognition of the earlier "combination," led to the grudging acceptance by Anglicans of the new arrangement. Dover had joined Hampton as a legally recognized Massachusetts town.

Exeter soon joined the fold. By the early 1640s, John Wheelwright's holy experiment in community development was in trouble. The original form of government still existed, but Wheelwright's influence over local decisions had been steadily eroded by the influx of new settlers and his own insistence on the maintenance of religious purity. Matters came to a head in 1643. Two groups, one led by Wheelwright and one by his antagonists, submitted separate petitions to the Massachusetts government for admission as a town. After lengthy discussions in which it became clear that the majority of residents opposed their pastor, the General Court rejected the Wheelwright petition, accepted the other, and in a gesture of reconciliation appointed as temporary town officials the few original inhabitants who had signed both petitions. The decision went a long way toward the restoration of harmony. It placed men of moderation in power and so infuriated Wheelwright that he gathered his disciples about him and left to found a new community near what is now Wells, Maine.

That left only the inhabitants of Strawberry Bank and nearby settlements on Great Island and the Atlantic Ocean without Massachusetts-sanctioned local governments. The situation seems initially to have bothered no one seriously. Although the General Court claimed jurisdiction and in 1643 included the area in newly-formed Norfolk County, it exhibited no further inclination to force itself on a population of settlers known to oppose its authority. The inhabitants themselves adopted a variety of informal combinations for self-government, through which Warnerton, Williams, and their allies at the Bank continued to manage local affairs.

In the mid-forties, however, patterns of government began to change. Warnerton was killed, probably in a drunken brawl while marketing some of Mason's goods at the French settlement of Fort Royal, and Williams either died or left. New leaders soon emerged, including John Pickering, former Laconia Company employees Henry Sherburne and Renald Fernald, and two merchants, John and Richard Cutt, who decided to move their trading activities from the offshore islands to the mainland. The new groups exhibited no sudden inclination to seek recognition from Massachusetts, but they did avoid open conflict and themselves organized an informal "town" which confirmed land grants, issued permits for cutting trees, and generally assumed civil authority.

Union with Massachusetts resulted from an unexpected internal political crisis. About mid-century Joseph Mason, a kinsman of Captain John and agent for his widow Anne, sailed for America to investigate the status of the family's New World estate. He soon discovered that the property had all but disappeared. The lands at Newichawannock were occupied by Richard Leader, who once had run the iron works at Saugus for the Massachusetts Bay Company but more recently had moved north, erected a large sawmill, and begun supplying timber for Piscataqua's growing export trade in forest products. The situation at

Strawberry Bank and Great Island shocked Mason even more. The cattle and stock-in-trade had been stolen, the tenants either had fled or insisted that family claims in New Hampshire were invalid, and most of the buildings erected in the thirties had been dismantled. Mason reported simply that he could find "nothing left but the bare lands and the monuments of ruin." Then he sued for recovery of the family estate in the highest judicial body available, the General Court of Massachusetts.

Joseph Mason's activities placed local residents in an uncomfortable position. Should the General Court decide for Mason, an unlikely but still possible development given past history, they would lose title to the land they occupied. When the Court responded positively to Mason's request that Leader's seizure of Newichawannock be declared illegal, Sherburne, Fernald, and their associates decided to move. In October 1651, they drew up a petition which noted Mason's presence, asked that Massachusetts either protect existing land titles or stop claiming jurisdiction over Piscataqua, recommended the laying out of a new township to include both the Bank and Great Island, and suggested that if the General Court in its wisdom chose to comply it should erect a local court to handle increasing problems of social disorder. The petitioners suggested persons who might qualify as judges, and selected Bryan Pendleton, a recent émigré with good connections in the Bay Colony to present their case. After lengthy negotiations and a last ditch effort by the disappointed Mason to prevent the petition's acceptance, the General Court gave its approval. It recognized the town of Portsmouth, which was defined to include all the territory south of the Piscataqua not part of Dover, Exeter, or Hampton, and passed a law which validated local land titles in existence five or more years and established the proposed court. About the same time residents on the Isles of Shoals agreed to a similar settlement and received a grant of town privileges. The decisions seem to have pleased just about everyone involved, except, of course, Mason. Massachusetts leaders congratulated themselves for having gained local acceptance of their jurisdictional claim to all the Piscataqua, and the inhabitants looked forward to developing both their property and their community institutions without fear of further external interference.

Thus by the middle of the 1650s settlers in the various New Hampshire plantations had adopted, with the help of Massachusetts, the town as the model of local government. The model proved highly successful. To begin with, it facilitated the process by which communal leaders were chosen and had their responsibilities defined. Each year townsmen gathered to elect officers. Although the franchise was limited to "freemen," a designation the precise qualifications of which were determined by the individual towns, freemanship was sufficiently wide-spread to give community residents the feeling that they controlled their own affairs. The towns had dozens of officers, each assigned specific tasks in accordance with Bay Colony laws and, as time passed, with local tradition. Perhaps most important, annual elections made possible the removal of any moderator, selectman, fenceviewer, constable, or other official who appeared corrupt or delinquent in the exercise of his duty.

The system also proved economical. In the old country a sometimes bewildering array of local taxes and fees had eroded individual and family income. The mechanics of town government tended to prevent this from happening again. Town meeting participants could reject any proposed expenditure not in accord with majority sentiment. Basic town expenses were kept minimal, since officials received no pay and towns "financed" most community projects by assessments in labor. For example, individual inhabitants were assigned responsibility for erecting and maintaining sections of the fence surrounding common fields and were expected to help in building the local meeting house and clearing town paths and roads. Taxes in cash or kind were few and in most cases were levied proportional to wealth.

Another benefit of town organization was an increased sense of physical security. Disease, natural disasters, or Indian attacks might occur at any time. Local officials could not prevent the first two, but they could and did afford help to individuals and families when trouble occurred. They made certain that those short of food received some from others with a surplus, and at a fair price; they organized relief for victims of fire and flood; and they assumed responsibility for cripples, old people, or children without families. As for Indian attacks, effective government reduced their likelihood. Town meetings passed regulations outlawing the sale of liquor to natives, and town magistrates arbitrated disputes involving natives. Most important, the town served as the basis for military organization and training. Every able-bodied male in each community became a member of the militia and was required by law to train regularly. Although such training was sporadic because of the generally peaceful relations with the few natives near Piscataqua—the only attacks occurred during King Philip's War—the militia continued to provide local self-protection.

Finally, town meetings and frequent informal contact between settlers and their elected officials provided a forum for resolving everyday community problems. When townsmen in Exeter became concerned about the potential depletion of timber resources, they passed restrictions on the cutting of oak and pine. A series of injuries to men and animals accidentally falling into uncovered saw pits resulted in regulations which reduced the danger. All four towns established ground rules for the distribution of common land, controlled the use of mill sites, and employed the instruments of town authority to preserve communal harmony. To be sure, disputes arose and mistakes were made, but the system proved sufficiently flexible to permit adjustments. Unpopular regulations could be forgotten or changed, and individuals with legitimate complaints usually received a sympathetic hearing. It is, in sum, not surprising that in the years after 1640, virtually all settlers in what soon became New Hampshire developed a strong commitment to the basic system of town governance.

Attitudes toward the civil authority exercised by Massachusetts were more varied. To a large extent, location and religion determined sentiment. Hampton's predominantly Puritan inhabitants thought themselves well served by Bay Colony jurisdiction, as did the citizens of Dover, where the leading resident, Richard Waldron, eventually became Speaker of the General Court. Exeter remained more aloof, in part because the terms of its "union" necessitated little formal involvement with Massachusetts. The greatest dissatisfaction existed in Portsmouth and the offshore islands, both of which contained a number of professed Anglicans and others generally ill-disposed toward interference in local affairs by their southern neighbors.

Conflicting attitudes toward "union" did not, however, alter the basic fact of Bay Colony jurisdiction over the region. The General Court had exempted some towns from specific laws defining freemanship and promised to use taxes collected in the area for local purposes but accepted no further limitations on its authority. It expected town officials to enforce properly enacted laws and tried to exercise even more direct influence through control of appointments to county courts.

Piscataquamen, understandably, battled to enlarge their own role in determining the outcome of deliberations in both the county courts and the General Court. More often than not they got what they wanted.

At the county level one thing Piscataqua residents wanted was local men on the bench. To a large extent laws and traditions defining the composition of county courts guaranteed such representation: each court included at least one General Court member (called the magistrate) and several associate judges who normally were chosen from among leaders in the area under court jurisdiction. Hampton settlers, for example, had been lumped with Salisbury and Haverhill in the act of creating Norfolk County and submitted their complaints to a court which contained a judge from each town. The lawmakers had also been wise enough to provide Dover and Strawberry Bank inhabitants with separate courts, which not only freed litigants from the burdens of lengthy travel to the county seat at Salisbury but recognized past animosities between the two plantations. The arrangement worked well as far as associate judges were concerned. The Hiltons, Wiggin, Gibbins, and later Waldron served in Dover and men of similar prestige at the Bank. In fact at one point in the early forties the General Court became so eager to establish a reputation for sympathy to local wishes that it even appointed Warnerton an associate, an action which no doubt elicited a few guffaws on his part. The requirement for a magistrate on the local court did cause problems, but not for Piscataquamen. Magistrates had to be drawn from among the assistants in the General Court, who were few in number and overworked; although appointed, they often failed to attend. That left the associates free to make decisions on their own and gave them a ready-made defense should they be accused of illegality. Massachusetts eventually stopped appointing magistrates and grudgingly acknowledged the virtual autonomy of the Piscataqua courts it had created.

Under these circumstances the courts functioned well. They settled minor boundary disputes, arbitrated dozens of civil suits involving claims of twenty pounds or less, ordered the incarceration of troublemakers and in general assisted the towns in preserving social and political order. Perhaps the most famous case involved an accusation of witchcraft made against a Portsmouth woman, Jane Walford, which was brought before associates Pendleton, Sherburne, and Fernald in 1656. They proceeded cautiously in the matter, and may well have been responsible for the eventual withdrawal of the complaint. In any case, when Walford later sued for defamation of character, the court awarded her five pounds damages and costs. The decision, like the court structure as a whole, met with broad community approval.

Piscataquamen had less direct involvement with the other major institution of Massachusetts governance, the General Court. Distance from Boston, the effectiveness of local government, and reluctance to become dependent on outsiders all contributed to an attitude which bordered at times on indifference. Exeter had no deputy in the General Court and never petitioned for one. Residents at the Bank were extended the right to representation early in the forties, a right reconfirmed in the negotiations which created the town of Portsmouth, but before the mid-sixties they rarely elected anyone. The men chosen after that date missed more sessions than they attended. Dover's habit of sending delegates regularly was the product mainly of Richard Waldron's political and economic ambitions, not broad community interest in colony politics. Among the four towns only Hampton seems to have assumed much fundamental responsibility toward the central government.

Despite the low level of interest in Massachusetts affairs, citizens not infrequently found it useful to ask the General Court for help in solving specific problems. Such requests normally involved minor matters. Area residents at one point obtained a law assigning marks to the individual towns for the purpose of identifying livestock. In 1658 a group of Portsmouth petitioners asked that an ad hoc group be established to settle a local land dispute in which the county judges had a vested interest. The General Court complied by asking the petitioners to choose one member, their opponents a second, and the Dover court a third. Occasionally town officials requested confirmation of their authority to settle disputes, or townsmen sought redress from what they considered unjust decisions at the local level. Individual New Hampshiremen also tried to influence the militia and judicial appointments made by the General Court.

By far the most important requests for assistance involved a single set of closely related problems: the unresolved conflicts over land ownership which remained from the first decades of settlement. The conflicts were of two types, those triggered by the efforts of the Mason family and purchasers under the Hilton patent to assert their rights to New World land, and those resulting from disagreements among

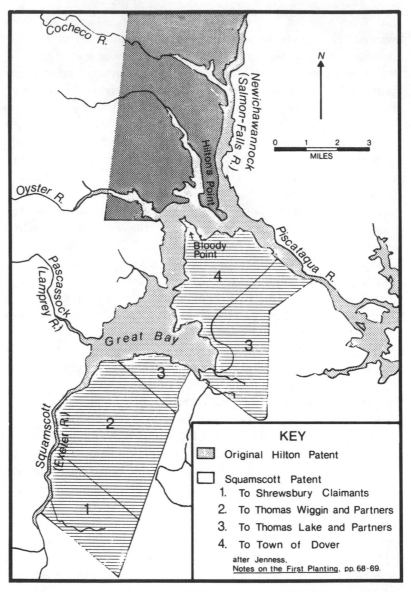

Boundary settlement stemming from the dispute over the Hilton and Squam-scott patents.

the four towns. Neither type of conflict could be handled satisfactorily by the town and county institutions of governance, for the stakes were too large and many local officials were themselves claimants. With the government at home disrupted by the Puritan Revolution the General Court offered the only possibility of making decisions that somehow had to be made. No settler wanted to spend a lifetime developing property without the security of a valid land title. Furthermore, most Piscataqua residents suspected that as far as land titles were concerned their interests coincided with the interests of Massachusetts magistrates. Both groups sought communal harmony and both disliked the idea of trans-Atlantic interference in their affairs. The suspicions proved correct. By the sixties the General Court had worked out a series of compromises satisfactory to the vast majority of regional inhabitants.

Few argued with the decisions regarding property rights of the Mason family. Joseph Mason and his supporters had threatened to dispossess homeowners not only at Strawberry Bank, but at Exeter and Dover as well. Indeed, he once posted public notices in the three plantations warning residents that they occupied land owned by Anne. Passage of the five years law by the General Court ended the threat for most, and the formal organization of Portsmouth made clear that townsmen throughout Piscataqua would control the future distribution of land. Even Mason himself could applaud some of the Bay Colony actions. The family received confirmation of its title to the mills at Newichawannock (and, by implication, to property it had improved elsewhere in the patent) and retained a residual claim to all ungranted lands in New Hampshire, a claim which subsequent heirs of the Captain pursued with some vigor. There is also some possibility the nomenclature "Portsmouth" was chosen to mollify Mason, for the family seat remained in the English city of the same name. Joseph's response to the entire package is not clear but he can't have been too offended. Soon after he received news of Anne's death he made peace with community leaders, took up residence in the area, and remained for more than a decade.

Disposition of the claims made under the Hilton patent took an entirely different course. Various claimants succeeded in efforts to gain firm title not only to the original grant but to a second area equally large. They did so largely through calculated cooperation with Massachusetts, careful manipulation of settler sentiment, and a series of negotiated compromises with the inhabitants of Strawberry Bank.

By the early 1640s the original patent obtained by Edward Hilton already had an elaborate history. Purchase by the Shrewsbury Puritans was only part of the story. Soon after the sale, Thomas Wiggin and his friends in Massachusetts conjured up a scheme to double the area claimed under the patent: they asserted that Great Bay and the Squamscott River, not the Newichawannock, constituted the main tributary of the Piscataqua, and they interpreted Hilton's grant to include not only the land surrounding the point where he lived, but a separate Squamscott patent to most of what is modern Newington, Greenland, and Stratham. A complex set of transactions during the thirties involving land in both areas left the validity of specific titles much in question. Thus, when the Shrewsbury patentees transferred civil jurisdiction to the General Court of Massachusetts the Court members assumed responsibility for arbitrating a number of territorial disputes.

It took more than a decade to satisfy all parties concerned. Settlers at Hilton's Point were told that the best way to confirm titles to the land they claimed would be formal union with Massachusetts, a suggestion that undoubtedly increased local support for the idea. But the creation of Dover, which was defined to include the property originally purchased by Hilton and his associates, did not resolve disputes stemming from land sales in the southern or Squamscott patent. During the forties and early fifties four parties emerged as major claimants. Dover inhabitants who had moved across the bay to Bloody Point (Newington) demanded inclusion of the land they settled within the limits of Dover. The other three claimants were a group led by Wiggin, a partnership managed by Thomas Lake, and a party of Shrewsbury men. After long and often bitter negotiations, agents from the General Court worked out an acceptable agreement. Bloody Point's linkage with Dover was confirmed, Wiggin and the Shrewsbury men divided land roughly conforming to modern Stratham, and the Lake partners accepted the remainder, which included much of present day Greenland as well as a strip between Bloody Point and Portsmouth. The members of the Lake group then sold most of the strip to town leaders at Strawberry Bank. By the end of the fifties controversies involving the Hilton and Mason patents appeared resolved.

Meanwhile the General Court had helped engineer a series of compromises which established precise boundaries for the four towns, a task made relatively easy by the abundance of unsettled land north of the Merrimack. Early in the forties the magistrates drew a line due west from a point three miles north of the river mouth to define Hampton's southern border. The recognition of Dover and Exeter led to an informal agreement, apparently negotiated by Wiggin, to have the Lamprey River separate the two towns. In 1652 Dover's northern limit was extended four miles above the falls at Newichawannock. Nobody felt the need to determine precise western limits to these towns, because fear of Indians and dependence on water transportation made inland settlement a remote possibility.

Only in one area did the determination of boundaries become difficult. The claims of the Squamscott patentees, the towns of Hampton and Dover, and settlers in the Strawberry Bank area overlapped at several points on the "neck," land south of the Piscataqua River and east of its Great Bay tributary. Conflict among Anglicans, Puritans, and those indifferent to church affiliation complicated the problem, as did memories of earlier troubles between Massachusetts authorities and residents in the area. The General Court moved slowly. It waited until the formal founding of Portsmouth to determine Hampton's northern border, then consulted deputies from both towns before deciding the issue. Sale of the strip by Lake and his partners clarified the southern boundary of the Bloody Point portion of Dover. The Court decided that the rest of the Squamscott patent should be part of Portsmouth, a decision in part dictated by the desire to isolate in one community dissenters from Massachusetts religious orthodoxy. That left one minor problem. Thomas Wiggin found himself a resident of Portsmouth, a situation he disliked for both political and religious reasons. Since Wiggin remained one of the Bay Colony's strongest supporters in the area, the General Court simply declared his extensive holdings part of Hampton. The boundaries of the four towns, with minor adjustments, remained fixed for the rest of the seventeenth century.

Cooperation with Massachusetts, then, played a key role in the process through which settlers ironed out their disagreements over land ownership. The ability to resolve such disputes amicably reflected a more general phenomenon, the gradual development in the years after 1640 of an effective pattern of governance in the area later set apart as the colony of New Hampshire. The presence of mutually reinforcing town, county, and colony authorities provided both the strength necessary to preserve order and the flexibility needed to adapt to New World conditions. Most residents, moreover, recognized their good fortune. When the citizens of Portsmouth in 1669 noted the "peace and quietness" of the times and the "favorable aspect of the government" since union with Massachusetts, they expressed sentiments widely held in the Piscataqua.

The settlers needed more than effective government to make their experiments in community building successful. Although personal motives for migrating to New Hampshire varied, just about everyone shared one aspiration: the desire to become economically secure, perhaps even prosperous. As individuals, families, and communities, the newcomers expected to work hard, to acquire and improve property, and in general to exploit the region's economic potential. The results of their efforts were impressive in absolute terms, even though Piscataqua's economic growth lagged far behind that of Massachusetts, New York, and Virginia. By 1680 population had reached more than 2,000, several residents had accumulated moderate fortunes, and the majority had attained an economic security unknown in the first decades of settlement. The area as a whole enjoyed self-sufficiency in agriculture and benefitted from rapidly expanding commercial activities.

Farming was organized on both a communal and an individual basis. Cooperative agriculture prevailed initially, especially in Exeter and Hampton. Town leaders designated certain areas—open land close to the village settlement when possible—as common fields. Although individuals tended specific plots within each field, many agricultural activities were community affairs. Everyone planted and harvested at the same time and was assigned responsibility for erecting and maintaining some portion of the fence used to protect crops from foraging animals. Officials made sure that the fences remained solid, that seed was kept for the following year's planting, and that citizens helped each other when grain shortages arose. Towns exercised similar control over the raising of livestock, an enterprise made attractive by the presence of numerous salt marshes. Animals were branded with the town symbol as well as the symbol of the individual owner. Local officials assigned pasturage, hired men to tend community flocks, and determined "stinting" privileges. The latter defined the number of animals each inhabitant could graze on the stubble left in common fields after harvest.

As time passed, however, community controlled agricultural production became less and less important. There had always been a few individual farms, some established by planters who purchased from agents of the various patent holders, others by men who simply squatted on land they found attractive. The success of several such enterprises, the realization that Indians posed little military threat, and the pressures of population growth all contributed to the gradual dispersion of settlement everywhere in the Piscataqua. Individuals sought and gained ownership of land distant from the fields where earlier they had labored in common. They felled trees, built either lean-tos or log cabins and eventually small frame houses, expanded the acreage under cultivation, and raised cattle, oxen, and hogs. Independent farms soon became the norm rather than the exception. Those who found opportunities limited in the villages moved out, thus making possible the consolidation of property holdings within the original areas of settlement. It is not clear how far this process had progressed by the time the English government made New Hampshire a royal colony, but the adjustments that had been made certainly helped increase agricultural output.

Meanwhile other forms of economic activity developed in the Piscataqua area. Town inhabitants could grow their own grain, but they needed mills in which to grind it. Permanent houses could be constructed much more efficiently if someone assumed responsibility for sawing the plentiful timber into usable boards and planks. From the beginning, therefore, community leaders encouraged the development of mill sites. In 1647, for example, Exeter granted land and water rights to Edward Gilman who, in return, engaged himself "to let the townspeople have what boards they need for their own use in the town at three shillings a hundred and what two inch planks they shall need for flooring at the same price"; other mill privileges were soon granted. In the late 1650s Portsmouth signed an agreement with two citizens to develop mills on South Creek and grind corn for the town in return for the right to cut timber from the commons. In some cases the initiative for establishing nonagricultural enterprises came more from ambitious groups of individuals than from town officials seeking to develop community services. Dover contained perhaps a half dozen sawmills within a generation of its founding, more than were needed in production of goods used locally. Both the Isles of Shoals and Dover had breweries which no doubt lent support to the reputation Warnerton and his associates had given the Piscataqua region. There is some evidence that Dover residents also ran a small tannery and a shipyard capable of building small frigates. One such vessel reportedly was constructed before mid-century.

Growth in agricultural production and the construction of mills led inevitably to a gradual increase in trade with those who lived outside the four towns. To a limited extent commerce with natives continued. Warnerton marketed stores among Abenaki tribes along the coast of Maine, as did other Portsmouth entrepreneurs. Richard Waldron and Peter Coffin, both of Dover, were the most successful traders. Supported by the Massachusetts government, they established a large trading post at Pennacook which remained active until Kancamagus led his people northward in the 1680s.

But trade with the natives never lived up to expectations. By mid-century it became clear to inhabitants of the four towns that demand for commodities easily produced in New Hampshire was far greater among their fellow Europeans. Some potential purchasers lived nearby. Norton's successful sale of Mason's livestock in the Boston area served as a model for others. Farmers in Hampton and, to a lesser extent, in Portsmouth and Exeter began shipping cattle and hogs southward where they were exchanged for cash or goods imported by Bay Colony merchants. Two other commodities found markets in the growing regional economy. Fish, either salted or dried at facilities on the Isles of Shoals and the mainland, was in heavy demand, especially during winter. Lumber products were exported to Plymouth, Boston, and Long Island Sound where local supplies began to run out by the 1660s.

The most lucrative markets, however, lay overseas. The third quarter of the seventeenth century witnessed rapid economic development in the West Indies. English and Dutch entrepreneurs produced increasingly large quantities of sugar, molasses, and other tropical commodities easily sold in Europe. New Englanders played a key role in this commercial expansion. They shipped fish and other foodstuffs to feed the Irish servants and African slaves. New Hampshire residents benefitted even more from the demand for forest products. Shingles, clapboards, barrel staves, and unfinished lumber cut from trees along the various Piscataqua tributaries could be sold for less in the islands than similar products produced from dwindling local forests. Several small ships constructed from Piscataqua oak and pine helped carry produce to and from the West Indies and provided employment for sailors who regarded Portsmouth or Dover as their home port.

At the same time trade directly with England and the European continent increased. The initial trade was largely in fish and was controlled by family groups on the Isles of Shoals. In the 1640s, the Cutt brothers and a few others began exporting lumber and naval stores as well as fish. The English-Dutch wars in the decades after mid-century gave the new trade an immense boost by making English shipbuilders at least partially dependent on New England for white pine masts and spars. By the 1660s naval stores had become such an important business that merchant houses in England became interested. One house sent over a representative, William Vaughan, who after assessing the situation married a daughter of Richard Cutt and quickly became one of New Hampshire's most successful businessmen. Community authorities assisted in developing the trade by passing regulations for the preservation of potential mast trees. Precise figures are unavailable, but it seems likely that during the 1670s about a dozen vessels loaded with naval stores left Piscataqua annually for delivery in England.

The expansion of regional and trans-Atlantic trade accounted in large part for a growing sense of economic optimism in the Piscataqua region. More than a few families and individuals lived primarily off the profits of trade or the wages paid by merchants and shipowners. Although most men and women continued to farm, to produce most of what they consumed, and to accumulate land in the expectation that their children would follow suit, they too benefitted from commerce. Land not needed for agriculture could be utilized for the production of timber and naval stores; fathers and sons could earn wages during the winter months by helping to cut and transport forest products; and trees once girdled, felled, and burned in the process of clearing land for farming could also be sold. The credits accumulated through indirect participation in regional and overseas trade enabled residents to purchase necessities not produced at home, ironware and firearms, for example, and occasional luxuries. In addition, all land values increased as economic opportunity attracted additional settlers; speculation in real estate provided still another means of augmenting the family estate. The mixture of agricultural and commercial activity thus provided New Hampshire townsmen with ample opportunity to expand their economic horizons.

"God has appointed mankind to live in societies first of family, secondly church, and thirdly commonwealth," a seventeenth century minister once wrote. Not all of New Hampshire's men and women considered themselves Puritans, but they shared the conviction that good communities were orderly communities and assumed that order could exist only within the framework of established social institutions. One of the reasons they sought effective government and labored so intensely to promote their prosperity was to create conditions in which desired social relationships could flourish. Past experience shaped their specific expectations. Like Englishmen in general, they hoped to form stable families and communities affording each person an established position according to a fixed set of standards: the "better sort" as measured by birth, wealth, ability, and moral conduct would assume responsibility for maintaining social order, all community members would obey rules and orders emanating from their superiors, and troublemakers would be reformed, denied the benefits of communal participation, or incarcerated. Religion served as a capstone to the entire arrangement. It provided the ground rules for measuring moral conduct, and provided an institutional framework, the church, through which social discipline could be exercised. The entire community could worship the Deity who ultimately determined the course of human events.

Social discipline had been difficult to maintain in the first quarter century of settlement. Families were the exception rather than the norm in the plantations founded by the Laconia Company, Mason, and Hilton, and by no means universal in Exeter and Hampton. Many of those whose status placed them in positions of authority, Neale, Gibbins, Warnerton, Underhill and Wheelwright, to site examples, moved on after a few years, thus leaving settlements without established leaders. The general pattern of migration, moreover, brought to New Hampshire men and women disinclined to accept the degree of social control exercised in communities elsewhere in New England, and created a religious mix of Anglicans, Puritans, and the unchurched. The various communal disputes of the thirties and early forties bear witness to the relative absence of an effective mechanism of social control, especially in Dover and the "neck."

Social disorder continued to plague communities in the region. Agents sent from Massachusetts to ride herd on the unruly inhabitants of the offshore islands complained about drunkenness, whoredom, and the general degeneracy of a population which included a large number of itinerant sailors and fishermen. Portsmouth experienced similar, though less serious problems. Unattached males looking for work came to Dover with such regularity that the town, in 1667, voted to fine inhabitants who kept boarders more than thirty days without informing the selectmen. Exeter once placed restrictions on employment of "foreigners," in part because their presence threatened the stability of community life. Population growth and the dispersion of settlement in all four mainland towns made it increasingly difficult for citizens to organize new communal institutions or to join in the activities of those already in existence. In addition, New Hampshire remained sufficiently remote from the center of Puritan authority to attract social and religious dissenters from both the Bay Colony and the Puritan regime in England. Their presence triggered a series of disputes which reminded townsmen that the maintenance of peaceable communities required constant vigilance.

Despite all this, social life in New Hampshire became increasingly stable in the years between 1640 and 1680. For one thing, an increasing percentage of the population lived within the framework of family discipline, where prevailing attitudes dictated that wives obey their husbands, servants their masters, and children their parents. Precise statistics are impossible to come by, but the broad pattern of change is clear enough. Adoption of the town form of government, the availability of land and certainty of titles, and commercial promise attracted men and women seeking a permanent location in which to raise their families. A new generation of children gradually reduced the earlier imbalance between males and females, thus further encouraging the formation of family units. Family relationships, moreover, proved valuable in the constant struggle to gain economic security. Sons and daughters cleared land, labored in the fields, and helped with the unending sequence of domestic tasks characteristic of agricultural life: bonds formed in childhood made brothers and other relatives reliable partners in trade. New World economic experience, in short, reinforced

A nineteenth century photograph of the Jackson family dwelling built in Portsmouth in 1664. The Jackson house is the earliest colonial structure still standing in New Hampshire. *Courtesy of the New Hampshire Historical Society.*

orthodox assumptions about the importance of family and guaranteed its effectiveness as an instrument of social control. The results were unmistakable: by the second half of the seventeenth century families dominated community life. One section of Dover counted fifty families among its two hundred and twenty inhabitants and used the count to justify its request for a separate minister. All four towns regulated the behavior of the few unmarried adults and used the judicial mechanisms of church and state to punish violations of family discipline. Even the Isles of Shoals were affected. There the combined influence of the Seeley, Kelly, Oliver, Cutt, and Endel families afforded the main element of stability to a set of social relationships which those concerned with community discipline considered most unsatisfactory.

The passage of time also allowed for the emergence of an indigenous group of community leaders. In many ways traditional criteria determined perceived success: men gained recognition and respect through occupation (ministers and magistrates were considered most important), family linkages, the acquisition of property, and the ability to serve effectively in communal roles. But additional developments helped shape the new elite. Since the Massachusetts government controlled appointments to a number of prestigious positions and influenced religious life in the Piscataqua, Puritans fared better than others in the competition for power. So did those who for whatever reasons proved flexible enough to adapt to the rapidly changing New World economic conditions. The restoration of the monarchy in England added a fresh ingredient to the mix, for it increased the political leverage of men whose ambitions had been frustrated by their reluctance to cooperate with Bay Colony authorities.

Local circumstances conditioned the specific processes through which patterns of community leadership developed. Most of the men who controlled affairs on the offshore islands were fish wholesalers who had established connections with merchants in Boston and England. In Portsmouth, the same group which filled the vacuum created by the termination of Masonian activities in the Piscataqua continued to make the best of their opportunities. The Cutt brothers, Sherburne, Pickering, Fernald, and Pendleton assumed political power after Warnerton died and retained it after union with Massachusetts. They served as deputies in the General Court and associates on the county court, gained election to town offices, received large grants in the distribution of community property, owned the local grain mills, and controlled much of Portsmouth's overseas trade. Immigration and death altered the composition of the group but not its nature. Elias Stileman, Nathanial Freyer, Richard Martyn, Thomas Daniel, William Vaughan, and the Reverend Joshua Moodey had become influential by the mid-seventies. Richard and John Cutt remained the most prominent figures, Daniel and Vaughan were married to Cutt daughters, and Moodey ministered to a Puritan church whose founding members included the Cutts, Stileman, Martyn, and Pendleton's son James.

A man, not a group, dominated in Dover. Richard Waldron, the scion of a well-to-do family of English Puritans, had purchased land from one of the Shrewsbury patentees in the mid-thirties and settled there permanently. Immensely able, forceful, and ambitious, he constructed mills, added to his land holdings, and gained control of trade with the Pennacooks; he may also have been responsible for organizing much of the shipbuilding activity for which Dover became locally famous. Waldron's influence in the community increased as rapidly as his personal fortunes. From the beginning he filled a number of local offices and sat on the county court. He first became a deputy to the Massachusetts General Court in 1654, served continuously for the next quarter century, and was chosen speaker several times. A man of uncompromising Puritan convictions, Waldron not only supported local religious life but used his economic and political power to ensure that others who did not share his convictions conformed to orthodox practices. By the 1670s the portion of Dover known as Cocheco had become something like Waldron's personal fiefdom, and citizens in the other areas of settlement rarely challenged his social authority.

Exeter and Hampton were more like Portsmouth. In the former the members of the Gilman and Hilton families skillfully exploited water power and timber resources to gain economic prominence, but enough others shared their success to prevent any single family or individual from dominating community affairs. Perhaps the most influential inhabitant was Samuel Dudley, the town pastor from 1651 to 1683, who exercised religious authority with judiciousness and sensitivity and also benefitted from the fact that his father, Thomas, had been a governor of Massachusetts. Hampton's elite included the Daltons, Husseys, Pages, Gerrishes, and Wiggins, all families with extensive land holdings, offices in town government, good Bay Colony connections, and

Puritan convictions. In both communities, as elsewhere in northern Norfolk County, political influence, intermarriage, and inheritance laws enabled the "better sort" to perpetuate their status from one generation to the next. And the "better sort," though they lacked the wealth and security of their gentry counterparts in England, gave the region a far more stable pattern of community leadership than had existed earlier.

The towns also managed to organize what most residents considered effective religious institutions. Effectiveness, from their point of view, had nothing to do with tolerance or the acceptance of diversity. It meant, in fact, just the opposite: the presence of an established church which exercised control over social life, served, along with town government as the focus of communal activity, and commanded the support of the entire citizenry. The town, not individuals, provided basic financing for the church; religious and political leaders both assumed that one of their main functions was to foster uniformity in belief and practice.

Efforts to create established religious order in the early plantations were far from successful. Lack of colonial commitment on the part of Leveridge, Burdett, Knollys, and Larkham, and conflicts between Anglican and Puritan settlers left Dover in chaos. The Reverend Richard Gibson, an Anglican, was employed at different times by both the Isles of Shoals and Strawberry Bank but so alienated the Massachusetts government that he found it wise to return to England. The first Puritan ministers who settled in the same communities fared no better. James Parker, for example, settled at the Bank in the early forties and even though he managed to trigger a short-lived spurt of interest in religious life, soon became discouraged and left. Most of the inhabitants, John Winthrop recorded in his journal, "fell back again in time, embracing this present world." Wheelwright's experience in Exeter paralleled that of Parker, the community simply refused to accept his continued religious and moral leadership. Even Hampton had its troubles. Stephen Batchellor, who helped found the community and came as its first minister, was dismissed in 1641 after confessing in public that he had tried to seduce a neighbor's wife. The virile old clergyman— he was eighty years old at the time of his dismissal—then began a series of lawsuits which continued to disrupt local affairs for more than a decade.

In time, however, conditions became more appropriate for the establishment of stable religious institutions in New Hampshire. The revolution in England and union with Massachusetts put Anglicans on the defensive and gave external support to those who wished to organize Puritan churches; migration from the south increased the number of such men and women steadily. Town governments provided apparatus through which meeting houses could be erected, ministers appointed, and taxes levied to pay ministerial salaries. Economic growth made taxes less and less burdensome, thus increasing the likelihood that they would be paid and that a popular minister would stay put. Good ministerial candidates for employment became available as Harvard College produced more and more graduates, a fact which town inhabitants acknowledged through generous donations to the institution. The emergence of a recognized social hierarchy also contributed to the development of stable religious institutions. Most members of the local elite were Puritans, and as individuals and families they stood to benefit from the preservation of a social order that established local churches would protect.

Hampton and Exeter experienced few problems after the early forties. The seacoast community replaced Batchellor with his less flamboyant assistant, Timothy Dalton, a man so committed to the town that he made it a major beneficiary in his will. A much sobered John Wheelwright, who had made peace with the Massachusetts government, returned from Maine to help Dalton in his declining years. When Wheelwright left to become the pastor in Salisbury, he convinced a young Harvard graduate, Seabury Cotton, to take his place. Cotton, the eldest son of Boston's famed clergyman, John Cotton, and the son-in-law of Governor Simon Bradstreet, was formally ordained soon after Dalton's death and served church and community well for the next half century. Hampton, as a result, gained a much envied reputation for social and religious harmony. So did Exeter under the leadership of Dudley. Although the town never supported its religious establishment as fully as its southern neighbor—Dudley sometimes found it difficult to collect his salary and at one point was embarrassed by a court suit accusing townsmen of "letting their meeting house lie open and common for cattle to go into"—no major religious conflicts disrupted community life.

Religious unity proved more difficult to maintain in Dover. The town continued to support the church which had been formed in the late thirties, erected a meeting house, hired a series of able ministers, and in general attempted to conform to existing religious norms, yet it faced two special problems. The first was the product of dispersed settlement. Bloody Point lay across Great Bay and so distant from the meeting house that residents had a ready excuse for not attending church services, an excuse they used with disturbing frequency. Oyster River settlers refused to pay taxes unless the town supported two ministers, one to serve their area. Although the town meeting in 1651 voted such a policy, a second permanent clergyman was never hired and the frustrated settlers eventually petitioned to become a separate town. Waldron then exacerbated tensions by using his influence with other members of the General Court to have the petition tabled.

Itinerant Quakers were the second problem. Massachusetts law provided stiff penalties against Quakerism, and magistrates enforced the laws with such vigilance that many friends sought refuge in the Piscataqua where dissenters from Puritan orthodoxy were more welcome. Some Quakers, especially those who moved across the river to Kittery, found what they sought, but three women who stopped in Dover did not. Waldron reported their presence to the General Court, received permission to punish them in accordance with current regulations, and did so by having them dragged behind a cart from town to town (he spelled out the exact route) and whipped in each. In a narrow sense the episode promoted religious harmony—the three women never returned—but a sufficient number of local residents disagreed with what they considered an unnecessarily brutal punishment to weaken respect for Puritan authority. Furthermore, a few other Quakers purchased land within the town boundaries, thus threatening renewed controversy.

In the long run, however, religious unity prevailed. Waldron finally realized that the community as a whole would benefit from a minister at Oyster River and accepted a compromise which exempted inhabitants in the area from the obligation to support the church at Dover's main settlement, providing they erected their own. The arrangement worked well for everyone involved. The Quaker problem neither disappeared nor became serious. The new arrivals kept their sentiments to themselves and agreed to pay taxes for support of the established Puritan church. Waldron, in turn, either had a change of heart or became so concerned about criticism of his past actions that he decided to leave well enough alone. From the mid-sixties on, he, the ministers, and other church leaders concentrated their energies on maintaining the quality of religious life among the orthodox majority.

Portsmouth leaders encountered even more serious obstacles in their attempts to establish a pattern of religious unity. The community, like Dover, contained several population centers, some nearly a half day's journey from Strawberry Bank. In addition, many inhabitants manifested little interest in any form of organized religious activity. Parker's hasty departure in the mid-1640s left the town without a resident clergyman and no one made a serious effort to replace him for the next decade. Union with Massachusetts stimulated the first internal efforts to obtain a settled minister. In 1656 leaders at Strawberry Bank, perhaps under pressure from the General Court, tried unsuccessfully to coax Dudley away from Exeter. Two years later they hired Joshua Moodey, a devout and energetic minister who agreed to preach regularly and to organize a formal church as soon as possible. Moodey, however, received only limited support. The outlying settlers appreciated his occasional visits but rarely travelled far to attend religious services. Many men and women at Strawberry Bank also hesitated to participate as fully in religious life as Moodey hoped. A full dozen years after his arrival in Portsmouth, Moodey had been unable to locate enough men of sufficient purity and conviction to found a church; at least twice he tried and failed.

Indifference was not the only factor limiting Moodey's influence. Portsmouth still contained men and women committed to the doctrines and ritual of the established Church of England and numerous others who, if forced to choose, preferred Anglicanism to Puritan congregationalism. For a time the situation caused no trouble: each family simply worshipped in accordance with its own convictions. But community leaders chose not to leave well enough alone. Soon after Moodey's arrival Anglicans were denied freemanship, and the Puritan controlled town meeting voted to outlaw some forms of Anglican worship. The men affected by these actions resisted as best they could. They refused to participate in Puritan services, informed associates in

England of their troubles, and when the home government sent a commission to investigate, signed petitions of formal complaint.

Yet the conflicts subsided, and Portsmouth gradually developed a religious life similar to that in the other three communities. Civil officials had been sufficiently frightened by the arrival of the commission to give up their campaign to impose religious orthodoxy on their fellow townsmen. Professed Anglicans, as a result, could worship as they pleased. Peaceful co-existence also worked to Moodey's benefit. Freed from the responsibility of trying to coerce or convert those who disagreed with him, the ambitious pastor could concentrate on establishing the church he so much desired. In 1671 he finally succeeded. A group of interested men held a series of meetings in which, according to Moodey, they read "each to other a reason of the hope that was in them, by giving account of their knowledge and experience that they might be satisfied one in another." Convinced of their mutual purity the group then successfully petitioned authorities in Massachusetts for formal church status.

The gathering and ordination which followed was the most impressive social occasion of Portsmouth's brief community history. Governor Leverett, several other Bay Colony magistrates, ministers from as far away as Boston, and a large crowd of local residents witnessed the ceremony which "embodied into a church by an explicit covenant" (Moodey's words) nine of the towns most respected citizens. The event was long remembered by those present, and for reasons of greater import than simple entertainment. The new church served as a fitting symbol of the entire process of civilizing the Piscataqua wilderness.

A half century after David Thomson established the first English settlement in what eventually became New Hampshire, the region contained four well-ordered and moderately prosperous communities. Formation of these communities was stimulated by the Old World tradition of town and village life, the example set by colonists in southern New England, Puritan religious ideals, and the practical need for cooperation in a constantly threatening environment. These same forces conditioned community development in Portsmouth, Dover, Exeter, and Hampton after their founding.

Towns retained their central importance in New Hampshire long after the 1670s, but as time passed their autonomy and control over individual lives eroded. The dynamics of erosion involved a complex group of changes the impact of which, for the most part, was gradual. One development, however, had an immediate and dramatic effect on community life. In 1679 imperial officials erected the royal colony of New Hampshire and created a provincial government to manage its affairs. Town and province soon came into open conflict.

4

THE ROYAL COLONY OF
NEW HAMPSHIRE

Late in 1677 a committee of the English Privy Council received "an Account of Land lying between Massachusetts and the province of Maine" from two agents appointed by the Bay Colony General Court. The "Account" described the region as "a small tract of land, which... by reason of the scantiness of its accommodations contains in it no more than four plantations or towns, the inhabitants whereof are but few in number and the generality of them of mean and low estates." Few citizens of Hampton, Exeter, Dover, and Portsmouth would have thought the description fair. From their perspective "accommodations" had improved constantly, perhaps even to a higher point than in the English villages many could remember leaving decades earlier. Two thousand men, women and children did not strike them as "few in number," nor did the general condition of individual estates seem "mean and low." The "Account," moreover, ignored completely the giant strides made toward the formation of civilized communities in the frontier wilderness.

But most of these same citizens would have forgiven the misrepresentation had they understood its purpose. The agents for the General Court were not trying to insult anyone. Quite to the contrary, they had written the "Account" as part of a carefully orchestrated campaign which had the full support of community leaders in the four towns. During the past eighteen months the home government had begun to express serious interest in the idea of separating the four towns from Massachusetts and placing them under a group of royally appointed officials. Only a handful of men, most of them Anglicans from Portsmouth, wanted that to happen. The vast majority were quite willing to admit weakness and poverty, if such admissions might help preserve the status quo.

Two closely related developments set in motion the series of events which made separation a real possibility. The first was the collapse of the interregnum government and subsequent crowning, in 1660, of Charles II, an Anglican monarch eager to increase the effectiveness of royal authority in America and decidedly unsympathetic to the growth of Puritan influence in northern New England. Renewed interest by the Mason family in its North American patents provided the second. Even before the restoration Robert Tufton Mason, the Captain's young and energetic grandson who inherited the rights to New Hampshire, had joined with agents of the Gorges and Godfrey families in petitioning parliament for relief from the usurpations of Massachusetts Bay in Maine and Laconia. The change in government encouraged Mason to pursue his interest still more aggressively. He and Edward Godfrey repeated their earlier plea, and Mason petitioned separately about his patent to New Hampshire. Royal officials, in turn, held a hearing on the petitions, a hearing which found these and other complaints about Massachusetts sufficiently convincing to recommend investigation. For that purpose the crown created a royal commission. Colonel Richard Nichols, an acquaintance of Mason, gained appointment as commission leader, and Samuel Maverick, a former Boston merchant with interests in New Hampshire and long standing grievances against the Massachusetts Bay government, was included in the membership. The commission received instructions to visit New England and "proceed in all things for the providing for and settling the peace and security" of the region. Soon thereafter, Mason deputized Nichols as agent for the family interests.

The commission members landed at Piscataqua in July 1664 and wasted no time in setting about their tasks. Discussions with established local leaders in Portsmouth and dissidents like Joseph Mason confirmed what they suspected, that Massachusetts had, in fact, assumed jurisdiction over settlements outside its charter boundaries. Nichols and his associates then took steps to undermine Bay Colony authority. They began by publicly announcing that the northern boundary of Massachusetts was a line drawn east and west from a point three miles north of the mouth of the Merrimack River, not, as the General Court had declared, three miles north of the headwaters of the river at the outlet of Lake Winnipesauke. Next the commissioners tried to drum up local support for the power they claimed as agents for both the crown and the original patent holders. In Maine they received sufficient encouragement to chance the formal appointment of a whole new set of local officials. The four towns in New Hampshire presented more difficulties. Maverick conducted hearings in Hampton, Dover, and Exeter, and learned first hand of the strong linkages between town residents and Massachusetts. Although Maverick told Nichols that he had been warmly greeted, it was clear to everyone that only Portsmouth contained a significant number of commission sympathizers. The commissioners therefore decided to move slowly. They asserted their authority by ordering the construction of harbor fortifications at Piscataqua and helped organize a campaign to petition for separation, but made no attempt to remove from power local and county officials appointed by the General Court.

That, however, was enough to spark a short-lived internal political crisis, at least in Portsmouth and Dover. The Cutt brothers, Stileman and Freyer, who served as selectmen in the former, panicked when they received orders from the commission and wrote immediately to Richard Bellingham, Governor of Massachusetts, requesting his "advice and counsel with all expedition upon what point of the compass it will be our safety to steer, so as not to hazard our allegiance to his Majesty, or our oathes" to Massachusetts Bay. They punctuated the letter with the plea "Haste! Post Haste!" The next day the same group reported further disruptions. The commissioners had presented in a public meeting a warrant for building the fortifications and lectured those attending about their independence from Massachusetts. Although the community remained about five to one against the intruders, support for their activities seemed to be growing: "our work," the Cutt groups concluded, "shall be to look up to God first, and yourselves nextly, for further direction." The response in Dover was similar. Waldron and his fellow selectmen agreed to let the commissioners present their warrant but argued against its acceptance and reported to Bellingham that the entire proceedings had been in violation of tradition and law because the commissioners had insisted that all adult males, not just freemen, be allowed to vote. Such "liberty," Waldron added, "we fear will be improved by our inhabitants in future meetings to our disturbances."

The petition campaign worried Puritan leaders as much as the fortification warrants. Abraham Corbett, a Strawberry Bank tavern owner who had been a vocal critic of local officials for some time, led the campaign. He collected signatures for two separate documents. One was from Portsmouth and complained that Moodey, the Cutts, Stileman, Freyer, and Pendleton not only "ruled, swayed, and ordered all offices, both civil and military, at their pleasure" but kept themselves in power by denying freemanship to Anglicans and distributing common land only to their fellow Puritans. The signers also asserted that they had not been allowed to receive the "common prayer sacraments" or rights of "decent burial" defined by English law. The second petition emphasized the unwanted intrusion of Massachusetts officials in the entire "eastward parts" and asked that the four towns be joined with Maine as a separate royal province. Corbett and his friends convinced a total of sixty-six men to sign either or both of the papers, quite enough to give pause to those whose authority was under attack. The lists, moreover, included men of known or suspected influence in England. The signature of Frances Champernowne, a nephew of Ferdinando Gorges who lived north of the Piscataqua in Kittery but owned a large estate called "Greenland" in the western half of Portsmouth, led both petitions. Edward Hilton also signed, as did a number of former Laconia employees and several young family heads engaged in overseas trade. All had connections with English merchants. Especially disturbing was the defection of Sherburne, Pickering, and Fernald's son Samuel, men who previously had acquiesced in union with Massachusetts. The petition campaign, then, seemed certain to cause further trouble. Already it had shattered the pattern of communal stability Puritan leaders had worked so hard to establish. Their only solace was the fact that no Hampton residents signed, and only five from Exeter.

Devising an effective strategy to combat the work of the commission proved difficult. At times the established authorities reacted with simple defiance. The Governor and Council of Massachusetts, for example, responded to the "Haste! Post Haste!" letter with specific advice to ignore the commissioners and refuse obedience to the warrant for building fortifications; later they had Corbett arrested for "tumultuous and seditious practices," then fined him and promised to keep him in jail until he posted bond for good behavior. The commissioners were never arrested but did encounter open hostility. Maverick complained of frequent insults and obtained depositions proving Richard Cutt had stated publicly of the commissioners that "a dagger should be put in their guts," or words to that effect. Generally the defiance was less overt. Nichols became so frustrated in his efforts to represent Mason that he turned the job over to Nicholas Shapleigh, a resident of Maine best known for his support of itinerant Quakers, and left for Boston. There his demands for information about Mason's property and an explanation of charter violations met, for the most part, with stony silence. The commissioners' final report described the behavior of Puritan authorities as "presumptuous," "refractory," "dilatory," and "impertinent."

But defiance constituted only part of the strategy. As tempers cooled and Puritans in both the northern towns and Massachusetts began to realize the potential seriousness of their plight, they decided to make gestures of compromise toward royal authority. The gestures took several forms. Cutt backed down and apologized for his remarks. The General Court passed resolutions proclaiming its loyalty to the crown, released Corbett, ordered the construction of fortifications at Piscataqua, and as a final act of good faith suggested to Joseph Mason that Massachusetts might support the family's claim to ownership of ungranted land in the four towns if the family, in turn, accepted Bay Colony governing authority in the area covered by the New Hampshire patent. Meanwhile community leaders had begun gathering evidence to counteract what they assumed would be a negative report from the commission. Signatures were collected in both Maine and New Hampshire on petitions of loyalty to Massachusetts Bay; those signing far outnumbered the sixty-six who had supported Corbett. Letters were written blaming the commission's own high handed behavior for the tensions evident throughout its visit. The General Court then made a packet containing the petitions, letters, and copies of its recent resolutions, and appointed agents to represent its case in England. There was nothing left to do but wait and hope for the best.

For those interested in maintaining the status quo, the best is exactly what happened. Neither Parliament nor the crown took any action. The plague, the great fire of London, and hostilities with the Dutch

so preoccupied the home government that the commission report and
petition for separation received little attention. Moreover, the attention
they did receive produced more criticism than approval. Lord Clarenden, the official most responsible for appointment of the commission,
had fallen from power and his successors felt they needed the support
of Massachusetts in defending overseas settlements from the Dutch.
The only group seriously interested in the commissioners' findings was
the Naval Board, whose members feared that the war would prevent
Denmark, an ally of the Dutch, from supplying further naval stores.
The Board held an inquiry to explore the possibility of developing
Maine and New Hampshire as alternate sources of supply, but lost
their enthusiasm after listening to testimony, provided mostly by
agents of Massachusetts Bay, which emphasized the area's limited production facilities and high labor costs, as well as the problems of
protecting mast ships from marauding Dutch seamen. The plan, which
Maverick may well have designed, was put aside.

The response of the government, in turn, gave Robert Tufton Mason
second thoughts about the wisdom of spending additional time and
money on the New Hampshire patent. Nichols had been unable to
accomplish anything as the family agent. His replacement, Shapleigh,
admitted that nothing could be done without crown confirmation of
the patent, and demonstrated more interest in his own future than that
of the Mason family. His one concrete suggestion involved the union
of Maine and New Hampshire under a government headed by, among
others, Nicholas Shapleigh. Joseph Mason's return to England in 1667
with first hand information about conditions in Piscataqua apparently
convinced Robert that he should shift tactics. He and Gorges tried to
peddle their patents to the Duke of Monmouth, who had expressed
interest in a New World fiefdom, but their assertion that £5000 in
rents could be collected annually in Maine and New Hampshire seemed
so obviously absurd that Monmouth rejected the proposal out of hand.
By 1671 Mason had become so discouraged he petitioned the crown
to trade his patent for the privilege of importing a small amount of
French wine duty free. Even that failed.

Meanwhile conditions in New England began returning to normal.
Most of the men who had supported the commission interpreted no
news as bad news and made whatever peace they could with their
antagonists. Puritan leaders breathed a collective sigh of relief, thanked

God for his protection, and renewed their declarations of loyalty to the crown. They also tried harder than before to avoid religious and political behavior which might lend additional credence to the accusations of corruption and disloyalty already on file in England. This mutual retreat from confrontation helped restore the general pattern of communal harmony disrupted by the arrival of the commissioners. Thus the first phase of the movement for separation ground to a halt.

The second and eventually successful phase began in 1672. Again, the prime movers were the royal government and Robert Tufton Mason. Charles II and his Privy Council reopened their campaign against Massachusetts after they learned that agents of the Bay Colony had expressed an interest in outright purchase of the Maine and New Hampshire patent. The Privy Council immediately ordered Gorges and Mason not to sell. It also drew up plans for another commission to visit New England, although renewed hostilities with the Dutch postponed implementation of the plans. The final termination of those hostilities in 1674 set the stage for more effective action. As part of a general administrative reform, the crown abolished the Council of Trade and Plantations which, under the Earl of Shaftsbury, had manifested decidedly pro-Puritan sympathies; and assigned responsibility for colonial affairs to a standing committee of the Privy Council itself. The new Committee on Trade and Plantations—soon dubbed the Lords of Trade—then announced an investigation into the entire state of governmental affairs in New England. Mason, to no one's surprise, was prominent among those expressing an interest in the impending investigation.

Mason's short term goal was royal confirmation of his title to New Hampshire, his long term goal the erection of a proprietary government over the four towns through which he would demand payment for land illegally seized in the past decades and develop a permanent source of personal revenue by renting unimproved land to new settlers in the area. Initially both goals seemed attainable. The Lords of Trade as well as the king himself had supported the development of proprietaries elsewhere in America. Mason had some influence with the Lords; he had also thought, as he later noted, that "the best and most wealthy" of New Hampshire's inhabitants wanted to separate from Massachusetts. The newly optimistic patent owner started by presenting an elaborate defense of his title to the government, a defense, incidentally, in which he grossly exaggerated the amount of money invested by his grandparents in their enterprise. When the document met with a favorable reception, Mason suggested that his ambitious and determined cousin, Edward Randolph, be appointed as commissioner to investigate complaints against Massachusetts. The Lords of Trade, mainly because no other candidates for the job appeared, accepted the suggestion. Mason then designated Randolph his personal agent, gave him instructions on how to proceed once he reached New England, and promised him ample rewards should the mission bear fruit.

In one sense the mission did, for Randolph encountered few difficulties in accumulating evidence that Massachusetts authorities had no intention of modifying their laws in accordance with the wishes and formal instructions of the royal government. In another sense, however, the trip to America proved disappointing. Randolph expected a warm reception at Piscataqua and received just the opposite. For one thing he found those who had organized support for Nichols and Maverick a decade earlier no longer helpful. Hilton had died, Corbett had left, and Champernowne refused to cooperate in part, perhaps, because his Portsmouth estate was now ably managed by Samual Haines, a devout Puritan and the deacon of Moodey's newly founded church. Equally important, King Philip's War had tightened the bonds of allegiance between inhabitants of the four towns and the government of Massachusetts. Everyone appreciated the military assistance recently provided by the General Court; they also knew that the infrequency of Indian attacks stemmed largely from the power and influence of Richard Waldron, one of the region's most outspoken advocates of Puritan hegemony. Randolph, as a result, could find few men to support either Mason or the idea of a proprietary, abandoned any plans he might have had to gather signatures on petitions for separation, and left the area. The changed nature of local opinion became even more apparent when Piscataqua residents were given the opportunity to petition for continued union with Massachusetts. The Portsmouth document, for example, contained the signatures not only of the Cutt brothers and their friends, but also of Pickering, Henry Sherburne's son John, and several others who earlier had asked for separation. All this undoubtedly convinced both Randolph, who arrived back in England in the fall of 1676, and Mason that they could not count on much American support for their scheme. Everything, therefore, depended on their capacity to influence the home government.

The two men went to work immediately. Randolph spent much of the winter drawing up a confidential and lengthy indictment of the Massachusetts government, an indictment he hoped would convince royal officials to seek an abrogation of the Massachusetts charter. Mason, for his part, pressed for a decision on the scope of his authority in New Hampshire. He also lobbied to make certain that Randolph's report received more attention than had the report of the Nichols commission. Mason discovered, much to his surprise, that the Lords of Trade wanted to pigeonhole the entire controversy. Apparently they had been convinced by agents from Massachusetts that Randolph was little more than an officious troublemaker. But the lords were not the only governmental group concerned with the colonies: the king, partly because he distrusted the lords, had asked a number of his closest advisors to serve on an ad hoc Committee on Foreign Affairs. Mason promptly turned to the Committee, which listened to Randolph's charges and ordered a formal hearing before the lords. Meanwhile the chief justices had promised a speedy ruling on the legality of the patents to Maine and New Hampshire.

Thus by the summer of 1677 it appeared as though the royal government would finally take action on the long standing conflict over land ownership and jurisdiction in the territory jointly claimed by Mason and Massachusetts. It is not clear what decisions the two cousins expected the justices and lords to make, but they must have been disappointed. The justices concluded that since Captain John Mason had never been granted the right to govern New Hampshire, his grandson's claim to a similar right had no validity. Power of governance, in fact, still lay with the crown. The decision quashed any hope for a proprietary. Equally important, the chief justices refused to rule on the matter of land ownership. Any such ruling, they asserted, must be made in New England courts where those who occupied the land in question could defend themselves. Mason was under no illusions about the meaning of the decision, for no presently existing Piscataqua court would accept his title. He might fare better if Massachusetts lost its influence over the area, but the lords also took care of that possibility. Although they listened to Randolph, they concluded his charges were exaggerated, refused to recommend proceedings against the Massachusetts charter, and said nothing about the seizure of power above the Merrimack.

Had Mason and Randolph accepted defeat graciously, there might never have been a colony of New Hampshire. But they didn't. Instead, they studied the decisions carefully, looked for openings to exploit, and devised a fresh strategy. The chief justices had ruled that the power of governance belonged to the crown, which could mean either the erection of a separate royal government in the area covered by the four towns or legalization of the status quo through a grant to Massachusetts of the authority it presently exercised. The former was clearly preferable, mainly because it would involve the creation of a number of offices and Mason felt certain he could influence appointments to those offices. The decisions of the Lords of Trade also left the two cousins room to maneuver. The lords had found enough substance in Randolph's charges to ask for a few minor changes in Massachusetts law. Randolph, predicting the General Court would ignore these requests, primed himself for a new round of accusations should his forecast prove correct and in the spring of 1678 informed the lords of his willingness to be of further service should they wish to reopen discussion of the "New England problem." By that time the Privy Council had received a petition from Mason and Gorges requesting a royal government for the territory included in their respective patents.

Fortunately, at least for Mason and Randolph, the various Massachusetts officials involved in the controversy did not know when to quit. The members of the General Court interpreted the lords' refusal to institute proceedings against their charter as proof of immunity to interference from the home government, and acted just as Randolph thought they would. The two Bay Colony agents in England, William Stoughton and Peter Bulkeley, went still further. In defiance of Privy Council orders, they helped negotiate the outright purchase of Maine from Gorges. Since the chief justices had acknowledged Gorges's right to government within his patent, the agents felt they could probably convince the lords to give Massachusetts formal jurisdiction over the four towns; the logic of geography, if nothing else, supported such a conclusion. Finally, Stoughton and Bulkeley obtained a copy of Randolph's supposedly confidential charges against the Bay Colony and demanded an opportunity to refute them directly. With both parties thus eager to renew hostilities and the fate of New Hampshire still undecided, the lords had little choice but to reopen hearings on New England. The lords may also have been influenced by naval officials still interested in preserving the forests of Maine and New Hampshire.

From the start, it was clear that Mason and Randolph had regained the initiative. The lords accused Stoughton and Bulkeley of stealing government documents, insisted that the purchase of Maine had violated, if not the law, at least the expressed intentions of the royal government, and seemed, according to the official minutes of the hearings, "very much to resent that no more notice" had been taken "in New England of those points which were so fairly, and with so much softness, intimated here to the agents." The end result was complete rejection of Stoughton and Bulkeley's petition requesting the extension northward of Massachusetts boundaries and a recommendation that *quo warranto* proceedings be instituted against the existing charter of Massachusetts Bay. Mason and his cousin could not have hoped for more.

At this point the interests of the two men temporarily diverged. Randolph sensed bigger game. He sought and obtained, after a personal appearance before the king, appointment to the newly created office of Customs Commissioner for New England, and began lobbying for a royal government in the entire territory covered by the commission. Mason congratulated his associate, but worried lest the idea of a separate jurisdiction for New Hampshire be forgotten in the movement for more general regional reform. Randolph's larger scheme, however, fell victim to a totally unexpected series of events. The so-called "Popish Plot" to assassinate Charles II disrupted the home government and triggered a wholesale reshuffling of membership on the various committees involved in colonial affairs. The Earl of Shaftsbury, who became President of the Privy Council as well as a member of the reconstituted Lords of Trade, used his heightened influence to engineer what amounted to a compromise settlement. Massachusetts would be given one more chance to mend its ways, but only within its charter boundaries; New Hampshire would be made an independent colony under its own royal government.

The plan took only a brief time to implement. In May 1679, the lords ordered Massachusetts to withdraw all officers from the four towns and summoned the gleeful Mason for consultation. The ensuing agreement accorded Mason much of what he sought: unimproved property in the original patent belonged to him, occupants of improved property would have to pay him six pence for each pound of annual income to obtain title to their land, and a royally appointed president and council would arbitrate disputes. But Mason did not get everything. The document establishing the new government, which passed the Great Seal the following September, specifically prohibited him from collecting back quitrents. It also indicated that royal officials had no intention of letting Mason control appointments in New Hampshire. The lords, in fact, solicited nominations from a number of sources, including a group of self-appointed "agents" from Massachusetts Bay and Plymouth, and decided to offer royal commissions to those already in positions of power. John Cutt would be offered the presidency; Waldron and five others selected from the established elites of the four towns were appointed councillors. The fate of Mason's land claims, then, would be in the hands of men known to oppose the idea of separation. Mason gained encouragement from one appointment, though. The Customs Commissioner for New England, Edward Randolph, would deliver the orders for erecting a separate government in New Hampshire and oversee their execution. In the context of threatened *quo warranto* proceedings against Massachusetts, a grudging acceptance of the orders seemed likely.

Subsequent events proved Mason correct. Randolph arrived in Portsmouth late that December, consulted briefly with Cutt, and convened the Council. The men attending found themselves trapped: acceptance of the commissions would facilitate the establishment of an external authority they did not want, and refusal might eventually cost them control over local affairs. Cutt, whom Randolph may have bribed by promising quick confirmation of his present land holdings, and John Gilman of Exeter decided to cooperate. Waldron led the opposition. The anxious Dover magistrate raced to Boston, the Reverend Moodey by his side, and was advised by leaders in the Bay Colony to resist. Upon his return home he convinced one other Council appointee, Portsmouth's Richard Martyn, to join him, and then went to work on Cutt and Gilman. The outcome remained in doubt for the better part of a fortnight, but Cutt finally forced the issue by publicly announcing his acceptance of the presidential commission. Waldron and Martyn then consulted with the ministers of the four towns, and after four days of prayer and debate, decided to offer a compromise. They would accept their commissions if Cutt and the other councillors promised to retain Waldron as head of the militia and designate him Cutt's "deputy." The latter office meant that Waldron would take charge should anything happen to the new president, a man whom everyone knew, in Randolph's words, to be "ancient and infirm."

That broke the deadlock. In mid-January the newly appointed royal servants of the crown took their respective oaths of office and set about the task of establishing a government in accordance with instructions from the crown. A few weeks later the members of the Massachusetts General Court announced acceptance of the change. "This Court," they resolved, "doth hereby declare that all commissions that have been formerly granted by the Colony of the Massachusetts to any person or persons that lived in the towns of Hampton, Exeter, Portsmouth and Dover are hereby withdrawn, and as to any future act made void and of no effect." For better or for worse, there now existed the royal colony of New Hampshire.

5

TWELVE YEARS OF TURMOIL

The new colony of New Hampshire was a risky undertaking for everyone involved. Authorities in England had no idea how well their attempt to strengthen imperial rule in a region dominated by Massachusetts would work. Virginia, the only other royal colony, had little in common with New Hampshire, and its apparent stability had recently been shattered by a series of internal rebellions. As for Robert Mason, his hopes for success had been compromised by the decision not to establish a full proprietary like the ones in Maryland, the Carolinas, and New York. The appointment as councillors of local men known to oppose validation of his land patent further exacerbated his anxiety. Those same local men and other inhabitants of the four towns were equally anxious. Who could tell what would transpire under the new arrangement?

Incompatible interests and the absence of established provincial institutions all but guaranteed that the first few years of New Hampshire's existence as a royal colony would be marked by political conflict. No one in 1680, however, could have predicted its intensity, complexity, and duration. Not only did Mason and local leaders work at cross purposes, but officials in England decided on an even bolder course of action than issuance of the Cutt commission implied. In 1682 they sent to New Hampshire a royal governor whose behavior alienated virtually everyone concerned with the new colony, and then they abolished the colony altogether as part of a short-lived experiment in regional governance known as the Dominion of New England. The Glorious Revolution in England and subsequent upheavals in Massachusetts and New York put an end to the Dominion; it also left the inhabitants of Portsmouth, Exeter, Dover, and Hampton uncertain about their future. Some wanted to rejoin Massachusetts, others to form their own combination, and still others to sit tight and await developments in England. The latter group prevailed, only to learn in 1692 that the new rulers had appointed as governor an English merchant who beforehand had purchased Mason's various patents to land in New Hampshire. The appointment promised still more conflict. All in all it was a period of extraordinary political turmoil.

From the start it was apparent that the Cutt commission would not prove an adequate vehicle for establishing effective royal authority in New Hampshire. The central problem was the composition of the Council. Cutt and Gilman may have had an initial disagreement with the Waldron faction about the wisdom of accepting appointment, but the disagreement stopped there. Once in office they took advantage of a loophole in the commission—a provision allowing the President and Council to appoint three additional councillors—by selecting political allies to fill the posts. All the new magistrates felt it their responsibility to see that the erection of royal government disturbed the status quo as little as possible. The status quo meant placing in positions of provincial and local control the same kind of men—Puritans with solid social and economic credentials—who had held office under Massachusetts, preventing Randolph from effectively enforcing his authority as the regional customs commissioner, and protecting land titles which Mason was sure to challenge. For the better part of two years the councillors were totally successful.

The terms of the commission made it easy for Waldron and his associates to accomplish the first of these tasks. They appointed all judges, justices of the peace, and militia officers. Within a few weeks they had issued commissions either to themselves or to other men they trusted. In addition, the councillors interpreted the commission in a manner which enabled them to gain total control of central authority within the colony. The document included a provision for a general assembly of elected deputies to assist the Council in framing a code of laws. Since imperial officials who drafted the commission had not been clear about the ground rules for enfranchisement, the councillors assumed that responsibility. They asked selectmen in the four towns for lists of nominees, then made the final choices themselves. Not surprisingly the voters, about half the adult male taxpayers, chose deputies sympathetic to the general goals of the Council members.

The tightness of the resulting system became evident when the

Council and Assembly met to erect a new legal code. The code, according to the commission, was to be derived from the set of English laws which Richard Chamberlain, a young friend of Mason who had been appointed Secretary to the Council, brought to Portsmouth. Chamberlain soon discovered the limits of his influence. When the councillors met they called in the Reverend Joshua Moodey for advice. Chamberlain objected both to the presence of Moodey, who in private correspondence he referred to as the "Arch Bishop," and to the minister's recommendations. It is not clear to what extent Cutt, Waldron, and Vaughan were influenced by Moodey, but it is clear they felt few compunctions about ignoring Chamberlain. The criminal code of laws they passed was copied almost verbatim not from English law, but from the strict Plymouth compilation of 1671. The civil code bore close resemblance to laws operative in Massachusetts. When the laws were sent to the Assembly for approval Chamberlain again pointed out the inconsistency between the proposals and the instructions in the commission. The Assembly, however, made few modifications. In fact, the deputies added insult to injury by announcing their disagreement with the whole idea of separation from Massachusetts. In conjunction with the Council, members then sent a letter to the king which referred to the "disadvantages likely to accrue to your Majesty's provinces and ourselves . . . by the multiplying of small and weak governments." They also informed the government of Massachusetts that they "should have heartily rejoiced" to remain under its jurisdiction.

Controlling Randolph necessitated even more open defiance of imperial intentions. By 1680 all of New England had become notorious for its unwillingness to abide by the various trade regulations and taxes, collectively labeled the Navigation Acts, passed by Parliament in the last quarter century. Merchants trading in the Piscataqua were no exception to the general rule. They ignored restrictions on the shipment of goods outside the empire, refused to carry required papers, and in general acted as though the region were what today would be called a "free port." One reason New Hampshire had been made a royal colony and Randolph had been assigned the dual role of delivering the commission and serving as customs commissioner was to make the Piscataqua a model for the effective administration of trade regulations throughout New England. The councillors, many of whom traded themselves, had no intention of letting the plan work.

For the better part of a year the Council members engaged in open warfare with Randolph and Walter Barefoote, his deputy. Randolph was informed that the government of New Hampshire did not recognize his commission and that he had no right to seize vessels in apparent violation of existing regulations. When vessels were seized—the number was somewhere between a half-dozen and a dozen—owners were urged to sue for trespass. In at least one case Randolph was found guilty and fined. Randolph and Barefoote, on the other hand, received little court support in their attempts to have captains and owners found guilty of customs violations. Randolph (who may not have been totally disappointed by what happened since part of his strategy was to gather evidence against Massachusetts in his long standing campaign to have the Bay Colony charter voided) soon quit and left for Boston. Barefoote, however, kept trying. Ordered by the Council not to set up office, Barefoote, a colorful and contentious individual who had long been at odds with the Puritan establishment, acted in defiance of the order. He was then hauled before the magistrates and fined for both his disobedience and his "insolence" in answering all their questions with the statement "My name is Walter." One of Barefoote's assistants fared even worse. When he tried to search a vessel owned by William Vaughan, the infuriated councillor beat him so badly with a cane it took him several months to recover.

The episode with William Vaughan brought a temporary halt to the customs enforcement campaign. Randolph's deputies bided their time awaiting instructions. The Council announced that it would assume responsibility for the regulation of trade and acted as though there were no Navigation Acts. It also wrote to England asking that the acts be declared inapplicable to the ports of Piscataqua.

Meanwhile the expected struggle over land titles began in earnest. The struggle was precipitated by Mason himself who, after learning that the Cutt code of laws had given the Council final authority over disputed titles, packed his bags and sailed for Portsmouth. Soon after his arrival the self-styled "Lord Proprietor" hired agents, announced his willingness to grant titles for an unspecified fee to those actually possessed of land, and presented his credentials to the Council. The councillors could not agree on a proper course of action. President Cutt, whose health had so worsened that he must have been primarily concerned with securing clear title for his children, urged accommodation while the Waldron faction advocated total rejection. According to Chamberlain, the Council at one point offered to compromise: it would collect funds annually from the towns and pay Mason an annual fee if Mason, in turn, would drop his claim. Nothing came of the offer, mainly because Cutt died. His death meant that Richard Waldron became acting president.

With the Council now in total opposition, Mason adopted different tactics. He instructed his agents to offer confirmation of existing titles at such nominal fees that those eager to erase any doubt about the legality of their ownership would accept, urged his supporters to vote for men of like sentiments in the upcoming provincial elections and hoped the results would enable him to gain in the Assembly what he had not gained in the Council. The strategy was doomed to failure. Despite Mason's offer, the vast majority of landholders refused to accept titles which implied that Mason had any right to ungranted land within his grandfather's patent. Furthermore, those opposed to Mason not only had compiled the original list of voters but also held local offices which gave them immense influence over the actual elections for assemblymen. In Dover, for example, Waldron served as town moderator, a position which permitted him to decide whether individuals met the franchise qualifications under the Cutt code. Mason attended the town meeting at which Dover's deputies were elected and witnessed what he and Chamberlain later described as the systematic exclusion from voting of those who supported his title. The two men probably exaggerated, but even they had to admit that the Assembly which convened in May 1681 proved as uncooperative as the Council. The deputies payed little attention to Mason's defense of his title, then voted to approve a Council-passed law confirming all existing land titles and town grants. Mason, frustrated and angry, repacked his bags and returned to England. His departure brought a temporary end to the disruptions triggered by delivery of the Cutt commission.

For the inhabitants of New Hampshire the second and most distressing phase of political turmoil began with the arrival in November 1682 of Edward Cranfield, a freshly appointed "Lieutenant Governor" of the province armed with a commission and specific instructions designed to thwart all resistance to royal authority. Cranfield remained in New Hampshire less than a year and a half, but his presence was long remembered. In that short period he managed simultaneously to remove from office the entire group of councillors, assemblymen, and judicial officials who governed before his arrival, to fill many resulting vacancies with men willing to uphold the letter of the law, to temporarily circumscribe the influence of Joshua Moodey and other Puritan ministers in the province, and to obtain court judgments against both smugglers and those whose land titles Robert Mason had challenged. Cranfield failed in the end to dominate the "unmanageable creatures" (the term is his) he had been sent to rule, but not from lack of effort.

The new turn of events stemmed largely from a growing awareness among the Lords of Trade that the Cutt commission had been a mistake. Shocked by the contents of the legal code and fully informed by Chamberlain, Randolph, and Mason of other provincial happenings, the lords began in the fall of 1681 a full investigation of New Hampshire. The evidence of "irregular" proceedings was so overwhelming that in December the lords reported to King Charles their belief that it would be necessary to send some imperial official "to settle the country." By the following spring they had decided on a specific course of action. They would cancel the Cutt commission, appoint a governor of the province instead of having the Council president serve as chief executive, and give the governor sufficient authority to control those determined to prevent reform in the colony. He would be authorized to veto all legislation by Council and Assembly, to remove councillors who proved uncooperative and replace them with men of his own choice, to choose from among the councillors his own deputy, to erect courts and appoint judges and sheriffs, to suspend the Assembly if necessary, and to settle disputes between Mason and landholders in the province. In general the governor was to seek the advice of his Council, to which Mason, Barefoote, and Chamberlain would be added, but be free to act without their consent. Cranfield's commission, which passed the Great Seal in May, incorporated these decisions.

The choice of Edward Cranfield to handle these heady responsibilities was the product of both policy and patronage. The king and his imperial advisors had decided to draw most of their colonial officials from the ranks of the army, in part to keep in government employment men who might be needed in time of war and in part to prevent the pattern of divided loyalties which in the past had so weakened the execution of royal authority in America. Cranfield, an army officer available for assignment, thus had attractive credentials. The lords may have learned of Cranfield through the committee secretary, William Blathwayt, who in 1680 had also been appointed auditor general for imperial revenues collected in the royal colonies. An efficient and shrewd bureaucrat, Blathwayt wanted someone in New Hampshire to make sure that his deputy in the province—about this time he appointed Chamberlain to the post—had some revenues to audit. It is more likely, however, that Mason suggested Cranfield and later obtained Blathwayt's backing. Before the governor left for Portsmouth Mason offered to pay him £150 a year for seven years out of quitrents collected in New Hampshire. Cranfield, eager to augment his own meager fortunes and confident in his ability to make landowners pay, accepted without hesitation.

For the first two months after arriving in New Hampshire, Cranfield hoped he would be able to manage affairs without serious difficulties. He did suspend Waldron and Martyn from the Council after Mason complained about their continued opposition to the proprietorship, but restored the two men when they apparently convinced him that the collapse of earlier compromise efforts had been Mason's fault. Moreover, the Assembly which convened in November 1682 readily passed a code of criminal law which the governor found satisfactory, mainly because it was based on English rather than Massachusetts tradition. Cranfield, in fact, wrote back to England that Chamberlain, whom he found both arrogant and incompetent, and Mason had been the major source of previous troubles. He may very well have suggested something similar to the assemblymen, for they voted a gift of £200 to their new chief magistrate.

Then the bubble burst. A series of events which included the refusal of a local jury to convict a shipowner detected smuggling, the disappearance of the vessel involved through the connivance of Councillor Elias Stileman, passage of laws by the Council and Assembly giving them the authority to appoint judges and control jury selection, and renewed resistance to the proprietorship, convinced Cranfield he had to take strong measures. He did just that.

The lieutenant governor first reorganized the government. He dissolved the Assembly. He completely reshaped the Council by suspending Waldron, Martyn, Stileman and other recalcitrants, and replacing them with men willing to accept reform. The replacements were drawn from two groups: merchants resident in the Great Island section of Portsmouth who had long resented Strawberry Bank's domination of community affairs and his few known supporters among prominent citizens in the other three towns. Cranfield and the Council, in turn, erected new courts, appointed several judges—Barefoote, for example, became the associate justice of the court of common pleas— and tried to gain even greater control of judicial affairs by having the sheriff, whom they appointed, determine which freemen should sit on juries. At one point the Governor and Council even passed a law making it illegal for selectmen to call town meetings without first obtaining permission from the local justices of the peace whom they, the Governor and Council, had appointed. On paper it was an extremely tight arrangement, one which Cranfield further buttressed by formally designating Barefoote his deputy governor.

With the institutions of provincial authority increasingly under control, Cranfield and his associates launched a massive campaign to make the citizens of New Hampshire accept royal authority. One immediate purpose of the campaign was to enforce customs regulations. Vessels entering port once again were searched and violators were brought to trial. Occasionally, though not always, the accused were found guilty. Equally important, the government took steps to make Great Island, where Cranfield, Barefoote, and many of the new councillors resided, the focal point of customs enforcement. The island was designated official port of entry, Stileman was fired as captain of the fort and replaced by Barefoote, and all entering vessels were required to stop there before proceeding upstream. Finally, the Governor and Council, which by now included Randolph, announced a series of commercial regulations designed to make life difficult for those suspected of past smuggling. No trader from the other New England colonies could use the Piscataqua without first purchasing a license; ships headed for Massachusetts could no longer stop in the region to pick up cargos of boards and timber. These regulations, of course, had other purposes—they were designed also to jar New Hampshire loose from its close economic ties to the Bay Colony, to make life difficult for men like Vaughan and Waldron who traded mostly through Boston, and to increase the personal income of customs collectors—but they were all part of the continuing effort to enforce the Navigation Acts in New Hampshire.

Another purpose of the campaign was to force acceptance of Mason's proprietorship. Initially Cranfield had urged Mason to give up his claim to common and improved property in exchange for title to unimproved lands, but by now his attitude had changed. The few leases which Mason and his agents had been able to arrange with landowners did not begin to provide the £150 annual income Mason had promised, and besides, the commission, Cranfield felt, empowered him to settle the general dispute once and for all. That meant attacking the source of the trouble, the large property owners like Waldron whose stubbornness had made compromise impossible. Mason instituted suits against Waldron, Stileman, a Great Island resident named George Jaffrey who had been in constant trouble with the customs, and dozens of others. The Court of Common Pleas, with a hand-picked jury and Walter Barefoote presiding, found all the accused guilty and ordered seizure of the property involved. In Jaffrey's case the decision was actually carried out. Government officials occupied his house and sold his goods at public auction; Cranfield issued an order freeing the one slave Jaffrey owned.

The reformers also wanted to gain some degree of control over religious practices in New Hampshire. Their motives were both personal and political. Barefoote, for example, had long opposed persecution of Quakers and two decades earlier had been responsible for releasing the women Waldron ordered dragged and whipped throughout the region. The deputy governor also believed that as long as the Puritan establishment remained intact, New Hampshire could never become politically independent. There existed, he once wrote the Lords of Trade, "a strict confederation between the ministers and church members of this province and those of Massachusetts Colony who rule," a confederation which gave the Bay Colony magistrates immense influence over their northern neighbors. Cranfield, Mason, Randolph and others held similar beliefs. They also found it inconceivable that as members of the Church of England they had no place to worship and that men who shared their faith had no access to clergymen willing to administer sacraments according to the Book of Common Prayer. The conspicuous presence of Quakers among those willing to accept Mason's proprietorship, and past cooperation among Vaughan, Waldron, and Moodey further convinced the reformers something must be done.

Late in 1683 the Governor and Council decided on a course of action. They passed a law ordering ministers in the province to admit to baptism all persons "not scandalous to Sacrament" as defined by the Church of England; any person refused such admission would no longer be obliged to pay taxes for church support. The order, if enforced, might have altered patterns of church membership throughout New Hampshire. Next the magistrates issued Moodey a direct challenge. They informed the shocked clergyman that Cranfield, Barefoote, Chamberlain, and one other councillor wished to receive Communion. When Moodey refused, the remaining Council members by a vote of four to two found him guilty of insubordination and ordered him placed in prison. Before he could be arrested the unrepentant minister departed for Massachusetts, as did the Reverend Seabury Cotton of Hampton. Meanwhile Cranfield suspended the two councillors who had voted against conviction.

Thus by early 1684 Edward Cranfield, other royal appointees, and provincial residents who chose to support them had joined in a well organized effort to destroy the pattern of established authority which had prevailed in the four towns for the past several decades. The organizers sought both personal profit and political power, but they also acted out of conviction that as Englishmen they should obey the dictates of the home government and no longer permit Puritan fanatics to oppress those who held different religious convictions. How optimistic the reformers felt when they launched the campaign is not clear. Cranfield was probably more naive than the others about the potential for effective local resistance—he was, after all, an army man not a politician—yet even he must have known that Waldron, Vaughan, Moodey, and their fellow townsmen would fight tenaciously to maintain as much of the status quo as possible.

Resistance took numerous forms. The most dramatic single episode was the abortive armed rebellion led by Edward Gove, a Hampton resident sufficiently prominent in town affairs to have been elected to the Assembly. Infuriated by the suspension of that body and convinced that God's kingdom in all New England, not just New Hampshire, needed saving, Gove began recruiting an armed band to march against the government. Cranfield learned of the activity, immediately issued warrants for Gove's arrest, and made plans to muster the militia. The governor, in fact, seems to have considered the turn of events a golden opportunity to discredit those opposed to his rule. He succeeded only partially. Nathaniel Weare, a Hampton justice of the peace and friend

of Gove, took matters into his own hands. Weare mobilized his neighbors and when Gove marched into town with a dozen or so followers
waving swords and pistols, disarmed the whole crew of potential rebels.
After swallowing his disappointment at having missed the action,
Cranfield proceeded to take advantage of the situation. He accused
Gove of high treason, ordered an immediate trial and for that purpose
erected a special court to which he appointed Waldron, Vaughan, and
Thomas Daniel. The evidence was so strong that unwillingness on the
part of the jury to convict (or refusal of the judges to pass proper
sentence) would provide additional evidence that his enemies should
be stripped of all power. Conviction, on the other hand, would discourage further resistance and buttress the governor's authority. The
jury did find Gove guilty of high treason and Waldron—with tears
in his eyes if tradition is correct—announced the required sentence of
death. But Cranfield never saw the sentence executed. His commission
outlawed capital punishment and included a provision requiring that
convicted rebels be sent to England. Gove eventually gained pardon
by the home government and returned to Hampton a free man.

Gove's rebellion, although it fed on the resentment felt by his
followers toward Cranfield and Mason, stemmed largely from the passion of a single man. Other forms of resistance were more general and
systematic in nature. The vast majority of New Hampshire residents,
for example, refused to accept the various court verdicts rendered in
customs and land tenure cases as anything which should alter their
customary behavior. Merchants continued to smuggle, refused to pay
fines when caught and convicted, and made life thoroughly unpleasant
for Barefoote and his deputies. Landowners paid no heed to Mason's
agents. Men hauled before the Court of Common Pleas and asked to
defend their title either remained silent or, like Waldron, challenged
the legitimacy of the court and its proceedings. Jaffrey rejected an offer
to have his case dropped and his house returned if he acknowledged
Mason's proprietorship. Citizens throughout the Piscataqua resisted
the temptation to buy at public auction the property of those actually
dispossessed.

The effectiveness of opposition to court judgments encouraged still
more widespread defiance. By 1684 even Cranfield and Council commanded little authority. When rumors of an impending Indian attack
circulated in the area Cranfield reconvened the Assembly and asked

militia leaders to support his request for money to purchase military supplies. They refused, and the deputies as a whole made clear not a penny would be voted for governmental services. The infuriated Cranfield dissolved the group. The Council then voted a tax bill, only to have residents withhold payment because the royal commission provided for Assembly approval of such bills. Other dictates of the Governor and Council, including those involving admission to baptism and administration of Communion, met with similar defiance. Some residents began to justify their actions by asserting that the commission itself was a forgery and that Cranfield had been sent not by the king but by his distrusted brother, the Duke of York.

Still another tactic used by those fed up with what one resident described as the "crew of pitiful curs . . . come to undo us both body and soul" was the threat of physical attack on anyone attempting to enforce the law. Cranfield, a short tempered and violent man himself, felt so unsafe in the spring of 1683 that he fled to Boston and remained three months hoping the home government would heed his request for military aid. Failure of the British to provide protection only increased the frequency of threats. Some were actually carried out. That fall and winter the chief assistant in the customs, the marshall of the province, and at least one councillor, received beatings. Cranfield apparently stayed free of trouble, but Barefoote and Mason did not. The former had his ribs broken and the latter his stockings and periwig singed when an irate landowner threw both men into the fireplace at the deputy governor's house on Great Island. The landowner, who happened also to be Barefoote's brother-in-law, became an instant hero in the region.

The deadlock between a government intent upon reform and a people unwilling to accept it lasted only a few months. Two closely related developments, the growth in England of opposition to Cranfield's management of provincial affairs and the governor's personal decision to seek his fortune elsewhere, brought an end to the crisis.

Home officials began to receive complaints about their recent appointee as early as the spring of 1683. Ironically, some of the complaints may have come through the very men responsible for Cranfield's appointment. Blathwayt was informed by Chamberlain that the governor's conduct, at first too compromising and then too heavy-handed, made it impossible for him to fulfill his responsibilities as deputy

I Robert Mason Esq Prop.r of y.e Province of New Hampshire doe make Oath,
that upon y.e 30.th day of Decem.r last, being in my Lodgings at y.e house of Walter
Barefoot Esq.r Dep.t Govern.r & seing Thomas Wiggins & Anth. Nutter of y.s Province
yeomen, talking w.th y.e Dep.t Govern.r I bid them welcome & invited them to stay
supper, after supper, upon some discourse Wiggins said, he & others had read the
Papers I had set up, but they did not regard them or value them at a Rush, —
for I had nothing to doe in y.e Province, nor had one foot of land therin, nor ever
should have, & withall did give very abusive & provoking language, so that I
comanded Wiggins to goe out of y.e Room, which he did not, but asked y.e Dep.t
Govern.r whose y.e house was Barefoots or Masons, the Dep.t Govern. told him y.t
y.e house & Servants were mine, & intreated him to be gone, & not to make a dis-
turbance, I then opened y.e door & took Wiggins by y.e Arm to put him forth, saying he should not stay there to affront me in my own house, Wherupon Wiggins took hold of my cravat & being a big strong man pulled me to y.e chimney
& threw me upon y.e fire, & lay upon me, & did endeavour to strangle me by gri-
ping my windpipe, that I could hardly breath, my left foot was much scorched
& swelled, my coat Perriwig & stockings were burnt, And had it not been for y.e
Dep.t Govern. who was all y.t time endeavouring to pluck Wiggins off from me,
I doe verily beleive I had been murthered. I was no sooner got out of y.e fire but
y.s Wiggins laid hands on y.e Dep.t Govern. & threw him into y.e fire, & fell upon him
so y.t two of y.e Dep.t Govern. ribs were broke, I did with much difficulty pull
Wiggins off y.e Dep.t Govern. Wiggins being risen upon his feet did again assault
me & y.e Dep.t Govern. & threw y.e Dep.t Govern. down, therupon I called to a Maid
Servant to fetch my sword, saying y.e villain would murther y.e Dep.t Govern.r
the Servant coming with my sword in y.e Scabbard, I took hold therof, but
it was snatched out of my hands by Anth. Nutter who was present in y.e
room & did see y.e assault made both upon y.e Dep.t Govern. & my self, & hindred
me from releiving y.e Dep.t Govern. Nor did y.s Nutter give any help or assistance to the Deputy Governor./

Robert Mason

Taken upon Oath the 8.th March
1685/6 before me
R Chamberlain Just P.

auditor and provincial secretary. Blathwayt probably relayed these observations to his friends among the Lords of Trade. Randolph too, seems to have become doubtful. He travelled back to England on the same vessel which carried Edward Gove, and although the details of their relationship remain uncertain, circumstantial evidence suggests Randolph developed sympathy for the convicted rebel. Gove might well have convinced the customs commissioner that the Navigation Acts could never be enforced in New Hampshire as long as Cranfield remained in power. Even if Blathwayt and Randolph said nothing, home officials had reason to be concerned. Gove's personal testimony and the record of his trial made clear that all was not well in New Hampshire. Cranfield's own correspondence, especially the letter which asked for military protection, must have raised questions about his capabilities. In addition, the lords had learned of the financial relationship between Mason and Cranfield. The relationship, they were sensitive enough to understand, bode ill for the establishment of effective royal authority in New Hampshire.

Home support for Cranfield grew still weaker as time passed. That fall Gove received a formal pardon, a pardon which quite apart from its legal implications could have been delayed had the crown been determined to support the governor. The following winter the Lords of Trade and the Privy Council received additional evidence in the form of depositions, signed by nearly half New Hampshire's adult male population, complaining that Cranfield, Mason, and their cronies threatened total ruin to the hardworking and loyal citizens of New Hampshire. The depositions could not be ignored. They had been gathered by William Vaughan and had the backing of Vaughan's English patron, the politically influential baronet, Sir Joshua Child. Nathanial Weare, who served as Vaughan's overseas messenger, accompanied the baronet to Whitehall and proved a willing and articulate witness. The case was strengthened by a subsequent letter in which Vaughan described, among other things, how he had been imprisoned for gathering the depositions. In July 1684 the Privy Council ordered a full investigation of Cranfield; the investigation completed, it removed him from office.

Meanwhile, in New Hampshire, the political crisis had already begun to subside. Cranfield himself was largely responsible. Aware that he was beaten long before home officials turned against him, impoverished, unable to command even the semblance of authority, and increasingly worried about his personal safety, the governor repacked his belongings and retreated to Boston. This time Cranfield had no intention of returning to New Hampshire. In May he wrote a Privy Council member and pleaded for a different appointment. Successful in his quest—he became the customs official in Barbados—Cranfield responded gratefully. "I esteem it the greatest happiness that ever I had in my life," he informed the Committee on Trade and Plantations, "that your Lordships have given me an opportunity to remove from these unreasonable people. . . . No man shall be acceptable to them that puts his Majesty's commands in execution."

Cranfield's departure initiated a brief period of political calm in the province. Barefoote and the other councillors made no attempt to enforce unpopular legislation and further contributed to communal peace by releasing Vaughan from prison. Mason, having gained judgments in his favor locally, wrote a lengthy defense of his conduct to the Lords of Trade and Plantations and awaited the outcome of developments in England. Residents throughout the colony who had fought so hard against the governor breathed a collective sigh of relief and hoped that the pardon of Edward Gove meant that the home government had become more understanding. Like Mason, they waited impatiently for news from overseas.

Different kinds of problems characterized the third phase of political disorder which followed the imperial decision to create the royal colony of New Hampshire. Trouble stemmed not from the formal organization of authority or the aggressive and arbitrary conduct of men who held provincial office, but from something quite different. Between 1685 and 1692 there was little effective provincial authority and frequent disagreement about the proper scope of town authority. Cranfield's old supporters struggled to retain some vestige of power. Those who before the Cutt commission had ruled under authority given by Massachusetts Bay tried to engineer a return to the status quo of the 1670s. Leaders in individual towns fought both among themselves, and against their counterparts in neighboring communities. In the end nobody won. The residents of New Hampshire, unable to resolve their own differences, stood aside while others determined the shape of their future.

It was some time before anyone in the Piscataqua learned for certain what fruit Weare's mission would bear or what the consequences of Cranfield's flight would be. The range of possibilities was broad. Cranfield might return with the armed protection he sought; a new lieutenant governor might be appointed; the home government might decide to forget about the idea of an independent New Hampshire; or the judgments made in Mason's favor by local courts might be sustained, altered or reversed completely. Sometime during the summer of 1685 dependable news began to arrive in Portsmouth. Some of it pleased the majority of inhabitants. Cranfield would not return. The Lords of Trade, in addition, found the discredited governor guilty of exceeding his authority in land cases. All past judgments were declared void and a single test case would be heard in England. The outcome of that test case caused still greater rejoicing. The English court found for the defendant thus leaving Robert Mason with a paper proprietorship but no title to specific land. But the rest of the news could not have been worse. The home government had made a series of decisions which promised not only to keep the four towns in turmoil but to spread disruption throughout all New England.

The first of these decisions, that of voiding the charter of the Massachusetts Bay Company, had been under consideration for some time and marked the culmination of Edward Randolph's efforts to convince his superiors that Bay Colony magistrates would never abide by the dictates of the royal government. The revocation itself worried New Hampshire Puritans, but subsequent events disturbed them even more. King Charles died and the Duke of York became King James II. James, a Roman Catholic, advocated a pattern of colonial reform which had as its model the vice-royalty system used by Spain to govern its New World possessions. The king lent his support to colonial officials who sought a single centralized government for all of New England, and when the Lords of Trade asked his advice on how the new government should be organized, announced his opposition to the whole idea of popularly elected assemblies. There should be a royally appointed governor, a royally appointed council, and courts run by royally appointed judges. The commission for the "Dominion of New England," drafted and approved in the fall of 1685, reflected these principles. The commission also indicated that as far as home officials were concerned, the only Piscataqua residents who could be trusted with authority were those who had supported Cranfield. The Council for the Dominion included Randolph, Mason, and John Hincks, one of the Great Island merchants the ex-governor had appointed to office. Few men in New Hampshire liked the new arrangement.

In the short run, formation of the Dominion of New England proved a blessing in disguise to the residents of Hampton, Dover, Exeter, and Portsmouth. Mason moved to Boston, as did Chamberlain who became the Dominion's Clerk of Courts. Randolph, his authority buttressed by the commission, concentrated on customs enforcement in Massachusetts Bay and forgot about the Piscataqua. The first governor for New England, a Boston merchant named Joseph Dudley, and his successor Edmund Andros found themselves so preoccupied with problems in the old Bay Colony that they paid little attention to events in the thinly populated and distant northern regions. The main actions taken by the Dominion government were the erection of a court in Portsmouth and the appointment of Hincks to replace the ailing Walter Barefoote as captain of the fort. Dominion authorities, moreover, seemed willing to cooperate with any individuals among the local elite who accepted their rule. Richard Waldron, Jr., for example, purchased several offices which left him with formal authority in Dover almost as great as that previously exercised by his aging father.

The Dominion, however, did not solve the basic problems of government in the four towns. For one thing no one could be certain whether New Hampshire still existed as a province. Dudley's commission suggested that it did not, but the Dominion government in establishing a separate court for the region used the term "Province of New Hampshire." Events of the past half decade, moreover, had created bonds among the towns which no external change could erase completely. When Chamberlain gathered up the provincial records and without informing anyone carried them to Boston, everyone became worried lest the records be lost or misused. Hincks, Barefoote, and several of their political enemies including one former councillor Cranfield had suspended, complained to the Lords of Trade. They styled themselves the "Council for New Hampshire," a term which must have made the lords wonder what exactly was happening in northern New England. How long the self-appointed group continued to function is not clear.

Local authorities experienced similar difficulties. Should they seek justice of the peace and militia appointments, and if they decided not to and were offered commissions anyway, should they accept? Whatever they did they came under attack, often by friends and neighbors who themselves found it impossible to sort out the pros and cons of co-operation with Dominion officials. Relations between central and local authority became especially confusing after Andros arrived. The new governor was an ex-army officer and like Cranfield—New Hampshire-men made the comparison frequently—expected obedience to his or-ders. Many town officials in Massachusetts refused to collect taxes levied by the Dominion government and withheld cooperation in doz-ens of less obvious ways. Andros, in turn, suspended the traditional right of selectmen to call town meetings, removed recalcitrants from offices he and the Council controlled, and instituted court proceedings against those who continued to resist. Although no officials in New Hampshire were affected, who could tell where Andros would strike next? The Dominion of New England, many concluded, was no more acceptable than earlier attempts to impose royal authority on the in-habitants of the Piscataqua.

Then, suddenly, the Dominion came to an end. Rumors that an army led by the Dutch monarch, Prince William of Orange, had landed in England to deliver its people from popery and slavery began cir-culating in New England sometime near Christmas 1688. The rumors were soon confirmed, and by the following April it was known that the rebellion, which the vast majority of Englishmen supported, had been totally successful: William, a Protestant, now reigned as the King of England. The success of what soon became known as the "Glorious Revolution" presented the people of Massachusetts with a golden op-portunity. Led by a self-appointed Council of Safety, they arrested Andros, Dudley, Randolph, and many other Dominion officials, voted to resume the former government (but not the charter), elected deputies to the Assembly, and reinstated councillors who had been removed from office by Dudley's royal commission. Increase Mather, a Puritan minister who earlier had sailed for England to protest both the loss of the charter and the behavior of Andros, pleaded with King William to accept recent changes. The new ruler had little choice but to agree, for England had just declared war on France and would need the full cooperation of Massachusetts in protecting its New World possessions. The resulting proclamation, which stated simply that those presently in charge should carry on until further royal instructions arrived, was read in Boston less than a year after citizens first heard rumors of the rebellion.

The collapse of the Dominion of New England left inhabitants of the four towns in an awkward position. Town government remained intact, but there was no provincial government and unlike Massachusetts, New Hampshire had no traditional charter which might serve as the basis for erecting such a government. Problems arose almost immediately. Justices of the peace hesitated to exercise the powers granted under the Dominion and met with resistance if they acted despite their hesitation. Leading citizens in the region debated among themselves about what to do: some wanted to have the towns form their own union, some wanted to petition Massachusetts for admission, and some wanted to wait and ask the crown for instructions. They agreed only, as Nathanial Weare later noted, that New Hampshire had neither "governors nor authority."

While the debate raged, tragic events occurred which gave leverage to the advocates of union. Indians attacked, initially at the village of Cocheco in Dover and later at Oyster River, killing or capturing over seventy people. Citing the need for a coordinated response to subsequent attacks, representatives from all four communities met to frame a temporary government. They drew up a plan which resembled more closely than anything else government established under the Cutt commission and sent it to the towns for approval. But the plan never was consummated. Hampton, the majority of whose inhabitants feared domination by merchants and lumbermen in Portsmouth and Dover, rejected the proposal and serious opposition developed in the other towns.

Failure to gain approval for a separate New Hampshire government left those deeply concerned about the absence of provincial authority with but one alternative: they must try to become part of Massachusetts. The idea was appealing for a variety of reasons. It was generally assumed that effective defense against attack by the French and Indians could best be organized by Massachusetts. Many civil and religious leaders with strong linkages to the Bay Colony still questioned the wisdom of making New Hampshire an independent colony and hoped that effective cooperation between the two colonies in the current crisis would encourage imperial officials to reconsider the decision made in 1679. Joining with Massachusetts might have the additional advantage of reducing antagonism between Hampton and the other three towns; the residents of Hampton had always been opposed to separation from their southern neighbors. These and other considerations soon convinced a group of Portsmouth's "prominent gentlemen" to take matters in their own hands. Led by Vaughan and John Pickering, the group drew up a petition for reannexation, collected over three hundred and fifty supporting signatures from freemen throughout the province, and hand delivered it to Boston. By the middle of March 1690, the governor, Council and General Court of Massachusetts Bay all had accepted the proposal.

Reannexation had the same general effect on New Hampshire as the Dominion of New England: it provided short term relief from threatened disorder, but no long term solution to the problems of governance experienced since arrival of the Cutt commission. The relief came in two areas. The Bay government quickly appointed three of the men responsible for drawing up the petition—Vaughan, Martyn, and Nathaniel Freyer—magistrates for the region and later approved a long list of civil and military appointments they and other local leaders recommended. In addition, the arrangement made possible more effective coordination of regional military activities. The individual towns forgot their differences long enough to agree that Vaughan should become their representative to the "United Colonies" a group founded to manage the war effort throughout New England. Vaughan, Martyn, and Waldron organized defenses in the Piscataqua area.

The problems which remained were also dual in nature. A large minority in the four towns held serious reservations about the temporary reunion with Massachusetts. Some objected to the whole idea, others to the fact that the organizers of the petition had gathered signatures but not sought approval of the towns as corporate entities, and still others to the decision by Bay Colony authorities to appoint three Portsmouth residents as magistrates instead of selecting men from all the towns. Resistance took several forms. A number of citizens refused to pay taxes levied by the Massachusetts General Court. The inhabitants of Hampton, where less than a third of the adult males signed the petition for reannexation, complained about a plot to subvert their traditional liberties and made clear their unwillingness to accept the judicial authority of Vaughan, Martyn, and Freyer. There were also suggestions that a second convention be held to make plans for an independent union. Reannexation, in short, failed to eliminate the bickering which had marked political life in New Hampshire for the past decade.

The second problem involved an even more important matter: the entire future of New Hampshire as an organized unit of governance. Vaughan and his associates had concocted a scheme which if successful would make permanent the union with Massachusetts. The plan was both simple and inexpensive. Increase Mather and other Bay agents in England seeking a new charter for the colony would ask to have New Hampshire included in the territory to be governed by the corporation. The agents could cite the petition for reannexation as evidence that New Hampshiremen both wanted and needed the protection of their southern neighbor, and explain to royal officials that sentiment in the four towns for continued independence was virtually nonexistent. With no one overseas to argue against annexation—Mason had died in 1688 and the planners naively assumed the Glorious Revolution had cost Randolph and Blathwayt their political leverage—the Lords of Trade might agree with the Massachusetts agents. And if the lords made their decision quickly, it would be too late for the men in New Hampshire who opposed union with Massachusetts to launch their own campaign.

The scheme, however, did not work. Vaughan and his allies in Massachusetts miscalculated badly when they assumed there would be little support in England for keeping New Hampshire independent. The new king had no intention of reducing the role of the crown in imperial matters and proved almost as distrustful of New Englanders as his predecessor. Randolph and Blathwayt not only remained in office, but manifested renewed interest in the Piscataqua as a beachhead of royal authority in New England. They found a powerful and energetic ally in Samuel Allen, an English merchant eager to exploit the possibilities of trans-Atlantic trade. Sometime in 1690 Allen made the decision to invest heavily in New Hampshire. He purchased the proprietorship from Mason's heirs, obtained a contract for supplying the Navy Board with masts, and approached the Lords of Trade with a proposal that he be made governor of all the territory included in Mason's various patents. For the better part of a year Allen and the agents for Massachusetts engaged in a running battle for control of New Hampshire. Allen won. The charter of Massachusetts, which passed the Great Seal in October 1691, did not include the four towns. The following January the Lords of Trade agreed to recommend that Samuel Allen be appointed governor of the still independent and royal colony of New Hampshire.

The news which trickled back from England shocked the inhabitants of the four towns. Although divided on the wisdom of union with Massachusetts, New Hampshirites were united in their feeling that nothing could be worse than to have the office of governor and the proprietorship held by the same man. What they knew of Allen himself only accentuated their anxiety. Reports from Mather and the other agents indicated that the new magistrate was resourceful, ambitious, and far more influential at Whitehall than, by contrast, Cranfield had been. In addition, there existed direct evidence that Allen would ally himself not with those leaders who had taken responsibility for regional affairs in the past several months, but with Cranfield's old supporters and men who had held office under the Dominion of New England. The new lieutenant governor, John Usher, was a former Dominion councillor who had been arrested and jailed in the rebellion against Andros, and one of the three men Robert Mason earlier had deeded a million acres in the Merrimack valley. The new Council, which Allen and Blathwayt probably chose, included three holdovers from the Cranfield days and excluded Vaughan, Weare, Martyn and Waldron. The composition of government under Samuel Allen clearly bode ill for the future of New Hampshire.

The year 1692, then, began much like the year 1680. But there was one major difference. In 1680 the inhabitants of the four towns were anxious but still uncertain about the consequences of having been selected to participate in the experiment of erecting a royal government in northern New England. Now the experiment was more than a decade old and from their point of view had been a total disaster. The intervening years had been marked by communal disorder and political turmoil even more extreme than the disorder of the 1630s. The long term effect of this collective experience is difficult to measure. It is tempting to speculate that attitudes toward government shaped during this period stiffened the determination of New Hampshiremen to control their own destiny and that this, more fancifully yet, somehow led to the American Revolution. It also could be argued that all parties involved, imperial officials, magistrates in Massachusetts Bay, and the men whose economic status and social standing made them natural leaders in the Piscataqua area, learned enough about the costs of political confrontation to become more receptive to compromise in subsequent years. Whatever the impact, one thing is certain: the men and women who lived in New Hampshire during these years yearned for more stable times.

6

TESTING TIME: WAR AND POLITICS IN "LITTLE NEW HAMPSHIRE"

The next quarter century proved even more difficult for Englishmen who lived in New Hampshire. The Indian attacks against settlements in Dover during the summer of 1689 were the initial skirmishes of frontier warfare which continued well into the second decade of the eighteenth century. The costs of war were immense: Eastern Indians and their French allies either killed or captured hundreds of inhabitants, the economy stagnated, and daily life in many parts of the colony was shaped by the constant fear of sudden assault. New Hampshire also experienced continued political disruption. Rapid turnover among imperial officials, the uncertainty of relationships with Massachusetts, renewed conflict between inhabitants and the proprietor, and internal factionalism all accentuated instability stemming from the war. Few New Hampshirites during this period had either the leisure or the inclination to record their innermost thoughts but they must frequently have wondered what sins they had committed to deserve such a fate.

Difficult as the times were for contemporaries, the 1690s and first decade and a half of the eighteenth century were years of fundamental importance to the future of New Hampshire. War and political conflict served as a crucible for testing the potential for a separate royal government north of the Merrimack. New Hampshire and its people survived the testing. When the war ended in 1713 the continued independence of the province was ensured: home officials considered their experiment in royal government a success, Massachusetts magistrates and all but a few Piscataqua residents accepted the idea of separateness, the proprietary no longer appeared threatening, and residents in the various towns had begun to develop a strong sense of common destiny. Optimism about the future of what one official labeled "little New Hampshire" existed as never before.

Restiveness among Native Americans along New England's northern frontier had been growing for some time. The various Abenaki tribes in what is now central Maine remembered the sporadic attacks on seacoast villages which, despite their efforts to remain neutral, had taken place during King Philip's War. Developments throughout the 1680s heightened tensions between the Abenaki and their English neighbors. Increased settlement, especially near the mouth of the Saco River, triggered a series of conflicts over fishing rights, livestock, and land ownership. The migration of the Pennacooks to Maine in mid-decade had a double impact: it increased the numerical strength of what New Englanders labeled collectively the "Eastern Indians," and it brought to Maine a group of young men embittered by loss of their traditional homeland along the Merrimack River. New England's own internal political troubles also contributed to the restiveness. Governor Andros had been negotiating with the Abenakis for a treaty which would guarantee them access to English goods, freedom from further Iroquois incursion, and protection against uncontrolled settlement. The Abenakis feared that his removal from office left regional authority in the hands of men intent upon the destruction of their entire culture. The manner in which the Massachusetts Bay government conducted subsequent treaty negotiations only reinforced their suspicion.

In the summer of 1689 the Eastern Indians took matters into their own hands by launching a series of surprise attacks against villages along the frontier. New Hampshire bore the brunt of the attacks. Led by Pennacook sachems, a large group of natives descended on an exposed and unprotected group of homes along the Cocheco River in Dover, killed twenty-three inhabitants, and captured another twenty-nine. Among those who lost their lives was Richard Waldron, Sr., whom the Pennacooks had never forgiven for violating the rules of hospitality years before. Oyster River suffered a similar fate later in the summer, although the number of settlers killed or taken into captivity totalled less than twenty. Smaller groups of natives threatened homes elsewhere in the Piscataqua.

Meanwhile the Eastern Indians had gained a powerful and dangerous ally. England's declaration of war against France in the spring of 1688 placed the Abenakis in a position of great strategic importance. English officials, both at home and in the northern colonies, saw the war as an opportunity to gain complete control of the profitable North American fur trade and to eliminate their main competitor for acquisition of unsettled territory in the New World by capturing Canada. Louis XIV had no intention of letting this happen; indeed, he confidently laid plans to expand his American possessions by capturing New York and seizing English posts in the Hudson Bay region. To carry out his territorial ambitions the French monarch appointed Count Frontenac as governor of Canada, instructed him to court native support among the Abenakis, and provided him with plans for a concerted attack on the northern frontier. The Abenaki were only too willing to cooperate. Already inclined toward the French—Catholic missionaries had long been active in Maine—the Eastern Indians accepted the guns and ammunition offered by the French and promised to continue fighting against the English. The fact that Iroquois tribes, traditional enemies of Algonkian speaking natives, were allies of the English further cemented ties with Frontenac and the French.

The conflict which pitted English settlers and the Iroquois against French colonists and the Eastern Indians lasted, with occasional lapses, for more than two decades. Neither side proved strong enough to destroy the other, but both had the means and will to make life miserable for their enemies, especially those who dwelled on the outskirts of settlement or were otherwise exposed to the possibility of attack. In the long run the natives suffered most. They did much of the actual fighting, lost population, witnessed the permanent destruction of many villages, and when peace finally came had little to show for their efforts. Although Europeans suffered also, they had the resources to survive and to emerge strong enough to engage in subsequent battles for continental dominance later in the century.

In a formal sense the conflict was two separate wars. The first, known in Europe as the War of the League of Augsburg but in the colonies simply as King William's War, began in 1688 and ended with the Treaty of Ryswick in September, 1697. New Hampshire was in constant danger throughout King William's War. In March 1690, less than a year after the disasters at Cocheco and Oyster River, a combined force of French and Indians destroyed the settlement at Salmon Falls, only a few miles up the Newichiwannock from Great

Bay. That summer more than thirty inhabitants lost their lives when Indians attacked in and around Exeter. After a short truce the raids began again. Between 1692 and 1696 Portsmouth was invaded four separate times with heavy loss of life; the various settlements in Dover fared even worse. Exeter and Hampton experienced less difficulty but were constantly alerted by reports of marauding Indians in the vicinity. The raids petered out after 1696 and came to a complete halt several months after Ryswick when magistrates from Massachusetts and New Hampshire signed a treaty of peace with the Eastern Indians.

The second phase of intercolonial fighting, Queen Anne's War, began in 1703, a year after England and Holland declared war on both France and Spain. New Hampshire was now better prepared. A well organized system of permanently manned garrison houses—fortified dwellings at key locations in each town—helped discourage the French and Indians from the massed assaults which had taken place so frequently in the 1690s. In addition, New Hampshiremen and other New Englanders became more aggressive in ridding the country of those who threatened its security. They sought out Indian parties before they had a chance to attack, destroyed the crops and villages of natives in Maine, and late in the decade organized a series of expeditions against French strongholds in Nova Scotia and Canada. They could not, however, protect the frontier completely. In 1703 Hampton experienced its first raid. The following year a group of marauding Abenakis and Pennacooks went after Richard Waldron, Jr. at his home in Dover, and although the provincial leader was not at home, killed several other colonists in the neighborhood. The raids continued until 1713, when news arrived that France, England and the other European combatants had agreed in the Peace of Utrecht to stop fighting. That summer the exhausted leaders of both English and Native American nations met in Portsmouth to sign a separate peace treaty.

Two and a half decades of mobilization and combat had a massive impact on New Hampshire. The war seriously retarded population growth. Estimates of population in early New Hampshire are at best educated guesses, but there is good reason to think that before the first attack at Cocheco the province contained over 3000 inhabitants and had experienced an annual growth rate of close to 8 percent since the establishment of royal government. During the 1690s growth all but stopped. Nearly three hundred residents lost their lives in surprise

Indian attacks and another hundred, many of whom returned, were carried off into captivity. Families abandoned newly constructed homes on the frontier and retreated to communities in southern New England. Births and new immigration barely made up for the lost population. The first years of the eighteenth century witnessed renewed growth, but at a modest rate. When the fighting stopped there were probably fewer than 4500 provincial inhabitants and the annual growth rate of the previous quarter century had been slowed to less than 2 percent.

Similar dynamics shaped the pattern of geographical expansion. Despite political turmoil, the 1680s had been marked by a gradual increase in land utilized for farming or lumbering. The northern parts of Dover and the land west of seacoast villages in Hampton experienced the largest amount of new settlement. King William's War reversed the process. Oyster River, which the enemy ravaged twice, was virtually abandoned. Settlers fled from freshly cleared acreage up the Newich- iwannock, Cocheco, Lamprey and Squamscott Rivers. The new town of Kingston, chartered in 1694 at the request of Hampton residents eager to take up land in the interior, remained uninhabited until the lull in fighting between the wars. There was some expansion during Queen Anne's War, but not much. The limits of settlement in Dover and Exeter never extended beyond the homesteads built in the eighties. In 1711 the small group of townspeople in Kingston complained that "the enemy now insults us as much as ever" and our circumstances remain "in a very low condition."

The war also had a major impact on economic life in New Hamp- shire. Agricultural production suffered for a number of reasons. The best land within existing areas of settlement had long been occupied, which meant that those forced because of the Indian danger to remain near the coast had to eke out a living on thin and rocky soil. Owners of more established farms often spent as much time on military duty as they did in the fields and, inevitably, productivity suffered. Con- ditions on the frontier were especially difficult. Planting and harvesting had to be done during the same months the natives were most likely to attack. To protect against the threat, men who otherwise would have been working stood guard, and fields located far from the garrison houses were abandoned. Even with precautions, farming remained dan- gerous. The diary of John Pike, a minister who left his parish in Dover for the duration of King William's War but returned later, includes the following entries: "John Church, sen., slain by the Indians as he travelled to seek his horse"; "Joseph Pittman slain by the Indians as he was guarding some mowers not far from the Oyster River meeting house"; and Maturin Ricker "killed in his field and his little son carried away." Pike also noted several episodes in which attackers destroyed livestock. It is impossible to assess the total impact of war on food production, but it must have been great. Throughout the period the colonists complained of shortages and were forced to import grain from regions less affected by the fighting.

The effect on New Hampshire's fishing business was even greater: the Anglo-French wars pushed into permanent decline an economic enterprise already in deep trouble. In the 1660s and 1670s the Isles of Shoals were the center of fishing in northern New England. The decision by leaders in the business to pursue other interests on the mainland, political division of the islands between Massachusetts and New Hampshire, and competition from fisheries in Newfoundland all tended to reduce the economic importance of the offshore center. War further reduced activity. Fishing along the coast of Maine and Nova Scotia became almost as dangerous as living on the inland frontier. Residents knew the islands would be impossible to defend should the French decide to attack and left for the mainland in large numbers. There was little incentive for anyone elsewhere in the region to take up the slack, for fishing would remain risky as long as international conflict continued. At the end of the war, the Isles of Shoals had fewer than a hundred inhabitants and fishing played a minor role in the provincial economy.

The impact of war on patterns of trade was equally dramatic, but different. In some ways trade suffered. The few New Hampshiremen who still exchanged goods with natives in the region could no longer do so. French privateers plied the waters off northern New England and captured an occasional vessel carrying goods from the Piscataqua. Local food shortages and a decline in lumber production caused by instability in the frontier reduced, at least during King William's War, the level of provincial exports. Imports declined also, for residents lacked the wherewithal to purchase or barter for commodities which earlier had been well within their means. And although the export trade picked up during Queen Anne's War, imports continued to be weak: taxation for the purpose of defending New Hampshire reached such a high level that people could afford little other than basic necessities.

War did, however, stimulate one dimension of New Hampshire's commerce. Conflict with the French forced British officials to become much more aggressive in developing the naval stores potential of the entire Piscataqua region. They gave gubernatorial appointments to Samuel Allen and William Partridge, both of whom were willing to invest heavily in the business, and when they proved ineffective sent agents to the region with specific instructions to recommend how the trade could be developed. Eventually the crown appointed a Surveyor General of the King's Woods to oversee the production of naval stores in New England. The settlers themselves were eager to participate. Money could be made—Jonathan Bridger, one of the investigating agents, estimated that masts worth £2000 in England could be obtained for £420—and the decline in other trade left local entrepreneurs with capital and energy to invest. Loopholes in existing law, furthermore, permitted the sale of masts outside the empire. When Partridge bragged that a shipment which cost him less than £300 cleared nearly the equivalent of £1600 in Portugal any residual skepticism about the business evaporated. Meanwhile, the provincial government had made clear its intention to cooperate by exempting from military service those actually engaged in the production of masts for the royal navy.

The almost total absence of trade statistics for the period makes it difficult to generalize about the naval stores industry during the war years. Some important details, however, are clear. Labor shortages, climate, and lack of interest on the part of hard pressed farmers prevented significant production of hemp, tar, or pitch despite the encouragement of both imperial and provincial officials. The major area of activity was the manufacture of finished wood products. According to the one available list of exported material, regional artisans provided English agents with masts, spars, bowsprits, yardarms, standards, and knees. Production and shipment of masts were by far the most important activities. Heavily guarded masting crews travelled as far into the woods as necessary to locate and harvest giant pines. The system of protection worked reasonably well (only two examples of successful Indian attack on men engaged in masting can be documented), and the monetary reward for success was sufficient to guarantee a ready supply of labor at every stage of production. Merchants in the Piscataqua shipped the finished masts overseas, sometimes in their own vessels but more frequently in specially designed "mast ships" owned by their English trading partners.

War affected the regional economy in one additional way: it accelerated the process which made Portsmouth the business hub not just of New Hampshire, but of all New England north of the Merrimack River. At the outbreak of hostilities Hampton, Dover, and Portsmouth all had about the same number of residents and Exeter, although smaller, served as an important center for the export of lumber. The towns developed differently during the armed conflict. Hampton continued to grow but remained a predominantly agricultural community with few external commercial relationships. Exeter and Dover barely held their own in population and witnessed a decline in their maritime commerce. Portsmouth, on the other hand, thrived. Population increased rapidly as families moved in from the frontier and the Isles of Shoals. The British government placed orders for a number of warships which guaranteed employment for many of the new arrivals. Privateering, the manufacture of finished products for the naval stores industry, construction of homes, businesses, and privately owned vessels provided additional economic stimulus. At various times New Englanders organized military expeditions against the enemy and used Portsmouth as a staging area; when that happened the town bustled with economic activity. Portsmouth thus benefitted from the very same conditions which so restricted development along New Hampshire's frontier and the coast of Maine. It was entirely fitting that the community was selected to host the signing of the peace treaty with the Eastern Indians in the summer of 1713. The town could well help sponsor the lavish ceremonies required on occasions of such importance, and local inhabitants had even more to celebrate than did others in the region.

A quarter century of warfare also affected social and religious life in New Hampshire. At no time in the experience of those living in the colony had the central institutions of family, community, and church been so disrupted. The disruptions were most serious along the frontier but were sufficiently strong elsewhere to make most inhabitants anxious about the very meaning of their lives. They responded by interpreting disruption as a test of religious commitment, and by utilizing the resources of family, community, and church to combat the disorder that surrounded them. Victory over the enemy meant more to New Hampshiremen than a cessation of hostilities. It meant that God had accepted their prayers, that life would become less burden-some, and that they finally were free to erect and enjoy the benefits of a more stable social order.

It was impossible to maintain normal family life throughout most of the war years. New Hampshire contained fewer than a thousand men capable of bearing arms. As a result virtually all family heads and older male children spent a large percentage of their time either man-ning the garrison houses, patrolling the woods in search of raiding parties, or guarding those who worked in the fields or cut timber. Sometimes men were drafted or volunteered to participate in the ex-peditions to attack the enemy in Canada or along the Maine coast. Most military duty was tedious business. Indians were difficult to locate, and guarding friends and neighbors when there was work to be done in the fields often seemed like a waste of time. Women left at home worried about their husbands; if they lived on the edge of settlement they worried still more about the possibility of attack. The spectre of captivity and a forced march into the wilderness haunted everyone exposed to the enemy. Families which abandoned the frontier underwent the painful process of resettlement. When a lull in the fighting occurred they sometimes returned home, only to leave again at the next outbreak of hostilities. And the high death rate from war related causes meant that many families, perhaps a majority, suffered some loss of life before the conflict ended.

Community and church life proved equally difficult to sustain. Most of the men who held positions of civil authority in the towns also served as militia leaders, and thus were absent much of the time. Churches experienced similar lapses in leadership because of the war. Attendance at both town meetings and religious services suffered, at least initially, because of general social disruption and the necessity of maintaining constant military alert. Marauding natives made it dangerous for residents to visit each other or to gather in larger groups to celebrate harvest, raise a neighbor's barn, or participate in any of the various communal rituals which punctuated village life in times of peace. At several points during Queen Anne's war inhabitants re-turning from such gatherings came under attack. The most serious problem was the strain military conflict placed on the capacity of towns to provide traditional services. Citizens had neither the time nor the money to clear roads, pay ministers adequate salary, and maintain fences in the common fields.

The psychological cost of all this—war, social and economic disruption, the sudden and unexpected death of loved ones, and disappointed personal expectation—must have been immense. How New Hampshire residents responded to their quarter century of trial is difficult to describe, for few men or women left written accounts of their experiences. But the surviving evidence does make some observations possible. Many inhabitants complained bitterly about the demands placed on them. Provincial authorities and local leaders were constantly buffeted by pleas for less taxation, reduced military service, and help in protecting personal property. A few colonists probably cracked under the strain: one Dover inhabitant, for example, moved into the woods and lived in a cave until killed by the Indians. The majority, however, were able to incorporate personal experience within a collective mentality which enabled them to accept what happened and maintain hope for the future. For them war with all its attendant troubles had larger meaning: it was, as Samuel Penhallow, a wealthy merchant who migrated to Portsmouth sometime in the 1690s and later wrote a history of the Indian wars noted, a "scourge for the punishment of our sins." The "bloody pagans" who were "as implacable in their revenge" as they were "terrible in the execution of it"—the words again are Penhallow's—served as God's instrument for reminding all New Englanders that they must put their house in order before expecting surcease from trouble. Evidence of God's displeasure went beyond the armed conflict itself. The outbreak of witchcraft in Salem, an epidemic of smallpox which struck early in the 1690s, and a series of natural disasters including a violent winter storm which destroyed much of the waterfront in Portsmouth all reinforced perceptions that, as Cotton Mather put it "the Great God who creates evil had further intentions to chastise a sinful people, by those who are not a people."

The solution, then, was to persevere in God's way until He became satisfied. And persevere most people did. What is most striking about the generation of New Hampshire residents who lived during the twenty plus years which spanned the start of the eighteenth century is the way in which they struggled against immense odds to adopt new forms of communal cooperation and to maintain traditional patterns of social and religious behavior. Far more families stayed on the frontier than left, and some reached even further out into the wilderness. Women assumed responsibilities for planting, harvesting, and on occasion protecting the home against Indian attack: the oft told story of Hannah Dustin, the Massachusetts woman who somewhere along the Merrimack killed her Indian captors and returned home to collect the bounty for their scalps, provides only the most dramatic example of courageous female response to the wartime crisis. Sons took over for fathers killed in combat or away on patrol duty. The garrison house system of defense and the need to protect those engaged in farming or lumbering involved elaborate planning. Despite the ever present danger, New Hampshirites resettled destroyed or abandoned villages, constructed new homes, held their town meetings, and joined together to celebrate their accomplishments.

They paid special attention to worship. The provincial government sponsored days for thanksgiving when Indian troubles subsided and days for fasting and prayers of humiliation when fighting resumed. Laws requiring church attendance were strengthened; public opinion and the warnings of local officials helped guarantee that inhabitants would obey the new regulations. Men on military duty sought God's help in locating the enemy, offered prayers of thanks if successful, and interpreted particularly fortuitous escape from disaster as a sign of divine interference on their behalf. Ministers throughout the province pleaded with parishioners to live according to the dictates of the Bible lest the forces of evil continue to threaten destruction. Deacons and other lay leaders delivered the same message at religious meetings held without the benefit of ordained ministers. In addition, communities as a whole put an extraordinary amount of effort into the task of maintaining organized churches as the central and most visible institution of religious life. Dover residents pleaded successfully with the Reverend John Pike to return to his flock. Exeter, which had been without a minister since the death of Samuel Dudley in 1683, not only recruited a replacement but paid him a generous salary and constructed a new meeting house for worship. Religious life in Hampton and Portsmouth also flourished.

Provincial inhabitants, then, had a ready explanation for the peace which came in 1713. Peace signalled the final success of their collective efforts to appease an angry God. With continued vigilance they could expect to grow in numbers, increase the area of settlement, prosper economically, and experience both the pleasures and obligations of a social existence uninterrupted by war.

The colonists had still other reasons to be optimistic about the future. During the war years a series of important developments affecting patterns of government in New Hampshire took place. The end result of these developments was the elimination of the major issue causing conflict both within and between the various towns, the erection of a far more stable and popular system of provincial authority, and removal of the proprietorship as a serious threat to landowners in the region. By the second decade of the eighteenth century, in fact, the vast majority of New Hampshiremen fully accepted both the structure of government and the men who held effective authority within it. Those old enough to recall the chaotic conditions of the 1680s had special reason to appreciate the new state of affairs.

The central political issue dividing the people of New Hampshire in the early stages of the war was permanent annexation to Massachusetts. Disagreements over annexation accentuated traditional geographical, kinship, and religious rivalries within the four towns, pitted men with economic interest in overseas trade against those with commercial connections in the Bay Colony, and was responsible for much of the tension between the citizens of Hampton and their neighbors. Equally important, the issue promised to affect the operations of provincial government under the commission granted to Samuel Allen. As long as union remained a political possibility its advocates would behave in a manner calculated to prove that New Hampshire lacked the internal cohesiveness to maintain an independent existence. Those who supported independence, on the other hand, would be tempted to cooperate with royally appointed officials.

Had the issue been decided in New Hampshire, there might be no Granite State for historians to write about. The outbreak of hostilities had already weakened the arguments for independence, for New Hampshire lacked the resources to organize effective resistance to the French and Indians. Moreover, experience under the Allen commission indicated independence meant just that. In 1693 Massachusetts asked New Hampshire to pay its share of expenses incurred in protecting the northern frontier, and the government, pleading poverty, procrastinated. The Bay Colony then withdrew its troops and the following year refused aid even after Portsmouth itself came under attack. Although magistrates in Massachusetts eventually changed their minds, New Hampshire leaders took advantage of the conflict to reopen the larger issue of independence. The newly elected Assembly formally petitioned imperial officials for annexation and town officials gathered over two hundred signatures in support of the petition. Despite the opposition of Lieutenant Governor Usher (Allen was still in England) the Council joined in the movement. Richard Martyn, representative from Portsmouth and Speaker of the House, then left for London to plead in person for what he and other provincial inhabitants considered a necessary change in the structure of regional government.

The decision, however, was not made in New Hampshire. Martyn received some overseas support, mainly from Massachusetts agents, but the Lords of Trade could not be budged. The Secretary of New Hampshire, a personal appointee of the governor, sailed from Portsmouth about the same time Martyn left and helped convince imperial officials that the petition represented still another effort by unmanageable religious dissenters to prevent the extension of royal authority in America. Allen himself appeared and reminded the lords of their original purpose in making New Hampshire a royal colony. The affair dragged on, Martyn returned to the Piscataqua, and near the end of the decade the lords recommended a compromise which guaranteed continued provincial independence. New Hampshire and Massachusetts would have the same governor (Lord Bellomont was selected for the post) but otherwise would remain separate. The decision, they made absolutely clear, was not one the British government planned to reconsider in the foreseeable future.

The citizens of New Hampshire responded to the decision with mixed emotions. Many, of course, expressed disappointment, but several considerations tempered their feelings. Resolution of the long standing conflict eliminated uncertainty about the permanence of King Charles's experiment in royal government and convinced everyone that for better or worse they must learn how to function as an independent entity. The specific terms of the new arrangement, moreover, made the idea of separateness more attractive than it had been at the outbreak of hostilities. A joint governor would be able to coordinate military defenses along the northern frontier, and the appointment of Bellomont

The official Seal of New Hampshire, 1692. From the center out the inscriptions read "Evil Be Who Evil Thinks," "God and My Right," and "The Seal of Our Province of New Hampshire in New England." *Courtesy of the New Hampshire Historical Society.*

suggested that home authorities had become more sensitive to the dangers of combining the offices of proprietor and governor. The increased importance of the naval stores industry also affected political attitudes: an independent government would be better suited to the development of direct trade with England than a government dominated by merchants and farmers in Massachusetts. And finally, experience during the past two decades had taught community leaders in the Piscataqua that even the most arbitrary and determined royal official could be prevented from controlling affairs in the colony.

Whatever the individual response, necessity dictated that men govern within the framework of provincial institutions established under authority of the crown. The institutions were the same ones created in New Hampshire by the Cutt, Cranfield, and Allen commissions, and were typical of royal governments throughout England's North American colonies. The governor or his lieutenant governor stand-in held ultimate executive authority, the limits of which were spelled out both by his commission and instructions drawn up by the Board of Trade. He ruled with the assistance of a royally appointed Council given a mixture of executive, legislative, and judicial responsibilities. The legislative responsibility was shared with an elected body of town representatives—local officials continued to decide who could vote in provincial elections—called either the Assembly or the House of Representatives. Relationships among the governors, councillors and representatives during the 1680s had been so antagonistic that little effective provincial authority existed. Although similar antagonisms continued to disrupt political life in New Hampshire as long as the commission of Samuel Allen remained in force, the provincial government as a whole became more effective in meeting the needs of its constituents. After the turn of the century controversy among the various branches of government all but disappeared, and royal authority functioned with even greater effectiveness.

The single most important factor affecting the level of political conflict was the behavior of the governor. In theory, the powers of the chief executive were immense. He could suspend councillors and appoint temporary replacements, decide when provincial elections should be held, convene, prorogue, or dismiss the Assembly anytime he chose, and veto proposed legislation; he also controlled the militia and in conjunction with the Council made both judicial appointments and decisions involving the general execution of provincial authority. The manner in which the various wartime governors chose to exercise their power, however, varied a good deal. Lieutenant Governor John Usher (1692–1697) and Governor Samuel Allen (1698–1699) acted much like Cranfield and their administrations, as a result, were marked by constant controversy. Lieutenant Governor William Partridge (1697–1698 and 1701–1702) and Governors Bellomont (1699–1701) and Joseph Dudley (1702–1715), on the other hand, cooperated so closely with leaders of the local population that all but a few New Hampshiremen accepted their leadership without complaint.

Usher experienced continuous frustration in his years as chief magistrate of the province. He had hoped to develop the proprietorship while serving, yet war made any effort in that direction both impolitic and unpractical. Like most colonial governors he thought appointment would enable him to increase his personal fortune. The Assembly, however, refused to pay him any salary and rejected many requests for reimbursement of expenses incurred in the line of duty. In addition, Governor Allen reneged on promises to pay him a stipend for management of the proprietorship. Usher tried to court the local gentry by appointing Waldron and Vaughan to vacancies in the Council— four men chosen by Allen and Blathwayt refused to accept their commissions—but the maneuver backfired. The new councillors not only refused to support his actions as governor but helped lead the annexation movement. Eventually Usher suspended them from office. Usher next turned to Cranfield's old supporters on Great Island. He appointed several residents to office, badgered the Council into incorporating the island as the separate township of Newcastle, and made Newcastle the seat of government. Although most island residents approved of the changes, the campaign only further alienated him from citizens elsewhere in the province. Usher also experienced difficulties as head of the militia. Governor Phipps of Massachusetts continued to issue orders through William Vaughan even though Usher had replaced Vaughan in command. At one point a local assemblyman and militia officer became so infuriated with Usher's efforts to assume military authority that according to one witness he "turned his britch upon the Lieutenant Governor . . . pist in his presence, and let a fart." Local merchants systematically defied efforts to enforce customs regulations. Usher fi-

nally gave up trying to manage the province. He spent more and more
time at his home in Boston, and as early as 1695 asked for a replacement. Shortly before leaving office he wrote the Lords of Trade that
his time as governor had been like "four years in Algiers captivity."

Samuel Allen's brief tenure as governor proved equally controversial.
Actually, the English merchant never intended to serve. He travelled
overseas for the express purpose of protecting the proprietorship and
fully expected that by the time he arrived Lord Bellomont would have
taken the oath of office. Bellomont, however, landed in New York and
remained there. The governorship was in the hands of Usher's replacement, William Partridge, a man whom Allen discovered had reappointed Vaughan and Waldron to the Council and decided to let local
leaders run the government. Both duty and self-interest, then, forced
Allen to take temporary command.

Allen encountered the same kind of resistance that had frustrated
Usher. Waldron, Vaughan, and one other councillor refused to acknowledge the legality of his commission. Two additional members
quit when Allen appointed Usher to fill one of the existing vacancies.
The Assembly, which Allen called into session in January 1699, ignored
his legislative requests, joined with rebellious councillors in petitioning
Bellomont for relief, and indicated it would not enter into any negotiations involving the proprietorship. The constables Allen appointed
to collect taxes either refused to do so, or met with such resistance
that Allen finally backed off and replaced them with men known to
oppose his governorship. Meanwhile, William Vaughan, whom Partridge had appointed Secretary to the Province, absconded with the
official records of New Hampshire. Samuel Allen soon became almost
as enthusiastic about his impending retirement as his political antagonists.

William Partridge, by way of contrast, thoroughly enjoyed his years
as provincial chief magistrate. Appointed largely through the influence
of Sir Henry Ashurst, agent for Massachusetts at Whitehall, Partridge
had no connection with Allen, Usher, or the proprietorship and thus
was greeted warmly when he arrived in Portsmouth with his commission as lieutenant governor. The new governor designate quickly
decided not to challenge local leaders. On their advice he postponed
publishing the commission and let a group of former councillors, led
by Waldron, Vaughan, and John Hincks, declare the governorship

vacant and assume responsibility for running New Hampshire. Partridge continued to take their advice while in office. He published his commission in November 1697, served the better part of a year until Allen unexpectedly showed up to replace him, and became chief executive again for a three year period starting in the summer of 1699. His main political actions were to remove Usher appointees from office and replace them with men recommended by the councillors, to reappoint Vaughan head of the militia, and to let the Council and Assembly manage things. Partridge spent most of his energy increasing his personal fortune. He asked for and received generous grants from a grateful legislature, and made still more money by aggressive marketing of naval stores. By the time he left New Hampshire—Bellomont helped get him fired by complaining that to give him responsibility for preserving the King's woods was like "setting a wolf to keep sheep"— Partridge had increased his net worth considerably.

Lord Bellomont's main impact on provincial government was to facilitate restoration of the same general conditions which prevailed during Partridge's first administration. Bellomont, who served also as governor of Massachusetts and New York and as military commander of all the territory previously under the Dominion of New England, simply did not have enough time to get deeply involved in the public life of New Hampshire. His only visit to the Piscataqua occurred in the summer of 1699 and lasted only eighteen days; he died in March 1701. Nevertheless, Bellomont accomplished a good deal during his brief tenure. His commission formally restored to the Council the group of Portsmouth community leaders who had usurped authority legally in the hands of Samuel Allen. In addition, Bellomont reorganized the judiciary and made a number of civil and military appointments: Hincks became Chief Justice of the new Superior Court, Waldron was made an Inferior Court Justice, and Vaughan gained a number of offices. Finally, Bellomont made clear his opposition to the proprietorship and may even have encouraged Vaughan and Waldron to institute proceedings against Allen in the Superior Court. His overall conduct while in the Piscataqua earned him a gift of £500 from the Assembly.

The administration of Joseph Dudley, the same man who earlier had served as the first governor under the Dominion of New England, lasted a dozen years and further convinced residents that royal govern-

Joseph Dudley, joint governor of New Hampshire and Massachusetts, 1702–1715. Artist unknown. *Courtesy of the New Hampshire Historical Society.*

ment could function smoothly in New Hampshire. As chief magistrate of both Massachusetts and New Hampshire Dudley had sufficient authority to manage the war effort effectively, but his political position was one of potential difficulty. Bay Colony leaders and their allies in the Piscataqua distrusted him from the start, and the imperial government further exacerbated the problem by reappointing Usher as lieutenant governor of New Hampshire. Dudley, however, managed to keep Usher in check, to gain the support of the Waldron-Vaughan group as well as their merchant rivals in Newcastle, and as a result to eliminate much of the political controversy which had disrupted the region for the past generation.

Controlling Usher proved easy. The lieutenant governor lived in Boston where Dudley could keep a close eye on his activities. Dudley, moreover, knew that Usher was on thin ice with imperial officials in England (at one point the Lords of Trade scolded him for the quality of his reports and advised him point blank "to write plain matter of fact and in such a manner as may be less obscure") and constantly cautioned his subordinate to avoid actions which might alienate those responsible for his appointment. Dudley may also have given Usher a portion of the permanent salary the New Hampshire legislature agreed to pay him. Unless he did, it is difficult to understand why Usher chose to remain in office during Dudley's entire administration.

Gaining widespread acceptance among those he ruled required more complex maneuvering. Dudley's basic strategy was to concentrate on his military responsibilities, to let the Council and House handle most legislative matters, to mediate factional disputes in the province, and to hope his overall conduct would gradually erode provincial distrust of royal authority in general. He succeeded on all fronts. Dudley's effective management of the militia during Queen Anne's War drew praise from all segments of the population and convinced the legislature to meet his frequent requests for defense appropriations. The governor gained support among the Waldron-Vaughan faction by encouraging Allen to compromise his proprietorship demands, and from Allen's few adherents by suggesting a settlement which would give them some return on their investment. Dudley's even-handed customs policy not only helped eliminate one source of factional tension, but convinced most Piscataqua merchants that enforcement of the Navigation Laws and active overseas trade were not mutually incompatible. Dudley used his influence over appointments to prevent any single group from dominating the Council or judiciary. And he found his efforts appreciated by the vast majority of the citizenry. In 1707, when Usher tried to engineer a change in the governorship, the Assembly petitioned the Lords of Trade to keep Dudley in office. They did so again in 1714 after Queen Anne's death threatened upheaval in officialdom throughout colonial America.

Governors Partridge, Bellomont, and Dudley, then, all helped to reduce the level of political controversy in New Hampshire. But governors by themselves could not make the whole structure of provincial authority operate effectively. Their commissions instructed them to rule in conjunction with Council and House, the infrequency of their actual presence in the Piscataqua meant that other provincial officials had to assume responsibility for managing such important matters as law enforcement and tax collection, and local conditions made cooperation with community leaders a political necessity. The twenty years following issuance of the Allen commission witnessed a gradual increase in the confidence and skill with which provincial magistrates as a whole functioned. By the last years of Dudley's administration both branches of the legislature had developed sufficiently to indicate that the system of shared institutional responsibility could serve New Hampshire well.

Several mutually reinforcing factors made the Council a potentially powerful agency of government. The various commissions gave its members a wide range of specific powers, including the right to exercise general executive authority in the absence of the governor. Since prevailing political assumptions dictated that councillors should be men of high social status, and the policy of the home government was to appoint leaders drawn from all the towns, the Council as a whole commanded a respect among the citizenry. A sense of public duty guaranteed that most men asked to serve accepted the offer. Finally, both tradition and the need for efficiency made Council members logical candidates for other civil and military offices.

The Council appointees fully exercised their potential throughout the war years. In the 1690s they successfully thwarted Lieutenant Governor Usher's best efforts to increase his personal influence over the affairs of government and for a brief period, led by Hincks, Freyer, Waldron, and Vaughan, assumed total executive authority. They also kept the Assembly, which beginning in 1693 included elected members from Newcastle, from challenging their power. Most of the time the Council met and acted independently. It also dominated the infrequent joint sessions: councillors drafted proposed laws before submitting them to the lower house for discussion, consulted informally not with the Assembly as a whole, but with those members they trusted, and terminated joint sessions which promised to cause trouble. Only on revenue bills did the House of Representatives act in full conjunction with the Council.

After the turn of the century the Council lost some of its leverage, but not much. The losses occurred largely because of Dudley's governorship. His active and effective participation in executive management reduced the freedom with which earlier Councils had functioned. Equally important, Dudley's unwillingness to let the Waldron-Vaughan faction dominate provincial politics cost the Council many of its experienced leaders: Waldron, for example, was not appointed until 1710 and by that time both Hincks and Freyer had quit. The Council, however, continued to exercise more control over the daily operations of government than any other provincial institution. Its members offered Dudley advice and made executive decisions in his absence, helped shape provincial legislation, sat as judges on most provincial courts, and occupied other important official positions. As time passed, moreover, the Council gained increasing public respect for the quality of its services. No longer could it be accused of utilizing its powers to favor a single group of provincial inhabitants.

Meanwhile, the lower house of the legislature grew in importance. Created by imperial officials because other colonies in America had developed similar institutions and because local representation in the operations of central government was a long standing English tradition, New Hampshire's Assembly had existed on paper since the arrival of the Cutt commission. But it accomplished little before the eighteenth century. Royal governors had few compunctions about proroguing or dissolving the House if it proved uncooperative; as a result sessions were both infrequent and brief. When the Assembly did meet, attendance was spotty. The House members as a group kept no institutional records separate from those of the Council.

The Assembly, however, held one key power: the provincial government could not raise revenue without its approval. During the administration of Governor Usher, House members began to see how effectively that power might be employed. They helped drive Usher from New Hampshire by refusing to pay him any salary, and discouraged his active participation in provincial affairs by rejecting many of the bills he submitted to cover expenses incurred in the line of duty. The Partridge, Bellomont and Dudley administrations further indicated that Assembly control of the purse could be put to good use. Well-paid governors tended to accept advice from those responsible for their good fortune and both councillors and governors needed funds to manage the war effort successfully. By the end of Dudley's term in office the Assembly not only determined the size of the provincial budget but authorized expenditures for specific purposes and helped audit the accounts of money actually spent by executive magistrates.

The Assembly also became better organized. In 1699 it adopted a set of formal in-house rules for the first time. The decreased frequency of elections—ten were held in the 1690s but only three in the last decade of Dudley's administration—reduced the turnover in Assembly membership and made it possible for a stable pattern of institutional leadership to develop. Representatives demanded and were given more responsibility for shaping provincial legislation. As a consequence joint sessions of Council and Assembly occurred much more frequently and lasted longer than before. The Assembly also began to hold more separate sessions. In 1711 it started keeping an independent "House Journal" to record its activities.

The growth of the Assembly, for obvious reasons, met with approval throughout the region. Since New Hampshire seemed destined to remain an independent royal colony, any check on the potentially arbitrary conduct of magistrates appointed in England would have been welcome. But more was involved. The fact that community inhabitants elected their own assemblymen and had someone to represent their special interests at the provincial level of government made the whole idea of royal authority more acceptable. If recent trends continued, the people of New Hampshire could look forward to playing an even more influential role in determining their political fate.

One additional development contributed to the growing sense of political contentment. For nearly a decade after the turn of the century provincial leaders fought a running battle with Samuel Allen and his son Thomas over the proprietorship, and emerged completely victorious. They convinced royal officials in New Hampshire to oppose the Allens, instituted and won legal suits in local courts, and through effective manipulation of the legal system successfully defended their case in England. Both Allens were dead by 1715, but even before then the proprietorship had been eliminated as a major source of controversy in the Piscataqua.

The first stage of the battle began when Allen personally assumed the governorship, tried to pack the courts with judges favorable to the proprietary, and instituted suits of ejectment against a number of landowners including Richard Waldron. He did not get far. Before the cases could be concluded Lord Bellomont arrived to take the oath of office. Bellomont had already talked with William Vaughan and concluded that development of the proprietorship would both alienate the population and inhibit growth in the naval stores industry. Allen tried to bribe the new governor but succeeded only in further convincing Bellomont to cooperate with provincial residents. In conjunction with the Council and Assembly he reorganized the courts and placed in key judgeships men known to oppose proprietary claims. Bellomont then wrote the Lords of Trade that "there never was, I believe since the world began, so great a bargain as Allen has had of Mason, if it be allowed to stand good." Bellomont soon left, but his actions bore fruit the following summer: the Inferior Courts ruled against Allen in each of the several suits he had instituted, and the Superior Court rejected his request for permission to appeal the cases in England.

The first stage of the conflict, however, ended in a stalemate. Despite the Superior Court decision Allen travelled to England, convinced the Privy Council to rehear the suit against Waldron, and took some satisfaction in the results of the rehearing. The assembled lords issued instructions which encouraged the proprietor to begin new proceedings. They also made it legally impossible for regional courts in New Hampshire to prevent local decisions in the case from being appealed to the home government.

The second stage was one in which both parties sought compromise. Allen's change in tactics stemmed as much from fatigue and failing health as anything else: he wanted to leave his son Thomas certain title to at least some land in the New World. The idea of a negotiated settlement also became more appealing to opponents of the proprietorship. The actions taken by the Privy Council implied that further legal confrontation might lead to a decision in Allen's favor, with unpredictable consequences for landowners throughout the settled parts of New Hampshire. Local leaders became even more worried about leaving their fate in the hands of home officials when lawyers for the proprietorship discovered that sometime in the 1690s the official records of Mason's earlier court victories had been destroyed and that either Vaughan or House Speaker John Pickering were the likely culprits. Destruction of official records was not something English barristers would take lightly. Finally, Bellomont's replacement, Governor Joseph Dudley, urged provincial leaders to moderate their stance, presented evidence that neither Allen nor the crown wished to disturb existing land titles, and warned both the Council and House that failure to negotiate would cost them his support in future controversy involving the proprietorship.

Dudley's "interposition," as Vaughan's son George described it, almost succeeded. In the spring of 1705 a combined group of town representatives and provincial magistrates agreed to accept Allen's title to all land outside the six settled towns, to allot him over 5000 acres within the towns in return for his quitclaiming all other such land, and to pay him a sum of money. Allen undoubtedly would have accepted these terms, but he did not have the opportunity: the very next day he died, apparently of natural causes, and provincial leaders decided to await future developments before renewing their offer. Many New Hampshirites must have shared the sentiments later expressed by Cotton Mather when he wrote "I cannot but admire at the providence of Heaven, which has all along strangely interposed, with most admirable dispensations, especially with strange mortalities, to stop the proceedings of the controversy about Mason's claim just in the most critical moment of it."

Renewed hostilities marked the third and final stage of conflict over the proprietorship. Thomas Allen lacked the flexibility of his father. Advised by Lieutenant Governor Usher to accept no compromise, Allen reinstituted legal proceedings against Waldron and after the expected defeat in provincial courts, appealed the case to the Privy Council. His antagonists accepted the challenge. Dudley, furious at both Allen and Usher, warned imperial officials that a decision in Allen's favor would create havoc in New Hampshire and seriously restrict utilization of regional timber resources. The Council and House hired George

Vaughan to represent Waldron in England, convinced Massachusetts to have its agents testify against Allen, and petitioned the home government. Provincial leaders, in fact, decided to risk further falsification of legal records. They hired someone to produce a fake Indian deed, the so-called Wheelwright patent, proving that residents of the Piscataqua held legal title to their land several years before Captain John Mason. The forgery was so cleverly executed it not only became part of official records, but remained undetected by historians for the better part of two centuries.

It was no contest in England. Thomas Allen possessed little influence with imperial officials, Usher's past conduct and personal stake in the proprietorship made his testimony suspect, and the legal ambiguities of the case left the Privy Council free to act on Dudley's advice. In 1708 it decided to let the decisions made in New Hampshire courts stand, and formally prohibited future ejectment suits. The battle over the proprietorship had finally ended.

Soon after the Peace of Utrecht George Vaughan, who remained in England after his successful defense against Allen's legal suit, addressed a lengthy memorandum to the Lords of Trade. The document contained many ideas about the management of all American colonies, but focused on New Hampshire. Vaughan offered specific recommendations about erecting defenses in the Piscataqua, developing the mast and lumber trade, and increasing regional population. Vaughan also suggested that the provincial lieutenant governor should be a native and by implication offered himself as a candidate for the post.

The memorandum written by Vaughan reflected a significant change in the way residents north of the Merrimack thought about themselves. At the outbreak of the war in 1689 Vaughan's father and most others in the region still resisted the idea of separation from the Bay Colony and found it difficult to imagine a future in which they willingly accepted the authority of magistrates appointed in England. Now they felt differently. Two and a half decades of experience under royal government indicated that forced independence had been a blessing in disguise. It had taught them how to coordinate civil and military activities among the towns and reduced their dependence on distant and sometimes demanding officials in Boston. It had permitted the growth of a system of internal authority in which their own elected leaders passed laws and determined the legality of individual taxation. Independence, moreover, had contributed to the development of a lucrative trade in naval stores, a trade certain to increase in importance as time passed. Few inhabitants, in short, possessed the slightest inclination to turn the clock back. They were New Hampshirites and accepted the fact.

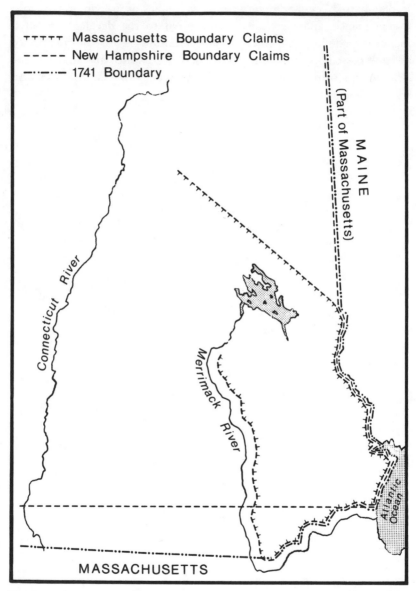

The boundary controversy between Massachusetts and New Hampshire.

7

PATTERNS OF GROWTH, 1715–1765

New Hampshire grew rapidly in the half century after the Peace of Utrecht. Favorable boundary decisions and continued military success against the French and Native Americans expanded the area available for settlement. Natural reproduction, immigration from the British Isles and West Indies, the boundary decisions, and the migration northward of many inhabitants from other New England colonies all contributed to a tenfold increase in the size of the population. The number of legally defined townships leaped from a half dozen to more than a hundred and fifty; the majority of these were sufficiently developed by the end of the period to be included in the provincial tax list. The economy also grew, both in productiveness and complexity. Large numbers of individual residents took advantage of opportunities in farming, lumbering, naval stores production, commerce, shipbuilding, and real estate speculation to accumulate sizable estates while the population as a whole became increasingly skilled in establishing and managing cooperative forms of economic activity. By the middle of the 1760s, in short, New Hampshire was a prosperous colony whose future looked as bright as its recent past. No longer did visitors to the province use adjectives like "little," "feeble," or "backward" to describe its condition.

New Hampshire Defined: Boundaries and Enemies

Before 1740 no one knew for certain where the borders between Massachusetts and New Hampshire lay. Both colonies accepted the Newichawannock and Piscataqua Rivers as the lower portion of the northeastern boundary, but agreement ended there. The Bay Colony insisted that above the source of the Newichawannock the line should run due northwest while New Hampshire argued as early as 1720 that the line ought to be drawn "a very few degrees westward of the north up into the mainland." Rich timberland and most of the White Mountains lay within the disputed territory. The southern and western boundaries were also the subject of controversy. Massachusetts claimed all land south and west of a line drawn three miles above the Merrimack, a claim which, since the river turns north thirty-five miles inland, included all of what now is the southwestern quarter of its northern neighbor. New Hampshire, on the other hand, felt the border should originate three miles north of the Merrimack outlet and proceed due west to the colony of New York. The two provinces also disagreed over the precise point from which the three miles north of the Merrimack should be computed.

Early attempts to resolve the conflict proved unsuccessful. In the 1690s Lieutenant Governor Usher, eager to define the limits of the proprietorship and to validate his ownership of land in the Merrimack valley, tried to negotiate a settlement, but could not get the anti-proprietary magistrates of Massachusetts to cooperate. George Vaughan, who succeeded Usher for a brief period after the end of Queen Anne's War, appointed a legislative committee which did meet with Bay Colony commissioners. The two groups, however, could not compromise their differences even though the issue of the proprietorship had become dormant. Vaughan's replacement, a Portsmouth merchant named John Wentworth, adopted different tactics. Wentworth, with the full cooperation of the Council and Assembly, abandoned the idea of direct negotiation, employed an agent to represent the province in England, formalized New Hampshire's boundary claims, and petitioned the crown for a favorable decision. That too failed. Massachusetts adopted similar tactics and the home government, uncertain how to proceed, did nothing for the thirteen years Wentworth remained lieutenant governor.

But resolution of the boundary conflict could not be postponed indefinitely. The central problem was jurisdiction of settlements above the great bend in the Merrimack. Early in the 1720s New Hampshire, in part to validate its border claims, incorporated the town of Londonderry within the disputed territory. Disputes between townsmen and colonists claiming title under competing Massachusetts grants began almost immediately. Conflict became more bitter and frequent after the Bay Colony erected the township of Rumford up the valley near the old Pennacook village in modern day Concord, and New Hampshire responded by making an overlapping set of grants. In 1733 Jonathan Belcher, the governor of both provinces, pleaded with the Lords of Trade to take action: "the borderers on the lines," he wrote, "live like toads under a barrow, being run into goals on the one side and the other as often as they please to quarrel.... They pull down one another's houses, often wound each other, and I fear it will end in bloodshed." Belcher (a Massachusetts man) once confessed that his native province was largely to blame for the inability of the two colonies to work out an amicable settlement, yet behaved in a manner guaranteed to prevent compromise. He supported the Bay Colony's interpretation of its charter, helped sponsor the granting of additional townships west of the Merrimack, and tried, albeit unsuccessfully, to prevent the New Hampshire Assembly from hiring a special agent to defend its case in London. Belcher may also have informed imperial officials that the simplest solution to the problem would be to have New Hampshire reannexed to Massachusetts.

Finally, late in the 1730s, the home government acted. It appointed a distinguished commission of officials from nearby colonies to investigate the local situation and conducted a series of Privy Council hearings in which agents from both sides could publicly defend their claims. John Thomlinson, an influential English merchant who represented New Hampshire at the hearings, won a complete victory for his new employers. The Privy Council not only accepted the commission recommendation that the border with Maine should run only slightly west of north, but in 1740 decided to draw a southern border which made New Hampshire several hundred square miles larger than even the Assembly had hoped. The boundary line would run three miles north of and parallel to the Merrimack until the river reached its southernmost point, and proceed due west thereafter. And to make certain there would be little delay in carrying out the decision the Privy Council fired Belcher, appointed another man governor of Massachusetts, and made Benning Wentworth—son of John and Belcher's main political antagonist in New Hampshire—an independent governor of the now enlarged colony. Wentworth did not disappoint his benefactors. Less than two years after he took the oath of office the eastern and southern borders had been surveyed and grudgingly accepted by authorities in the Bay Colony.

New Hampshire as described by agents for Massachusetts in the boundary controversy, and George Mitchell's survey of part of the boundary as determined by imperial authorities in 1741. *Both photographs courtesy of the New Hampshire Historical Society.*

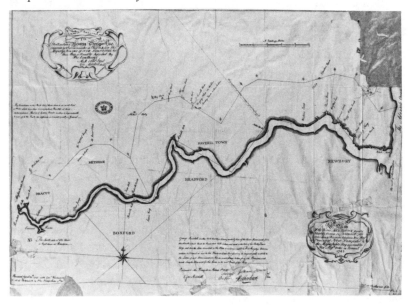

Buoyed by these successes, magistrates in New Hampshire made further efforts to expand provincial borders. Wentworth, blithely assuming that all of what ultimately became the state of Vermont lay within his jurisdiction, began granting townships west of the Connecticut River and despite protests from New York, which claimed title to the same area, continued the practice until the last few months of his twenty-five year administration. Renewed war with the French and Indians delayed settlement of the western boundary until the mid-1760s, and although by that time the news from England indicated that imperial authorities would decide in favor of New York, no one could be certain about the final outcome. Whatever the outcome, New Hampshire residents could be thankful for their previous territorial gains. The province would remain several times larger than the original New Hampshire granted to Captain John Mason.

Boundaries, of course, are legal constructs and define limits only to those who accept the authority of officials determining the boundaries. The treaties which terminated Queen Anne's War gave the English nation effective control over the southern parts of New Hampshire, but as settlement pushed northward it was inevitable that conflict between the English and their foreign enemies would arise. Abenaki bands still occupied villages along the eastern frontiers of the province, hunted in the upper reaches of the various river systems, and resented the continued intrusion of Englishmen into the mainland. The French provided an even greater potential threat. Embittered by past failures in the competition for New World hegemony, leaders in both Europe and Canada were eager to prevent further expansion of English settlement. Nothing had happened to erode the natural alliance between the French and Indians.

Open warfare erupted three different times in the half century after the Peace of Utrecht. Dummer's War, named after the lieutenant governor of Massachusetts who helped organize it, lasted from 1722 to 1725, all but eliminated the Abenaki as an effective fighting force, and made New Hampshire's eastern frontier safe for future settlers. Twenty years of subsequent peace were shattered in the mid-1740s by King George's War, which had a dramatic impact on villages in the upper Merrimack and Connecticut River systems. Although the French and English signed a truce in 1748, both continued to prepare for what one historian has called "the climactic struggle for empire," more commonly known as the French and Indian War. It began in 1755, ended in a complete military victory for the English, and, since the resulting peace negotiations transferred ownership of Canada to Great Britain, freed New Hampshire from further foreign obstruction to northward expansion.

Dummer's War was the final phase of the long standing struggle between New Englanders and the Eastern Indians. The treaty signed in Portsmouth during the summer of 1713 put a temporary halt to open hostilities but did not resolve the basic conflict over land rights along the coast of Maine. By 1720 relations between Massachusetts and the Abenaki had seriously deteriorated, largely because the Bay Colony sponsored settlements along portions of the coast the Indians thought had been left under their control. Led by the Jesuit priest Sebastian Rasle and armed by the French in Canada, the natives threatened to attack the intruders. The English, in turn, decided to destroy the enemy once and for all. In 1724 two hundred militiamen, including many from New Hampshire, descended upon the largest Abenaki village in Maine and killed over eighty Indians; they also killed Rasle, who had barely escaped an earlier attack. Other wartime events affected New Hampshire directly. Several times the Indians attacked and killed isolated homesteaders in the upper Piscataqua watershed. To combat such depredations the provincial governments offered bounties of up to £100 for the scalp of each native killed by volunteers. The policy was responsible for the episode known as Lovewell's Fight. Shortly before the war ended a party of scalp-hunters led by Captain John Lovewell ambushed a native community on the upper Saco River just east of the eventual border between Maine and New Hampshire. Although Lovewell miscalculated the strength of the Indians and along with several others lost his life, the raid convinced the native population in the region to move elsewhere. The migration was so complete that in 1730 a New Hampshire official wrote: "There are no Indians in this province that we know of." The growing number of crude homes, cleared fields, and lumbering operations along the colony's northeastern frontier reflected the security of the region after the conclusion of Dummer's War.

King George's War differed both in its origins and in its impact on New Hampshire. Hostilities began not because of regional tensions between natives and the colonists—the Council, for example, had just accepted an Indian proposal to establish a trading post south of Lake Winnipesauke—but as a by-product of conflict between Protestant England and its Catholic rivals on the continent. France took advantage of the hostilities once again to harass New England's northern frontier and to expand its general influence in North America.

New Hampshire participation in the war was of two kinds. The province provided men and ships for the siege of Louisbourg, the French fortress on Cape Breton Island at the mouth of the St. Lawrence River. The success of the undertaking in 1745, which was planned and conducted mainly by New Englanders, boosted morale throughout the region and helped limit subsequent military activities of the French and their Indian allies. New Hampshire was also forced to defend its newly expanded frontiers. It did so by constructing a string of forts and garrison houses from the Maine border to the town of Rumford and down the west bank of the Merrimack (Massachusetts built a similar set of fortifications still further west), by organizing regular patrols, and by reinstituting a policy of bounty payments to volunteers who killed Indians on their own. The system worked better than it had during the earlier period of Anglo-French conflict. Although some recently founded villages between the Merrimack and the Connecticut had to be abandoned, few New Hampshire inhabitants lost their lives. At one point about thirty men stationed at Fort Number Four in what is now Charlestown repulsed an invading force of nearly three hundred French and Indians. The raiders never did feel confident enough to attack settlements along the upper Merrimack.

New Hampshire defended its frontiers even more effectively in the French and Indian War. The only settlements which had to be vacated lay along the Pemigawasset, a northern tributary of the Merrimack which reached into the foothills of the White Mountains. And despite frequent marauding expeditions down the Connecticut River valley, the enemy killed or took captive fewer than fifty provincial inhabitants in the seven years the conflict lasted. Yet the impact of the war on the province was huge. Each year New Hampshire provided several hundred soldiers for the fighting, most of which took place in disputed territory between New York and Canada; in 1759 the number of enlisted men, quite apart from those serving within the province, reached nearly a thousand. Robert Rogers led the most successful of the military groups from New Hampshire. His "rangers" not only did invaluable scouting for the English armies, but near the end of the war successfully attacked the Indian community of St. Francis where many of the frontier raids had originated. Hundreds of natives were slaughtered in the surprise assault. The next year, 1760, the English captured Montreal and for all intents and purposes the French had been beaten. The Treaty of Paris, signed in 1763, made Canada an English possession and the northern frontier of New Hampshire safe for future settlement.

Population Growth

Meanwhile the size of New Hampshire's population had begun to soar. Natural reproduction accounted for much of the increase. The typical couple in eighteenth century New England produced at least four offspring who reached adulthood, and there is no reason to think New Hampshire varied significantly from the regional norm. Although some children left the province, by far the larger number remained, married someone in the neighborhood, and continued the process started by their parents. The only serious interruption to the pattern of internal growth occurred in the mid-1730s when an epidemic of "throat distemper," which modern medical historians have tentatively identified as a combination of diptheria and scarlet fever, killed about fifteen hundred inhabitants, most of whom were under sixteen years of age. War resulted in a few hundred additional New Hampshire deaths, but by that time the population was about 25,000 and large enough to absorb the loss without significant diminution of the general rate of natural increase. That rate, in fact, may have become greater by mid-century as the ready availability of land and changing social mores encouraged men and women both to marry earlier, and to remain in the province once married.

New Hampshire also received a steady stream of overseas immigrants. Many of the new arrivals came from England. The expansion of direct trade between the Piscataqua and ports in the home country convinced several merchant entrepreneurs to settle with their families in Portsmouth. English sailors, attracted by the relatively high wage scale in New England, jumped ship to remain in America. Although many later returned to their seagoing life, a good number became permanent provincial residents. Some of the British troops sent overseas to fight against the French deserted and began working in New Hampshire. There was little return migration to England.

The British West Indies served as an additional source of immigration. Through most of the seventeenth century labor on the islands had been provided by white indentured servants, many of whom, upon completing their term of service, became landowners and sugar producers. By the end of the century land had become so expensive and economic opportunities so limited that former servants left for the mainland: most went to the Carolinas or Virginia, but trade with New England guaranteed that some would end up in New Hampshire. Many of the approximately six hundred black slaves who lived in the province by the mid-sixties also came from the West Indies. Familiarity with the English language made them more attractive to potential purchasers—who were looking for house servants, not fieldhands—than slaves brought directly from Africa.

The single largest source of overseas migration, however, was Ulster, the portion of northern Ireland occupied mainly by men and women of Scottish descent. Late in the second decade of the eighteenth century a large group of Presbyterian "Scotch-Irish" purchased land in the lower Merrimack valley from owners claiming title under the forged Wheelwright patent, asked for and received permission from New Hampshire's provincial government to settle in the region, and quickly established the thriving community of Londonderry. Led by the Reverend James MacGregor, the Scotch-Irish were hard-working, well-organized, and much like the original founders of Plymouth and Massachusetts Bay, united by a heritage of past religious persecution. The success of the original enterprise attracted additional migrants: by 1730, according to one royal official, over a thousand Scotch-Irish lived in the province and constituted one-tenth of the total population. The pace of overseas migration from Ulster slackened after mid-century, but remained sufficiently strong to fuel settlement in several townships in the Merrimack valley and further west.

Migration from southern New England provided the final major source of population growth. Between 1710 and 1760 the combined population of Massachusetts, Rhode Island, and Connecticut leaped from about 100,000 to over 400,000. Land, good farming land especially, became increasingly scarce and expensive. Young adults eager to establish their own homesteads found it difficult to buy sufficient acreage for a good farm in their native provinces and began looking elsewhere. New Hampshire had much to offer. It contained a seemingly limitless supply of good timber and an adequate amount of fertile soil, the provincial government both encouraged settlement and promoted the formation of town governments with which they were familiar, and land could be leased or purchased at a reasonable price. Equally important, the land was accessible. The Piscataqua, Merrimack and Connecticut river systems made the transportation of personal belongings to the interior relatively easy and the marketing of any future surplus commodities even easier.

Migration, which had been reduced to a trickle during the wars with the Eastern Indians, picked up markedly in the second quarter of the eighteenth century. The initial wave brought farmers from Massachusetts and Rhode Island into the undeveloped parts of the older towns and the newly granted townships of Chester, Rochester, Barrington, Canterbury, and Nottingham. Men and women from the same area also began moving up the Merrimack valley, some into townships incorporated by New Hampshire, others into the lands granted by the Bay Colony. The boundary decision not only transformed nearly a thousand colonists who thought they were Massachusetts residents into New Hampshirites—only a handful found the change objectionable enough to move back across the border—but helped accentuate the number of new arrivals. There was less uncertainty about the validity of land titles, and much of the acreage recently awarded to New Hampshire lay adjacent to existing Massachusetts settlements. Even renewed Anglo-French hostilities failed to seriously blunt the pace of migration into much of New Hampshire. The effectiveness of provincial defenses made the region east of the Merrimack safe from attack by raiding French and Indians.

A second wave of immigrants from southern New England began moving up the Connecticut River valley late in the 1730s. Before war broke out a village had been established more than thirty miles north of the Massachusetts border, and the Ashuelot, an eastern tributary of the Connecticut River, had several clusters of homes along its shores. Many of these frontier towns were abandoned in the mid-forties but reoccupied as soon as the fighting stopped in 1748. Migration up the river, most of it by previous residents of Connecticut and western Massachusetts, continued at a moderate pace even during the French and Indian War. Peace triggered an unprecedented surge of new settlement. By 1765 the provincial government had granted more than two dozen townships on the eastern side of river valley alone and many more west of the Connecticut. Thousands of potential immigrants purchased land in the new towns and either moved or started making plans to move.

Shortly after the war ended the first formal New Hampshire census was taken. Entitled "A General Account of the Number of Inhabitants of the Several Towns in the Province of New Hampshire appears by the returns of the Selectmen from each place in the year 1767" by an obviously delighted provincial secretary, the census made clear how rapidly population had grown in the past half century. The tabulated returns, which did not include figures from the towns granted west of the Connecticut, indicated that New Hampshire had nearly 53,000 residents, about evenly divided between women and men. The actual total may have been significantly higher.

Town Founding

Growth in the number of New Hampshire townships was even more extraordinary. Today there are over 240 such legal entities; 60 percent were erected in the period between 1715 and 1765. Behind the growth, of course, lay the rapid increase in the number of actual or potential inhabitants, the vast majority of whom accepted without question the desirability of organizing themselves into the kinds of self-managed communities with which they were familiar. But other factors were involved; ten times as many people did not need twenty-five times as many towns in which to settle. The demands by outlying inhabitants of existing towns that they be allowed to manage their own civil and religious affairs accounted for some of the change. Several communities had their origins in the early competition between Massachusetts and New Hampshire to sponsor settlement in the disputed territory along their common borders, and the boundary decision itself resulted in the formation of more than a dozen new townships. The economic ambitions of entrepreneurs who controlled the provincial government also played a key role in the growth. One reason towns were founded was to place valuable timber and farmland in the personal possession of

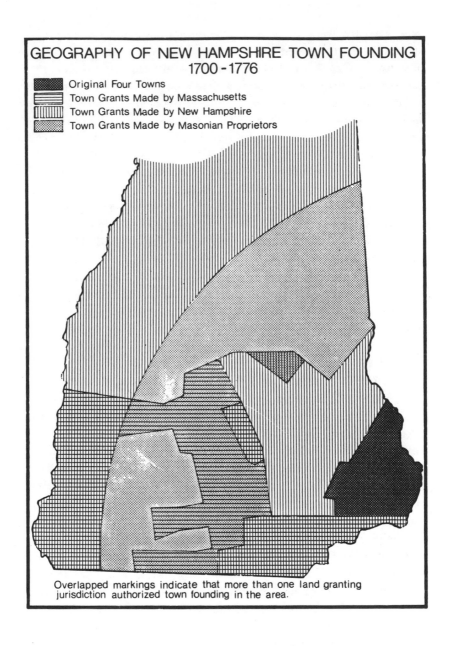

GEOGRAPHY OF NEW HAMPSHIRE TOWN FOUNDING
1700-1776

Original Four Towns
Town Grants Made by Massachusetts
Town Grants Made by New Hampshire
Town Grants Made by Masonian Proprietors

Overlapped markings indicate that more than one land granting
jurisdiction authorized town founding in the area.

those who did the granting, and since magistrates shared the largess with others in the province there was little public criticism of their behavior. Two additional factors fueled expansion. Speculators throughout New England sought proprietary rights to proposed new townships in New Hampshire, anticipating a profit from quick resale. Finally, the province adopted an aggressive expansionist policy at the end of the French and Indian War. By 1765 the government had established forty-one additional townships east of the Connecticut River in territory known to lay within provincial boundaries. Still more were granted west of the river.

It is difficult to generalize about the process of town founding. Although the Governor and Council chartered most towns in accordance with royal instructions, in some instances private landowners did the initial granting. Many townships possessed the right of self-government when established but many did not, and in a few the question was left hanging. The Massachusetts and New Hampshire governments, individual investors, surveyors, and the men who settled the land all played important roles in shaping town boundaries. Original grants often were declared invalid and the towns rechartered. Anyone who attempts a systematic reading of New Hampshire local histories quickly learns how varied were the origins of individual towns within the state.

Nevertheless, some broad configurations may be drawn. Four basic patterns characterized town founding in the period between 1715 and 1765. One involved a sequence of subdivisions within the original boundaries of Portsmouth, Hampton, Exeter, and Dover, and paralleled a process which had taken place earlier in many eastern Massachusetts townships. Most towns formed in this manner began as separate church jurisdictions; when erected into towns they were immediately granted the governmental privileges of their parent communities. Newcastle and Kingston had been incorporated before 1715. Seventeen more towns were founded in the region during the next half century and three others after that.

Initially, the splitting off process was both lengthy and controversial. In the case of Hampton Falls, for example, it began in 1709 with a petition by inhabitants south of the main river in Hampton for the right to choose their own minister. Despite protests from other town residents the government eventually formed a parish—the institution existing both in England and in Massachusetts—in the section where the petitioners lived. Soon the parish took on civil as well as religious functions. In 1717 town authorities tried to tax parish members for school support but were told by the Council they could not. Shortly thereafter the Council voted to give Hampton Falls virtually all the privileges of a town, including the right to representation in the Assembly. Again there was opposition from outside the parish. Continued jurisdictional conflict produced a subsequent resolution that the parish had town privileges "without exception"; Hampton Falls was formally incorporated in 1726. Separation of the Oyster River section of Dover took even longer. As early as 1669 inhabitants asked to become a town and were still asking sixty years later. Oyster River was finally incorporated as Durham in 1732.

As time passed, however, the people of eastern New Hampshire became more accustomed to seeing their towns divided. The provincial government helped by regularizing the process. It adopted a policy of approving all petitions for separate parishes if the petitioners seemed numerous and prosperous enough to support a church, and if the separation made geographical sense. It clarified parish rights, granted formal town incorporation as soon as conditions warranted, and helped settle any conflict over boundaries. Townsmen themselves became less opposed to subdivision. Experience indicated that smaller townships were easier to manage and less subject to civil and religious conflict. The lessened need for services balanced the loss of tax revenue. In any case, the legal responsibility for erecting parishes and incorporating towns lay with the Governor and Council; the leaders of any single community lacked the power to alter general policy.

The second pattern originated in the boundary controversy with Massachusetts. Rochester, Londonderry, Pembroke, Bow, and several other townships granted by New Hampshire in the 1720s owed their existence in part to the desire of New Hampshire officials to establish jurisdiction over disputed territory. The Bay Colony was even more aggressive. It granted several sets of what ultimately became New Hampshire towns in the region between the Connecticut and the Merrimack. The so-called "Narragansett" grants, given (at least in theory) to veterans of King Philip's War or their descendants, included three towns along the west bank of the Merrimack. Four towns were chartered on the east bank of the Connecticut, and nine more stretched along the northern frontier between the two watersheds. A number of individual town grants were also made. The general policy of the New

Hampshire government was to accept the boundaries defined by these Massachusetts grants once imperial officials determined that the region lay within its jurisdiction. In some cases the Governor and Council simply regranted the land to the same group of men named in the original charter, in other cases chose a completely different group of men, and in still others decided to include both old and new proprietors. Only in a few instances were Massachusetts grants totally ignored.

The boundary controversy was also responsible for the founding of over a dozen towns which neither province had chartered before 1740. Most of these lay along the newly drawn southern border, which cut through a number of communities already settled and incorporated under Massachusetts auspices. Inevitably problems arose. A few diehard settlers wanted to fight the decision in court, and of those who accepted New Hampshire authority some advocated the retention of old boundaries while others asked the Governor and Council to draw new lines. Controversies also arose over the establishment of church parishes. Provincial magistrates, eager to limit disorder in the region, tried their best to arbitrate these disputes. They accepted the existence of intercolonial parishes, responded quickly to petitions for the formation of new parishes, incorporated towns as soon as local residents made clear what they wanted, and in general moved as expeditiously as possible to integrate new residents into the existing structure of government. Within a decade Southhampton, Newton, Plaistow, Salem and several others had been added to the growing list of incorporated New Hampshire townships.

Special conditions were responsible for the founding of one town. The old Massachusetts town of Rumford and the New Hampshire town of Bow overlapped. Shortly before mid-century the proprietors of the latter, who included the governor and many of his close political associates, instituted suit against settlers in the former for recovery of the disputed acreage. *Rumford vs. Bow* became the most closely watched legal case in northern New England, for it was widely assumed that the outcome would determine the fate of all competing grants made by the two provinces. The Bow proprietors won first in New Hampshire courts and later in England when Rumford landowners, led by the Reverend Timothy Walker, appealed the decision. Once the legal battle ended in the early 1760s, the two parties compromised their differences and to celebrate the agreement recommended that what remained of

Rumford be incorporated as the town of Concord. The provincial government accepted the recommendation.

Resurrection of the old Masonian claim to all land within sixty miles of New Hampshire's coastline was responsible for the third town founding pattern. Sometime in the 1730s John Tufton Mason, a descendant of the captain and current holder of the long dormant patent to New Hampshire, appeared in Boston. Bay Colony magistrates considered the arrival most fortunate, for the existence of Mason's claim might be used as an argument against what they considered the inflated territorial ambitions of their rivals in the boundary dispute. The young man, who called himself a mariner, was flattered by all the attention, sold the patent to a group of agents representing Massachusetts, and agreed to serve as a witness before the Privy Council. But the scheme backfired. Mason not only failed to testify—solicitors for the colony thought raising the issue would be considered an "artifice"—but while in England sold his patent again, this time to agents of the New Hampshire government. The patent eventually ended up in the possession of twelve wealthy and influential New Hampshire entrepreneurs who styled themselves as the "Masonian Proprietors."

The Masonian Proprietors, who could grant rights to the soil, but not to government, managed their investment judiciously. Meeting first in 1748, they quickly issued quitclaim deeds to all towns in the purchase either chartered or incorporated by New Hampshire, gave all other settlers title to the land they occupied, and set about the task of developing the remaining acreage. Proprietary policies were so generous and so conducive to provincial growth that neither the government nor the public at large had reason to complain. Instead of selling the land, the proprietors granted township charters to petitioning groups who met their approval, and sometimes provided seed capital for cutting roads and erecting mills. They required original grantees to meet certain conditions lest they forfeit their rights and frequently regranted the land to more energetic developers if the conditions were not met. The only profit which accrued to the proprietors came from the increased value of the plots in each township they reserved for themselves. In the nearly forty years the Masonian Proprietors remained active they granted thirty-seven townships. More than half of these grants came before 1765; by then several of the resulting settlements had also gained formal incorporation.

The fourth process by which a large number of townships came into existence was the chartering by provincial authorities of what historians have labeled "speculative proprietorships." The proprietorships served a variety of functions: they enabled the government to establish jurisdiction over territory which already had been or might be claimed by magistrates in neighboring colonies, provided a convenient vehicle for rewarding men whose cooperation provincial authorities sought, helped relieve the pressures created by a rapidly expanding population, and gave speculators throughout New England an opportunity to invest in the future of the province. The Governor and Council, like the Masonians, required town proprietors to develop the land within a specific time period and sometimes regranted townships when the holders of original proprietary rights failed to meet charter conditions. Of the towns in New Hampshire founded by the mid-1760s, over fifty began as proprietary grants by the Governor and Council.

The provincial government made its initial proprietary grants between 1720 and 1722. The first four—Chester, Nottingham, Barrington and Rochester—were an imaginatively conceived experiment in utilizing the township as a device to promote both geographic expansion and economic development. Rochester helped validate New Hampshire's claims along the eastern border with Massachusetts, and parts of Barrington had earlier been granted by the Bay Colony. Barrington contained bog iron which the proprietors, with the assistance of the provincial government, planned to develop. Moreover, the four towns included large stands of valuable timber. In 1711 the home government had passed regulations reserving all mast trees on public lands for use of the crown. Since the land in each of the newly granted towns belonged to proprietors listed in the charters, it fell under private ownership and thus became exempt from imperial regulation. Indeed, economic opportunities in the four frontier towns seemed so promising that provincial authorities made certain they would gain a share of future profits. Lieutenant Governor John Wentworth and several of the councillors who chartered Barrington, for example, were among its 272 proprietors as were most of the elected assemblymen. Wentworth was one of two men receiving more than a full square mile.

The experiment proved successful. Despite the delay caused by Dummer's War, many proprietors moved into the townships and others either leased their property or sold their rights to those who expressed willingness to become residents. The ironworks probably never did get built, but farming and lumbering flourished. In 1727 the Governor and Council erected seven additional townships in the territory between the Merrimack and Piscataqua. They experienced no difficulty locating inhabitants willing to pay the small fee required of all participating proprietors.

The bulk of subsequent proprietary grants by the provincial government came in the 1760s. By that time the various adjustments necessitated by the boundary decision had been made, settlement had begun to spread beyond the limits of the Masonian patent, and the defeat of the French and Indians seemed likely. Even before the Treaty of Paris was signed, the Governor and Council adopted a policy of chartering townships in territory between New Hampshire and Canada. The townships differed from the earlier proprietary model only in that the number of proprietors was smaller—sixty-five to seventy—and that grantees came mostly from outside New Hampshire. The provincial authorities were so eager to establish jurisdiction in the region they employed agents to peddle the townships in Connecticut and Massachusetts. The practice worked well: by mid-decade land as far north as modern day Lancaster had all been granted, and there were over 150 legally defined New Hampshire townships.

The Economy: Expansion, Organization, and Prosperity

All this—extended borders, war, population growth, and the founding of many new townships—helped shape the course of economic development in eighteenth century New Hampshire. The central features of that development were rapid expansion in the level of economic activity, the gradual introduction of more varied and complex forms of economic organization, and an overall increase in the individual standard of living. Expansion took place in every significant area of the economy: agricultural output soared, the production of non-food items multiplied several fold, both internal and external trade flourished, and the level of capital accumulation, investment, and speculation increased. The organizational changes included refinement of the proprietary as an instrument for land development, the appearance of a far more integrated and flexible system for marketing goods, and the increased use of the provincial government to coordinate and stimulate the economy as a whole. It is impossible to measure standard of

living with any precise yardstick, but economic historians have estimated that in the years between the Peace of Utrecht and the American
Revolution the real income of the average colonist (slaves excluded)
probably doubled; circumstantial evidence suggests that New Hampshirites benefitted fully from the general pattern of prosperity.

Growth in agricultural production, of course, stemmed mainly from
the tenfold increase in population. The vast majority of both natives
and immigrants assumed responsibility for producing the food they
consumed. Men, women, and children all participated in the annual
cycle of spring planting, summertime tending of crops, fall harvest,
and the yearlong task of caring for livestock. Agricultural surplus was
used to purchase a few exotic groceries like rum, tea, spices, and sugar.
Need and tradition dictated that even those with income from other
sources—artisans, ministers, storekeepers, and lumbermen—engage
in some farming.

Other factors contributed to agricultural growth. Per capita production increased for a variety of reasons. Men spent a good portion
of their time clearing the land in the initial years of homesteading but
as time passed devoted more of their energy to planting and harvesting.
Farmers learned which crops grew well in local soil and which did not;
they shared their accumulated experience with neighbors and gradually
became more skilled in their occupation. Technological innovation,
though limited, also helped increase production. Equally important
the percentage of relatively "mature" farms within provincial boundaries
grew. In 1715 much of settled New Hampshire lay open to attack and
the general state of agriculture had been adversely affected by a generation of continuous frontier warfare. Fifty years later most farms had
been in existence for decades and despite some reduction in soil fertility,
were as a whole more productive. Finally, the second period of Anglo-
French warfare stimulated agriculture instead of retarding it. The presence of British armies in the northern colonies provided a guaranteed
market for surplus commodities. Demand for foodstuffs became so
great, in fact, that for several years New Hampshire became a net
importer of flour, grain, and pork.

Non-food production increased, if anything, more rapidly. Much
of it took place within the individual household as the men in the
family, having cleared sufficient acreage, spent a greater percentage
of time on home building and the manufacture of both farm implements

and furniture; the women produced cloth and finished wearing apparel. The Scotch-Irish in Londonderry and neighboring communities were especially aggressive in the development of household manufacturing. By the mid-1720s they had gained the reputation for producing an excellent grade of linen; with the cooperation of regional merchants they sold goods throughout the colonies and in international markets as well.

Some individuals and families made household manufacturing their primary form of economic activity. There always had been men skilled in blacksmithing, shoemaking, and other specialized activities, but in the decades after the Peace of Utrecht the proportion of artisans in the population as a whole gradually increased. Newcomers to the colony needed their services, and the increase in agricultural surpluses gave inhabitants the wherewithall to pay for commodities produced by others. In the older and larger communities artisans began to hire assistants to help increase production, and after a period of apprenticeship the assistant gained sufficient skill to move out and establish his own shop. Some artisans became general retailers in the communities they served by marketing the goods received in exchange for their products as well as the objects they manufactured.

The major source of expansion in non-food production, however, was not the individual household. The expansion stemmed from the widespread exploitation of New Hampshire's abundant timber resources both for domestic consumption and for export. Throughout the colony entrepreneurs gained permission from either proprietors or town authorities to construct sawmills along the numerous brooks and rivers. More than two hundred such mills existed by the 1740s and the number continued to grow in the next quarter century. The lumber—most of it pine—produced in these mills became the basic building material for homes, barns, and wharves in places as far away as the Mediterranean littoral. By the 1760s the annual production of pine boards was nearly twenty million board feet. And lumber was by no means the only wood product manufactured in the province. In the Piscataqua and elsewhere hundreds of men were occupied in the production of barrel staves, shingles, hoops, clapboards, and drainspouts.

The most sophisticated use of timber resources involved the manufacture of ship components and shipbuilding itself. Some of these activities had taken place in the seventeenth century, but production increased several fold in the fifty years after the Peace of Utrecht. Masting, a term which encompassed the cutting and shaping of spars and bowsprits as well as masts themselves, reached its maximum level by the early 1740s and remained there for two decades before declining in the 1760s. The production of oak plank declined earlier. Shipbuilding experienced a steadier pattern of growth. Although no precise figures are available, circumstantial evidence suggests that both the number of vessels built and their average size continued to rise until well after the end of the Anglo-French wars. The economies of Portsmouth, and to a lesser extent Exeter and Dover, boomed as the number of sail manufactures, ropewalks, and shipyards increased. Artisans skilled in producing ship components found the demand for their services on the rise. The Piscataqua as a whole became one of the major shipbuilding regions in all of North America.

Inevitably, as the inhabitants of New Hampshire produced more and more goods not used in their own homes, trade played an increased role in the provincial economy. Much of the trade took place within individual villages and townships. The average farming family was not the self-sufficient economic unit so commonly romanticized in popular literature about colonial America. To the contrary, farmers depended heavily on the labor and surplus commodities of their neighbors. The diaries of men like Matthew Patten of Bedford make clear the nature of that dependence. Patten provided services for others, traded items almost weekly, and recorded the details of every transaction so there could be no doubt about what obligations remained unfulfilled in the complex pattern of exchange which marked his life. Regularly scheduled fairs broadened the scope of commerce within towns. Initially the privilege of holding such fairs had to be granted by the colonial governor. Hampton Falls, for example, obtained approval from Governor Belcher for an annual day of "public trading" in 1734, eight years after the town had been incorporated. But as time passed the usefulness of such public trading became so apparent that the privilege became an assumed right. Most of the proprietary charters granted after 1740 included a provision that as soon as fifty families were settled, the town should "have the liberty of holding two fairs annually" and should "also have a market opened and kept one or more days in each week." The appearance of privately owned stores added to the opportunity for local commerce.

Trade among inhabitants of different towns also increased rapidly. The construction of roads and bridges which freed inhabitants from their earlier dependence on water transportation made such trade possible, and the ability of residents throughout the province to pay for goods imported from England or colonies elsewhere in America made it profitable. In the 1740s Samuel Lane, a Stratham tanner and shoemaker, marketed his goods in Portsmouth, on the Isles of Shoals, and in nearby Exeter and Greenland. The Great Bay area, the Merrimack valley between Rumford and Londonderry, and lower Connecticut River valley had developed thriving regional economies by the 1760s.

Overseas trade capped the entire structure of commerce and provided the single most dynamic element in New Hampshire's economic growth. The Piscataqua served as the center for overseas trade, and since both imperial and provincial officials kept records of entering and departing vessels, reasonably accurate estimates of the quantities of goods involved can be made. Despite the presence of some fish and other foodstuffs, forest products dominated the export trade. Shipments of pine lumber climbed from a quarter million board feet annually in the 1690s to nearly two million feet annually in the 1730s; by midcentury the total had reached the six million figure and in 1768 nearly double that amount left the Piscataqua for the West Indies alone. The number of barrel staves and shingles exported increased at a similarly dramatic rate. Shipments to naval stores grew steadily until the 1740s, then began to level off as the supply of large trees available for masts declined and a greater percentage of manufactured ship components were used to build ships locally. It is not clear how many vessels constructed in New Hampshire were themselves sold in England and the West Indies, but the total must have been large enough to constitute a significant component of overseas exports. Smaller quantities of finished furniture, drainspouts, joists, houseframes, and even firewood appear in the shipping records.

The proliferation of exports gave New Hampshire merchants the credit with which to purchase more goods from traders in other colonies, the West Indies, and England. Salt was the largest single import item; from 1695 to 1752 the annual quantity rose from 100,000 to nearly 1,000,000 pounds. Sugar, molasses, rum, wine, pork, and flour were also important. As time passed, the list of non-food items grew larger and more varied. Textiles, finished clothing, nails, tallow, ironware, glass, lead, and dozens of other items all were imported in increasing quantities. Incomplete records and the frequency of smuggling make it impossible to determine the relative value of exports and imports, but the two must have been in some kind of rough balance. New Hampshire merchants never became as heavily indebted to their overseas counterparts as did, by contrast, many plantation owners in the Chesapeake.

Increased production and commerce, in turn, made possible the accumulation of capital for investment and speculation. The opportunities for such activities were many. The farmer who saved even a few pounds could and with greater and greater frequency did buy additional land, hoping later to sell it for a profit. Proprietary rights cost as little as a hundred shillings—about fifty times the prevailing daily wages—and the steady influx of immigrants almost guaranteed that such rights could be marketed with relative ease. Successful merchants and others with greater resources not only speculated in land but sometimes assumed development costs in newly founded communities. In the older towns, Portsmouth especially, men used their surplus capital to build wharfs, shipyards, and commercial buildings. Hundreds of individuals became either full or part owners of vessels engaged in maritime trade. At the beginning of the eighteenth century less than a third of the ships departing the Piscataqua were owned by New Hampshiremen; the percentage more than doubled in the next sixty years. Some investments, of course, proved costly—saw and grist mills could be washed away during spring freshets, ships were lost at sea, and not all land could be sold at a profit—but economic conditions as a whole remained sufficiently promising to encourage continued risk taking.

In the seventeenth century, the mechanisms of economic organization were relatively simple. Families produced goods for personal consumption and had little need to develop ways of marketing their surplus beyond the communities in which they lived. Men engaged in overseas trade either did so on an individual basis or relied on more experienced Boston merchants as middlemen. The town served as the most effective unit of economic regulation: it distributed land, granted mill rights, organized exchange of commodities, and in general tried to protect against the possibility of economic disaster. There were, to be sure, exceptions to these generalizations. The production of naval stores required more elaborate planning and organization than did other forms of economic activity and war forced both the provincial and imperial governments to interfere in the pattern of town autonomy. But for the most part simplicity remained the central feature of provincial economic organization.

The eighteenth century was marked by the development of more varied and complex forms of economic organization. One major innovation involved the use of the proprietary to stimulate growth. Conceived initially as a solution to the problem of establishing provincial jurisdiction over territory where few if any settlers existed, the proprietary was economic not governmental in nature. Town proprietors collectively had the right to distribute land, and assumed responsibility for settling the township and providing necessary economic services like road clearing and the erection of grist and saw mills. Individual proprietors responded to the mixed patterns of opportunity and obligation in a variety of ways. Many sold their rights to others, for a quick profit if possible. Others leased their land. Still others did little except pay their portion of development costs and wait for the value of their property to rise. Many men moved to the frontier and became residents as well as proprietors. Eventually the settlers, both proprietors and non-proprietors, grew large enough in number to assume the right of self-government.

The proprietary system proved remarkably successful as an instrument for promoting geographical and economic expansion. The key to that success was the flexibility it gave to those with the time, energy, and capital for land development. In many cases the new township was settled by younger men from an old town who as a group purchased proprietary rights, planned their migration in detail before moving, and maintained close contact with their "parent" community after their trek into the wilderness. Thus the Oyster River portion of Dover sired Canterbury and several towns became satellite communities to the Scotch-Irish in Londonderry. In other cases a single individual bought up a large portion of the newly granted township and took responsibility for fulfilling charter conditions. Sampson Stoddard did so in Fitzwilliam and Acworth, Benjamin Bellows in Walpole, Samuel Chase in Cornish, and Josiah Willard in Winchester. In still other cases the proprietors in neighboring grants joined together to stimulate regional settlement. Proprietary managers in Lebanon, Hanover, Hartford, and Norwich, for example, jointly arranged for construction of a road northward from the older settlement in Charlestown. Furthermore, the one major problem experienced with the proprietary—indifference on the part of those granted township rights—was easily solved. The provincial government could and frequently did repossess townships where little or no progress had been made. Repossessed townships were then regranted to a new set of proprietors. All in all, it is difficult to imagine a system of land distribution and development which could more effectively have stimulated economic expansion in New Hampshire than did the proprietorships.

The way in which goods were marketed also underwent gradual change. The old mechanisms of trade—private bartering, public sales on town regulated market days, and opportunistic importing and exporting of commodities—remained important, but less so. One new feature was the introduction of paper money. The provincial government emitted notes in 1709; the presence of a flexible medium of exchange so facilitated commerce that assemblymen voted for several subsequent emissions. At one point in the 1730s when tension between Governor Belcher and the Assembly seriously reduced the supply of public currency, a group of Portsmouth merchants began issuing private money. Notes from the other New England provinces also circulated in New Hampshire. Whatever the source, the presence of paper significantly reduced dependence on bartering.

Paper money also contributed to the decline of community control over marketing and the rise of private merchandising. The problem with town fairs and market days was their restrictiveness: trade simply became too important to limit to a few days a month. Private entrepreneurs—most began by turning one room in the ground floor of their house into a store—were always eager to do business. General traders first appeared in the Piscataqua. By the end of the Anglo-French wars dozens of stores existed in the interior. The owners of these stores purchased their goods from and sold commodities to merchants in Portsmouth, Newburyport, Boston, and Hartford, Connecticut. Thus New Hampshire steadily became more integrated into the economy of New England as a whole.

Another innovation was regional advertising. Beginning in the 1720s Piscataqua merchants utilized Boston newspapers—all of which

Water color rendering by an unknown artist of the Sheafe family warehouse in Portsmouth. The warehouse, built before the mid-eighteenth century, remains standing today in Prescott Park, Portsmouth.
Courtesy of the New Hampshire Historical Society.

had subscribers in New Hampshire—to announce the availability of goods for sale. Advertising became easier and more effective after 1756 when Daniel Fowle, a Boston printer in trouble with Bay Colony magistrates, moved to Portsmouth and commenced weekly publication of the *New Hampshire Gazette*. Fowle's newspaper prospered, in part because he was an energetic entrepreneur, but also because merchants in New Hampshire found advertising in the *Gazette* increased their sales markedly. The newspaper soon had subscribers in every eastern New Hampshire town and contributed significantly to the development of a regional economy on the Piscataqua watershed. Massachusetts newspapers played a similar role in the Merrimack valley.

A different set of organizational innovations took place in the structure of New Hampshire's export trade. The business became more complex, more specialized, and less dependent on capital and management from outside the province. As the volume of trade increased rapidly and forests near the coastline became depleted, it was necessary for exporters to develop relationships with suppliers far in the hinterland. Similarly, the increased volume of trade made it difficult for the same man to be a ship captain and exporter. Long absences from Portsmouth in the former role hindered his affairs in the latter role. By the end of the 1720s individual merchants had begun to form "houses," the contemporary term for small groups of clerks, ship captains, and others joined together for the management of overseas trade. Often, though not always, members of the group were related by birth or marriage.

The arrangement worked well. Because houses established permanent connections with similar organizations in the West Indies and England, trade as a whole became more stabilized and predictable. Some merchants utilized their overseas linkages to obtain favorable contracts. Mark Hunking Wentworth, for example, gained a dominant position in the mast trade through his relationship with the English merchant John Thomlinson. Equally important, at least for the economic development of New Hampshire as a whole, the new pattern of organization helped free Piscataqua merchants from financial dependence on their counterparts in England and Massachusetts Bay. By mid-century more than half the vessels involved in Piscataqua trade were New Hampshire owned and a large percentage had been built in the province. And of the ten most active Piscataqua traders, seven lived

Money in four different denominations printed in 1737 by the provincial government. *Courtesy of the New Hampshire Historical Society.*

in the province. No longer did outside entrepreneurs gain the major portion of profits from New Hampshire's export trade.

Another major shift was the increased role of provincial authorities in regulating and stimulating economic development. Even though the imperial government provided ground rules for both overseas trade and some kinds of internal economic activity, and towns tried to control local affairs, the governor, Council and House were in a better position to affect what actually happened in New Hampshire. The governor either directly or indirectly determined how seriously imperial regulations would be enforced. As Surveyor General of the King's Woods, charged with responsibility for enforcing Parliament's white pine policy, Benning Wentworth made little attempt to inhibit exploitation of New Hampshire's forest resources. Similarly, neither he nor his predecessors clamped down on notoriously lax customs officials. The Governor and Council together distributed land, established the basic responsibilities of town proprietors (the Masonian group made certain its standards did not differ significantly from those of the provincial government) and as the highest judicial authority in New Hampshire decided how seriously violators of provincial regulations would be punished. Those regulations were the product of deliberations in which House members as well as the Governor and Council participated. Since many of New Hampshire's most successful and aggressive entrepreneurs became representatives, it is not surprising that the House urged passage of literally hundreds of acts designed to promote economic development. Many of its recommendations became law. In addition to the money emissions there were bills authorizing road and bridge construction, bills encouraging sheep raising and hemp growing, bills defining the rights of both millowners and farmers threatened with flooding if milldams were constructed, and bills designed to maximize profits from overseas trade. During the eighteenth century economic development became an overriding concern for a larger and larger percentage of New Hampshire inhabitants. Few had cause to complain about lack of cooperation from their provincial government.

Economic expansion and innovation brought increased prosperity to the citizens of New Hampshire as a whole. Visitors to Portsmouth in the 1760s frequently commented on its many fine mansions, churches, and commercial buildings. Village centers in towns throughout the southeastern parts of the province contained numerous large and well maintained frame houses; taverns, active markets, and carefully fenced fields added to the general appearance of communal well being. Even the inhabitants of newly settled townships had much for which to be thankful. Unlike earlier frontiersmen they could count on the availability of imported commodities like salt, rum, and ironware and many had sufficient capital to employ others in the arduous task of carving out a homestead in the wilderness.

Not everyone, of course, shared equally in the benefits of growth. All communities included men who because of physical disability, misfortune, poor work habits, or other personal limitations had acquired little property and lived on the edge of poverty. The widows of such men often had to be cared for by town officials. Portsmouth, like other large colonial seaports, harbored a floating population of intermittently employed sailors who also required public maintenance. In the interior were significant numbers of single young men engaged in cutting mast trees or other forms of lumbering whose wages, if the complaints of colonial ministers can be believed, ended up mainly in the cash boxes of local tavern keepers.

At the other end of the scale were individuals and families with sufficient wealth to support a style of living well beyond the means of the average citizen. The very rich, like the very poor, were concentrated in Portsmouth. There the Wentworths, Jaffreys, Sherburnes, Atkinsons, Pierces, and many other successful merchants led an exclusive and expensive social life centered in their homes near Strawberry Bank. They hired architects to design these homes, sponsored an occasional theatrical or musical performance, commissioned artists to paint individual and family portraits, and sent many of their sons to Harvard. Most other communities also contained a recognized economic elite, though outside the Piscataqua wealth generally came more from land ownership than from success in trading. The homes and living habits of the rural elite were less ostentatious than those of their urban counterparts.

The vast majority of residents, however, were neither rich nor poor. By the 1760s most of the "middling sort," a term used often by contemporaries, lived in frame houses, had sufficient capital to invest in acreage not used for farming, produced enough surplus to have cash for an occasional luxury purchase, and were as a whole quite satisfied

Four products of increased economic prosperity. The clock, made by David Blasdel of Massachusetts, was owned by Josiah Bartlett of New Hampshire and is probably similar to the clock Samuel Lane owned. A New Hampshire cabinet maker, John Kimball, made the desk. The silver salver belonged to Theodore Atkinson, a wealthy Portsmouth merchant. The object with the Reverend Timothy Walker's name on it is a pocketbook. *All four photographs courtesy of the New Hampshire Historical Society.*

with their economic accomplishments. Samuel Lane of Stratham was one such individual. A tanner by trade, Lane set out on his own at the age of twenty-one with nothing but a small amount of leather given to him by his father. He tanned leather, made and sold shoes, invested in both land and livestock, built a house with the help of hired labor, and before he turned thirty took pride in the purchase of his first clock. A few years later he had become sufficiently prosperous to build a house addition. When it was finished Lane held a party. "Had my Father and Mother and all their fourteen children together at my table," he noted with pride in his diary.

Hundreds of other men and women in mid-eighteenth century New Hampshire felt similar pride in their accomplishments. They were the direct beneficiaries of the geographic expansion, population growth, founding of new towns, and increase in economic opportunity that had occurred since the Peace of Utrecht.

8

SOCIAL INSTITUTIONS: FAMILY, CHURCH, AND COMMUNITY IN A CHANGING WORLD

The basic structure of society shaped during the first century of European settlement in New Hampshire remained intact for the rest of
the colonial period. Men and women continued to function in families,
churches, and units of government of which the town was of greatest
daily importance, and to assume that individual acceptance of legitimate authority exercised at all three levels was the best protection
against social disorder and immorality. Moreover, those with responsibility for maintaining the effectiveness of family, church, and polity
worked hard to fulfill their obligations. The Bible, tradition, and their
own sense of duty dictated they do so.

Rapid growth after the Peace of Utrecht, however, produced serious
strains within this basic social structure. Problems arose not so much
in individual households—families, in fact, may have been strengthened by the course of events—but in religious and communal institutions. The churches experienced a number of difficulties. There were
not enough capable pastors to serve all the new towns, and individual
congregations were buffeted by the "Great Awakening"—a massive
evangelical revival which took place in all of North America during
the 1730s and 1740s—by the loss of members to other faiths, and by
a decline in the general level of religious commitment among inhabitants. At the same time towns lost some of the cohesiveness they
possessed at the start of the century. Demographic change made community management more difficult, eroded the authority of town officials, and in many places produced a distressingly high level of religious and political conflict.

Family and Household

Family governance, the colonists believed, was one key to a properly ordered society. All individuals were expected to reside within a household dominated by a sense of mutual obligation and acceptance of clearly defined authority. Husbands ruled their wives, parents their children, and masters their servants. Custom and law defined both the limits of authority and the responsibilities of all household members. Those guilty of defying traditional patterns of discipline could be, and often were, punished by church and state officials.

At least one dimension of family life, the relationship between women and men, remained virtually unaltered throughout the colonial period. Evidence of female subordination in mid-eighteenth century New Hampshire is sketchy, yet compelling. In many churches women sat apart from men and retired when the congregation met to discuss policy. Women, of course, could not vote in town and provincial elections. Wives often were described by their husbands in formal and impersonal terms. The diaries of Samuel Lane, for example, include such entries as "I married a wife," and "I hired journeymen when I wanted help to save my weakly wife the trouble of a great family"; not once did Lane use his wife's given name. Daughters fared the same as their mothers. They received little or no formal education and were not expected to share the responsibilities of public leadership. When Lane drew up his will he left his most important books to his sons; his daughters had "liberty" to read the books only if they requested it "of their brethern." A visitor to Portsmouth noted that "women come not into company, no not so much as at dinner." Perhaps the best summary of women's expected role in life was made by an anonymous provincial poet who wrote late in the 1750s:

Small is the province of a wife,
And narrow is her sphere in life,
Within that sphere to move aright,
Should be her principal delight.

The parent-child relationship remained reasonably intact also. Tradition dictated that daughters serve the household until married, and that sons both work for their fathers until the age of twenty-one and care for their parents when they grew old. Most daughters had no choice but to accept the norm. The main exception seems to have occurred when a surplus of daughters in the household made the presence of some superfluous. In such cases the daughter, with permission of her parents, might "hire out" to a neighbor and work for wages. Many sons did labor for their fathers until twenty-one. The practice was so widely accepted that the provincial government compensated fathers for loss of services if an underage son were wounded or killed while in the military. Sons, furthermore, often signed formal contracts to provide for one parent should the other die, to care for handicapped or elderly relatives, or to assume other family responsibilities. Eldest sons, who by custom received larger portions of family estates, generally accepted the greater portion of such obligations.

There may, however, have been some alteration in this generally stable pattern. Teenage sons who were unhappy with their parents encountered little difficulty finding a job if they left. They could go to sea, sign on with a masting crew, or in time of war join a military regiment. The ready availability of land made sons less dependent on parents for the wherewithall to establish their own household. Because New Hampshire had no law requiring the publication of marriage banns, and ministers in several communities—Hampton Falls and Chester especially—were notorious for their willingness to conduct quick marriages, young couples sometimes eloped in defiance of parental wishes. How frequently such events occurred can only be guessed, but it is clear that many adults in the province thought something had gone awry. "Young people grow uncommonly loose, rude, vain, and ungoverned," lamented one observer in 1757, "and if restrained by their superiors immediately list into the war, and so get clear of their parents." In the mid-1760s the provincial government passed a law prohibiting single persons "of either sex, under the age of twenty-one" from living "at their own hand." Justices of the peace were given the authority to place them under "some orderly family government."

Whatever the degree of erosion in parental authority, there can be no doubt that master-servant relationships underwent significant change in the eighteenth century. The change was of two kinds. White servitude declined in importance. Few indentured servants moved to the province after the Peace of Utrecht, and of those who did a good number abandoned their masters. The unwillingness of servants to remain, in turn, made potential masters hesitant to invest in indentures. A similar though less pronounced development took place in the institution of apprenticeship. Parents, unable to hire labor cheaply, became more reluctant to apprentice their own children to others and when they did, demanded more of the child's future master. Children who were apprenticed often chafed at their servitude and threatened to leave unless adequately rewarded. The absence of kinship ties in most master-servant relationships further weakened the sense of mutual obligation. By the 1760s white servitude played a far less important role in provincial social and economic life than it had in the seventeenth century.

Black servitude, on the other hand, increased in importance. There were very few Africans in New Hampshire in 1715; the census taken fifty years later listed over six hundred slaves and a number of free blacks also living in the province. Affluent merchants owned the largest number of slaves—a third of the black population resided in Portsmouth—but ministers, prosperous farmers, and others with sufficient capital to afford the investment also became owners. Black servants could be easily identified should they run away, and unlike many whites, they seemed willing to accept household authority. Slaves lived in more than fifty New Hampshire towns when the wars with France ended, and ownership of African servants had become a status symbol throughout the province.

Families, no matter what happened to relationships within the household, retained their central role in the organization of society as a whole. Individual success was very much a function of birth. The child of indigent parents normally remained poor and struggled to eke out a spare existence in a harsh world. Families of the "middling" sort produced moderately ambitious children satisfied with their station in life, willing to accept traditional family responsibilities, and capable enough to fulfill them. Wealth and high social status tended to beget still more wealth and high social status unless the offspring lacked the personal qualities to take advantage of their opportunities. There were, of course, exceptions to the rule, but pronounced changes in family status from generation to generation were rare in eighteenth century New Hampshire.

In part this stability stemmed from the way in which individuals were educated. Despite laws requiring all towns to maintain grammar schools (the initial legislation was enacted in 1693) few children in colonial New Hampshire ever had the opportunity to attend publicly sponsored educational institutions. Many towns simply ignored the laws and the provincial government made no serious attempt to enforce them. When schools were built towns encountered problems in finding competent schoolmasters: New Hampshire contained few formally educated residents, the pay for teachers was much lower than for common laborers, and the average student manifested little interest in academic work. Those hired to teach rarely stayed long. Exeter had eleven different schoolmasters in the 1730s alone. Several towns had the embarrassing experience of discovering that recently hired instructors had absconded with school funds.

Under these circumstances parents assumed direct responsibility for seeing that their children gained sufficient skills to make their way in the world. Parents normally taught what they knew. Sons of farmers learned how to manage a farm. Parents did have other options since they could apprentice a son or hire a tutor to train their offspring academically. But taking advantage of these options required more sacrifice than most were willing to make. The ambitious child could insist that he be allowed to learn a trade different from his father and threaten to leave otherwise, but custom and normal familial affection discouraged such rebellion. There was a much higher degree of occupational continuity in eighteenth century families than there is today.

A second reason for the central role that kinship ties played in colonial New Hampshire society had to do with the structure of community life. Every town had its own pecking order, and family, more than any other factor, determined an individual's social status. Elites tended to become self-perpetuating. The family composition of Portsmouth's merchant aristocracy changed little in the eighteenth century; clusters of "leading" families existed in all the other old communities in New Hampshire. The situation along the frontier was more fluid, but not much. In many new townships a single man commanded such economic power and local prestige that his sons and relatives could not help but benefit from their association with him. In others the original settlers all came from the same level of society and it took longer for status differentiation to emerge.

A variety of economic factors also contributed to the continued importance of the family. The high cost of hired labor made farmers more dependent on their children than they would have been in a labor-rich economy. The proprietary form of land distribution—virtually all the land in the township came under private ownership before actual settlement—frequently meant that a family moving into the wilderness found itself temporarily without neighbors and had to rely almost exclusively on its own resources. The difficulties merchants encountered in locating dependable agents and clerks encouraged them to train sons and relatives for those jobs. And increased demand for artisan services made it possible for the craftsman to use not one, but several sons in his business.

Finally, family remained important because people wanted it to serve as the focal point of their lives. It always had, and nothing in the colonial experience altered that expectation. If anything, the inhabitants of mid-eighteenth century New Hampshire had more reason to emphasize family, for a complex set of developments had begun to erode the authority of both church and community, the other two major social institutions of which they were part.

Churches, Ministers, and Congregations

In the spring of 1763 the *New Hampshire Gazette* printed an article about public resistance to the payment of local taxes. The writer, who called himself "Timothy Meanwell," offered a solution to the problem. Since ministerial salaries ate up a good portion of such taxes each community should be asked to vote on a resolution that all ministers "be henceforth totally and finally dismissed." There had been a time, "Meanwell" admitted, when such a resolution "doubtless would have failed had it been put to the test," but those times had passed. In virtually every provincial community the combination of "men who never, or rarely" went to church, those who loved "money above all things," and those who disagreed with their ministers' religious beliefs would produce a majority for dismissal. Fired ministers should then be encouraged to set up retail liquor establishments where they would have ready access to those needing instruction and could ply their trade without cost to the public. "Meanwell" concluded by remarking that all critics of local taxation unwilling to accept his proposal should "stop their mouths as close as a bottle of ale and never so much as mutter out the least complaint."

"Meanwell" jested of course—neither the provincial government

nor individual communities would have dared follow his recommendations—but the jest had bite to it. Church attendance in New Hampshire had become irregular; a significant percentage of provincial inhabitants did seem increasingly eager to avoid any financial commitment
to the support of ministers; and theological disagreement, rare in the
first third of the century, had disrupted many congregations. Moreover,
what one man described as "the multiplicity of tippling houses" did
pose a threat to traditional patterns of social discipline. Several communities, in fact, had taverns but no settled minister. Since the majority
of the colonists still believed that a properly ordered and moral society
depended in large part on the effectiveness of church authority, these
were disturbing developments.

The law reflected general acceptance of two broad principles. The
Custom and law defined popular expectations about the organization
of church life in eighteenth century New Hampshire. Custom, the
product largely of past linkages with Massachusetts and continued
heavy immigration from southern New England, dictated that all towns
should erect a meeting house for public worship and hire a properly
trained Protestant clergyman to serve as a "settled" minister. The
minister and townspeople with whatever religious qualifications they
agreed upon would be full members of a formally established church
run by deacons and elders. All residents, whether or not they enjoyed
full church membership, should attend the religious services held regularly in the community meeting house. The church itself helped
maintain discipline in the community, and pastors, if they fulfilled
the potential of their office, provided both spiritual guidance and
effective leadership for the community as a whole.

The law reflected general acceptance of two broad principles. The
first was that traditional patterns of worship should be encouraged by
the provincial government. Legislation passed in 1693 and reenacted
later without significant change gave town freemen the right to choose
a settled minister and town officials the right to tax inhabitants for
his support; it also legalized local assessments for defraying the cost
of meeting house construction. Other laws, some temporary and some
permanent, exempted deacons and elders from military service and
ministers from a variety of public responsibilities. New town charters
required proprietors to set aside at least two parcels of land for religious
purposes, one for the meeting house and another for personal use of
the settled minister. Many governmental pronouncements on other

matters contained language urging residents to support religious life in the colony.

The second principle gave individuals and groups some freedom of choice in the specific form of worship they wished to adopt. New Hampshire had what historians call a "multiple establishment": the system was "established" in that the state required all citizens to financially support some organized religious denomination, and "multiple" because the state did not attempt to dictate the specific denominational identification of ministers and congregations. Multiple establishment had its origins both in ideology—"liberty of conscience," as the legislation of 1693 put it, had gained grudging acceptance throughout the English speaking world—and in practical considerations. Practicing Anglicans and Quakers already lived in the province and the industrious Scotch-Irish who began arriving in the 1720s all were Presbyterians. Any law denying these dissenters from the congregational norm the right to practice their own faith would have met with royal disapproval, triggered internal religious conflict, and inhibited population growth.

In many ways the combined force of custom and law produced the kinds of religious activities considered essential to the functioning of a well-ordered society. Inhabitants, for example, constructed meeting houses throughout the province; by the mid-1760s the total had reached well over fifty and some of the larger towns had two or more. The buildings varied a good deal in size and degree of opulence, but all were financed by the people they served. The erection of a meeting house, in fact, became a major public symbol of communal accomplishment and provided those who contributed time, labor, and money to the task with an immense amount of satisfaction. Congregations usually celebrated completion of the work by holding a large communal dinner. Seating arrangements in the meeting houses reflected the social status of individuals and families.

The inhabitants also joined together in formally established churches. The process took place most quickly in townships settled by organized groups from communities in Massachusetts and Connecticut where a church already existed. In such cases the migrants simply transferred their membership to the new church. Frequently, as in the case of Upper Ashuelot (Keene) a minister was hired in the initial stages of settlement. In townships where the first settlers had less previous

Exterior and interior of the Sandown, New Hampshire, meeting house, built in 1773–1774. Original photographs by the Historic American Buildings Survey. *Courtesy of the New Hampshire Historical Society.*

association the process of church founding often took much longer. Despite this, the overall record was impressive. According to the best available tabulation sixty-six churches had been organized in New Hampshire by 1765; more than thirty others were founded during the next decade.

In addition, public worship became a normal part of the weekly routine in most communities. The minister delivered either one or two Sunday sermons and sometimes preached in the middle of the week. The average resident knew his Bible and paid close attention to both the minister's textual interpretations and his attempts to relate biblical content to everyday life. Church attendance had the added advantage of providing social entertainment. Groups of inhabitants gathered before and after the formal service to discuss recent developments in the province, catch up on local news, and comment on the weather. The pleasures of such gatherings undoubtedly helped ameliorate any displeasure the individual parishioner may have experienced in listening to the minister or paying local taxes for his salary.

Church meetings served an additional purpose: they provided an effective format for members to perform other communal functions. Frequently the goal was to punish aberrant social behavior. Deacons and elders normally determined the guilt or innocence of accused individuals, but the church as a whole participated in the disciplinary process. It was customary for the person judged guilty to confess and apologize in public, and refusal to do so normally resulted in at least temporary social ostracism. In many places the church as a collective entity decided how the guilty should be punished. Punishment ranged from simple admonishment—given, in one concrete case, to James Doake of Londonderry for failure to "respect and honor" his parents— to formal excommunication. Another common activity in church meetings was the collection of funds to help those in need. The same group that admonished James Doake raised money to ransom a town resident captured by natives and did the same for a farmer whose two cows had been killed by a falling tree.

The church experience of many eighteenth century New Hampshire residents fit with their expectations in still another way. Most ministers served both their congregations and communities well. They provided spiritual and moral guidance for individuals, mediated disputes, helped organize communal activities, and in general tried to manage their affairs in accordance with the traditions of their profession. Frequently, and especially along the frontier, ministers knew more about medicine and law than anyone else in town and offered advice in these areas. Ministers also tutored children and in several cases acted as school-masters for the entire community. Many pastors assumed they should remain with their churches unless dismissed, and did remain even when tempted to take advantage of professional opportunities elsewhere. Congregations and communities, in turn, sometimes became so attached to their religious leaders they found it difficult to imagine communal life in their absence. One example illustrates the point. In the spring of 1763 Daniel Wilkins, the settled minister in Amherst, threatened to leave if the provincial government approved a proposed alteration of town boundaries in the region. The town argued in a hastily drawn up petition to the General Assembly that "If our Minister leaves us . . . we shall be thrown into the utmost confusion and a quarrel will commence that will be handed down from generation to generation and never end, and it is easily seen that such quarrel and confusion will affect the government as it will obstruct the future growth and prosperity of the town." The Assembly apparently found the argument convincing and rejected the proposed change; Wilkins continued to serve Amherst until illness forced him into retirement.

Finally, acceptance of religious denominations other than Congregationalism worked reasonably well. The Scotch-Irish formed Presbyterian churches in the communities they settled and whenever possible hired ministers educated at the University of Edinburgh or at the College of New Jersey, which Presbyterians in the Middle Colonies had founded in 1746. Quaker families, who lived mostly in the towns north and west of Great Bay, erected a central meeting house in Dover and were granted exemption from payment of ministerial taxes in the various towns they inhabited. A group of Portsmouth residents established an Anglican church in the 1730s. With the help of friends in England they not only built Queen's Chapel, but convinced the Reverend Arthur Browne, then preaching in Rhode Island, to become their pastor. Other Anglican churches were established later. Residents of Newton formed the first Baptist church in the province shortly after mid-century. In 1765 a number of people professing allegiance to the doctrines of Robert Sandeman, a Scottish theologian, began worshipping in Portsmouth. Congregationalism, to be sure, remained the dominant form of religion in New Hampshire but any group of men and women with the time, money, and energy to establish a different denominational church could do so.

Much of church life in eighteenth century New Hampshire, then, proceeded smoothly in accordance with tradition and law. But not all church life. Ministers and congregations as a whole faced a set of closely related problems which complicated their lives immensely. Some of the problems were the product of local conditions, some reflected regional change, and still others trans-Atlantic developments. Success or failure in attempting to resolve these problems had a permanent impact, not just on the churches themselves, but on the entire structure of provincial society.

To begin with, church members often experienced difficulty hiring pastors. The specific nature of their difficulties varied from community to community, but the problem itself did not change. Frontier townships offered few amenities to young ministers looking for jobs, so they tended to go elsewhere. Portsmouth, at least early in the century, had such a bad reputation at Harvard that the faculty hesitated to recommend any but inferior candidates. One professor was reported to have said that a student of his, though lacking either "character" or "abilities," might prove satisfactory to the townspeople "for he could make a very handsome bow, and if the first did not suit, he'd bow lower a second time." The north parish in Portsmouth still invited the student to preach. He rejected the invitation, as did several others. The records of churches elsewhere in New Hampshire include frequent entries reporting similar rejections. Moreover, as time passed the problem of finding ministers intensified. To help alleviate the shortage, Governor John Wentworth in 1769 granted an ambitious Connecticut minister named Eleazar Wheelock a charter to found Dartmouth College. The college, however, produced few graduates during the colonial period. In the early 1770s twenty different churches in the province still had vacant pastorates.

Once a church managed to hire a minister, there was always the possibility he might prove unsatisfactory. Approximately forty ministers were dismissed by their congregations before the American Revolution. Many of these were young candidates whom the churches had invited to preach on a trial basis, but others had contracted with their communities for permanent employment. Because of this contractual arrangement dismissal often became a messy business. Hugh Adams of Durham managed to alienate his congregation which he labeled as "exceedingly viscious, disorderly, and unruly," refused to accept the advice of his fellow clergymen to give up the ministry, and when finally dismissed continued to preach in the town. The church in Canterbury discovered that its newly installed pastor had a past record of both adultery and theft; even then the church members tried to keep him, but pressure from ministers elsewhere in the province forced them into a formal dismissal. In other cases getting rid of an unsatisfactory minister caused little difficulty. The minister in Epping left willingly when accused of sexual misbehavior. A Newcastle clergyman who had impregnated his servant and tried to seduce several other parishioners left for England rather than face trial for his behavior.

Churches also faced the task of keeping a satisfactory minister happy with his station in life. Although most pastors accepted their commitment to a specific church as permanent—dozens served twenty years or longer during the colonial period—some did not. William Shurtleff, who had been with the Newcastle church for nineteen years, left abruptly when invited to the south parish in Portsmouth. The pastor in Nottingham accepted a post in Massachusetts even though his church refused to dismiss him and the town proprietors launched a formal complaint with the council of regional ministers which had responsibility for mediating such disputes. James Scales moved from Canterbury to Hopkinton after fifteen years. Ministerial reasons for abandoning a church varied in each case. Some left for financial reasons, some because they had been involved in theological disagreements with their congregations, and some because they decided to leave the ministry altogether. After mid-century more and more competent young college graduates trained as clergymen decided on more lucrative careers in commerce and law.

Difficulty in hiring and keeping good ministers was only one of the problems faced by churches in colonial New Hampshire. Many churches found their internal proceedings disrupted by frequent disputes. Sometimes the disputes pitted the minister against his congregation, sometimes the congregation against itself. Whatever the nature of the conflict the resulting disharmony left a bitter residue which infected church life thereafter.

Many disputes involved payment of the pastor's salary. Detailed contractual negotiations between ministerial candidates and the town or church officials who employed them occurred routinely, but once the original contract had been arranged most congregations assumed the matter was settled once and for all. Ministers, on the other hand, often asked for renegotiation. Periodic inflation eroded real income, bigger families than planned brought increased expenses, and a generally rising standard of living in the province made ministers regret having asked so little initially. Most tried to augment their income by investing in real estate, teaching, and utilizing whatever other talents they had, but salary remained their main financial resource so they demanded their contract be changed. Rarely did renegotiation proceed smoothly.

Theological disputes also occurred. They involved a number of doctrinal matters, but when most acute focused on the fundamental question of how men and women could know they had been chosen as one of God's elect. Disagreement about "conversion," "justification," and "sanctification," all terms used to describe an individual's religious condition, disrupted virtually all Congregational and some Presbyterian churches. By the mid-1740s the disruption had become so widespread that a large group of concerned ministers organized an annual convocation in order to, in their words, "guard the Churches against everything that might shock their foundations or corrupt their doctrine." And although the trouble subsided after mid-century, it never disappeared entirely.

For the first forty years of the eighteenth century a quiet orthodoxy prevailed in New Hampshire churches. All members wanted to be saved, but knew their ultimate fate lay in the hands of God. The most they could do was to act morally, worship regularly, and hope they would be judged accordingly. Moral conduct and faithful adherence to church ritual provided evidence of sanctification but not of justification. That came only with conversion, a psychologically powerful experience the precise nature of which no one could describe and the timing of which no one could predict. Should an individual claim conversion but not act sanctified, church officials would not accept the conversion as valid. Most churches were divided into two groups, communicants who participated fully in church ritual and those who had been baptized but not admitted to communion. The requirements for obtaining communicant status normally included proof of conversion.

Orthodoxy came under attack in all of North America during the fourth and fifth decades of the eighteenth century. The attack was led by clergymen who stimulated religious enthusiasm—the movement as a whole was known as the "Great Awakening"—partly through their evangelical style of preaching, and partly through their insistence that old doctrine had to be modified. Justification, they argued, required nothing more than a personal commitment to God. Commitment could be made at any time, had little to do with sanctification, and did not depend on the past moral conduct of an individual. The sacrifice of Christ had purged all men and women of their innate sinfulness; freed from their burden good Christians had only to acknowledge the beneficence of God to reap the rewards of their faith. Many new preachers also insisted that every converted individual have full access to church ritual and that only the converted could comprehend the true meaning of Scripture. The colonists labeled this set of theological beliefs "New Light," and the traditional set "Old Light."

Although elements of New Light doctrine may have been preached in New Hampshire earlier, the first general exposure came during a visit in 1740 by the charismatic English clergyman George Whitefield. Whitefield, who toured America several times and prompted religious controversy wherever he travelled, was disappointed by his initial reception. He noted after one sermon that he had "Preached to a polite auditory, and so very unconcerned that I began to question whether I had been preaching to rational or brute creatures," and left the province shortly. But Whitefield's presence stimulated others. Churches in many communities invited New Light clergymen to deliver sermons, the established ministers in a few towns began conducting New Light services, and itinerant New Light preachers without permanent employment appeared before receptive audiences. Sometimes the results were dramatic. Nicholas Gilman, an intense Harvard graduate who gained notoriety throughout New England for his activities, described one meeting in Durham as follows: "We continued in religious exercises all night. Had the presence of the Lord with us in a very wonderful manner.... What shown forth and made the deepest [impression] on my soul was a marvelous display of the manifold wisdom of God in man's redemption by Christ . . . . We held on . . . sometimes praying, then singing, exhorting, advising, and directing and rejoicing together in the Lord. It seemed the shortest and was, I think, the sweetest night that I have ever seen." When Whitefield returned to New Hampshire in 1744 the Great Awakening was in full swing. "A more visible alteration I never saw in any people," he commented about the congregation he had addressed in 1740, "I could scarcely believe I was preaching to the same persons that behaved like rocks and stones four years earlier."

The impact of New Light theology and preaching on individual churches in New Hampshire varied a good deal. Several, including those in the upper Merrimack valley where the Reverend Timothy Walker kept matters under tight control, seem not to have been significantly affected. In many other churches the New Light preferences of an already popular minister helped stimulate a revival in interest in religion broad enough to discourage Old Lights from taking any decisive action. A few congregations, however, experienced serious internal rifts. In Stratham the church members found their regular minister, Henry Rust, much too conservative, invited two different New Lights to preach, and despite the opposition of Rust hired one of the two as an associate minister. The most distressing confrontation occurred in Exeter. About a third of the inhabitants had New Light preferences and became incensed when their Old Light minister, John Odlin, not only tried to have his equally conservative son Woodbridge hired as associate and heir apparent to the ministry, but met the travelling Whitefield at the town borders and ordered him to stay out of town. Although Odlin Sr. eventually relented and let Whitefield lecture in the meeting house, the New Lights left the church, hired their own clergyman, and after a long delay gained recognition as a separate parish.

Understandably, most ministers in the province felt threatened and offended by theological innovation. They commented on the undisciplined response of residents to New Light preaching, complained about the disruptive influence of itinerent clergymen, and worried about the moral state of a society gone mad. One minister reported that Gilman's Durham congregation "made all manner of mouths, turning out their lips . . . as if convulsed, straining their eyeballs and twisting their bodies in all manner of unseemly postures." In 1747 Odlin and others organized a general meeting which seventeen ministers attended. Previous ministerial convocations had been mostly social affairs, but this one was different. It condemned "ignorant persons who set themselves up as teachers," formed a permanent council to check on the theological beliefs of all ministerial candidates in the province, appointed a special committee to investigate Gilman, and passed a lengthy resolution describing the "divers errors in doctrine" lately propagated "contrary to the rules of peace and holiness." Among the list of doctrinal errors cited were the belief "that morality is not the essence of Christianity," the belief "that God sees no sin in his children," and the belief "that sanctification is not evidence of justification." The theological battle lines between Old and New Lights were clearly drawn.

Neither side, however, won the battle. The influence of the New Lights gradually declined after mid-decade. Whitefield left the province; external pressure, self-doubt, and poor health forced Gilman to resign his Durham pulpit (he died in 1748); itinerant preaching all but disappeared; and churches looked increasingly askance at ministerial candidates whose theology seemed too unorthodox. At the same time many established ministers were sufficiently disoriented by the Great Awakening to change their ways. "Some of them that were strangers to true and vital piety before," one observer commented in 1745, "became now acquainted with it, and others that were grown in a great measure dead and formal were quickened, stirred up, and had new life put into them." How long the quickening lasted is anyone's guess, but in a few individual cases the lessons learned during the revival may have stuck. Enthusiasm and theological debate, after all, had bolstered church attendance; controlled they might continue to stimulate religious commitment.

The churches in New Hampshire experienced one additional difficulty which, although related to the concrete problems of finding good pastors and resolving internal disputes, transcended these problems in long range impact. Provincial society became increasingly secular, just as it did elsewhere in North America. Inhabitants cared less about their religious condition, more about their economic success and personal pleasure. The effective authority of ministers, deacons, and elders eroded to such a point that many churches stopped trying to discipline their members for social misbehavior. After the Great Awakening public declarations of faith decreased: in one congregation over twelve hundred citizens were baptized but only thirty-six admitted to communion. Opposition to payment of ministerial taxes increased and more than a few residents joined whatever church required the smallest financial sacrifice; many managed to avoid any payment at all. Circumstantial evidence suggests that attendance at public worship declined, in some churches precipitously.

Secularization had multiple origins. The rapid pace of economic expansion provided both opportunity and excitement which absorbed the energy of colonists and the trans-Atlantic trade attracted a seafaring clientele notoriously lax in religious commitment. Before mid-century New Hampshire had experienced a series of disasters only religion seemed able to explain: frontier warfare with heathen enemies lasted until the mid-twenties, an ominous and destructive earthquake occurred soon thereafter, an epidemic of throat distemper which killed nearly a third of the children in New Hampshire peaked in the 1730s, and war broke out again in the following decade. After mid-century, however no major natural disasters took place, and success against the French and Indians indicated that God looked with favor on his chosen people. Religious controversy also took its toll. If ministers themselves could not agree on proper doctrine and conduct, what were laymen to believe? Many inhabitants reacted against the excesses of the Great Awakening, yet continued to find the old ministers, as one man observed, "stale and unsavory" to their "palates." The presence of the Scotch-Irish, whose customs permitted behavior considered immoral by traditional Puritan standards, may have encouraged defiance of Congregational authority. Finally, many inhabitants learned through experience on the frontier they could manage quite well outside the framework of formal church discipline. Barrington, for example, was settled in 1737 and thirty years later when the population had grown to more than a thousand still had neither a minister nor a church.

Whatever the explanation, few residents who gave serious thought to religious practices in the province doubted that important changes had taken place. Some applauded the loosening of doctrinal and institutional authority, suggested that liberty of conscience gave individuals the right either to worship or not to worship, and worried not at all about the moral condition of society. Others did just the opposite. They linked declining religiosity to the prevalence of "vice, immorality, worldly-mindedness, drunkenness, oppression and profaneness"—the words are from Samuel Lane's diary—and awaited God's punishment for the collective sins of a degenerate people. The attitudes of the vast majority fell somewhere between these two extremes.

The Towns: "Peaceable Kingdoms" and their Problems

The town was the third major social institution affecting the lives of individuals. Towns had first been established in the 1630s and immediately became the single most important form of communal organization. They helped protect citizens against the total collapse of social order during the 1680s and, in general, proved so useful that almost nobody in New Hampshire—or elsewhere in New England for that matter—ever questioned their fundamental worth. Towns served a number of purposes. They were the primary units of political and military organization; they stimulated the founding of religious institutions; they helped to promote local economic prosperity; they provided essential social services; and they gave individuals a sense of communal identity. Inhabitants were trained to accept the authority of local officials and to guard against behavior which might threaten communal cohesiveness. Well managed towns, the colonists assumed, would be stable and harmonious. Ministers occasionally used the term "Peaceable Kingdoms" to symbolize the possibilities of town life.

At times and in places the towns in eighteenth century New Hampshire manifested many characteristics of the idealized peaceable kingdom. Settlers elected town officials skilled and sensitive enough to gain almost unquestioned acceptance of their authority. Townsmen respected their pastor and managed to solve individual and family disputes before they became too disruptive. Provincial law provided guidelines which helped promote stability. The responsibilities of moderators, selectmen, constables and other town officials were clearly defined, as were the ground rules for voting and assessing taxes. Equally important, the provincial government made little effort to enforce laws which, if enforced, might have caused communal disagreements. As a rule towns ran their own internal affairs in accordance with whatever mix of tradition, law, and pragmatic problem solving seemed appropriate given the immediate circumstances. Virtually every town in eighteenth century New Hampshire enjoyed extended periods of overall peacefulness.

These same communities, however, suffered through periods of disharmony quite inconsistent with the peaceable kingdom model. Internal town disputes were the direct product of both internal population growth and the dispersion of settlement. The disputes pitted individual citizens against town officials, competing religious and political groups against each other, and in the newer communities inhabitants against the town proprietors. All too frequently—at least for those who lamented disorder—the towns found it impossible to resolve their internal disagreements and turned to the provincial government for help. The lower house of the Assembly, which handled most local matters, tried to arbitrate disputes even-handedly, but its decisions inevitably disappointed many. As a result conflict lingered on, town officials found it difficult to maintain the peace, and individual residents increasingly felt free to ignore or defy men in positions of communal authority. A growing population of what one provincial law described as "beggars, thieves and strollers" who moved from town to town further eroded community discipline. Towns, in short, experienced problems fully as serious as those affecting the churches.

By the middle of the 1760s a dozen New Hampshire towns held more than a thousand inhabitants. The population of Portsmouth was approximately 4500, of Londonderry 2500, of both Exeter and Dover between 1500 and 2000, of Somersworth, Newmarket, Barrington, Durham, Chester, Hampton Falls, Epping, and Brentwood between 1000 and 1500. More than another dozen communities had populations close to a thousand. Earlier in the century many of these towns had been larger but lost population when the provincial government divided them into two or more separate communities.

Size created two major kinds of problems. In most cases population increase meant greater cultural diversity, and diversity threatened communal cohesiveness. The history of Barrington provides a classic case. Settled originally by Congregationalists, the town soon attracted a number of Quakers, Anglicans, and if the petition drawn up by a group of anxious residents is accurate, "Separatists from all denominations of Christians." Londonderry and several other Merrimack valley towns contained a mixed population of English and Scotch-Irish inhabitants: the former chided the latter by calling them Irishmen—the term had negative ethnic connotations—and the latter accused the former of arrogance and intolerance. The population of Portsmouth included wealthy and powerful Anglicans, hundreds of transient seamen, and more than a few Puritan descendants concerned about the moral impact on society of both these groups.

Increased population also complicated the task of maintaining traditional public services. A few town poor could be supported easily; many town poor required the construction of an alms house. An elaborate network of town roads placed additional burdens on highway surveyors who, like other town officials, received no pay for their work. Clustered building necessitated the organization of community fire protection: in 1758 the provincial government added firewards to the list of legally sanctioned town offices. The prevention and detection of crime became more difficult, especially in communities with large transient populations. Portsmouth, of course, encountered the greatest amount of trouble in maintaining the quality of its public services, but problems had begun to crop up in the other sizeable towns by the 1760s. Then, as now, large communities proved more troublesome to manage than did small communities.

Population dispersion affected towns even more intensely. The central reason for this dispersion was the simple fact that small plots of land clustered around a central or nuclear village made farming more awkward than did much larger plots scattered throughout a township. The timing and form of dispersion, however, varied from place to place. In the older towns settlement did not spread much beyond the central villages until the first set of Anglo-French wars came to a close, then citizens obtained grants of common land and moved outward. Many of the towns founded in the eighteenth century distributed the land initially with the intention of creating a central village, but quickly switched to larger "range" plots of a hundred or more acres when it became clear that the idea of a village had lost much of its appeal. In these as well as the older communities dispersion made possible the concentration of land ownership inside the original village; those who stayed bought land privately from those who left. The towns organized by speculative proprietors sometimes did not even start as nucleated villages. The proprietors divided the township into huge range plots of approximately three hundred acres (a single lot for each proprietary right) and let private buying and selling of land shape the ultimate pattern of settlement. In these communities the initial population was widely dispersed.

Whatever its specific origins, scattered settlement within townships caused all sorts of community tension. Inhabitants in outlying sections complained about the location of the meeting house, and when the time came to build a new one tried to have the location moved. Road construction and maintenance became the subject of frequent controversy. In towns which voted to hire a schoolmaster citizens argued about where he should conduct classes. Residents distant from the meeting house sometimes formed their own church, petitioned for relief from town taxes, and eventually sought incorporation as a separate parish or town. Several groups of outlying inhabitants asked to be annexed to a neighboring community. In general, townspeople in the older sections of a community resisted anything which would undermine their control of local affairs or increase their taxes.

The concrete disputes linked to demographic change were many. Inevitably town officials who struggled to fulfill their traditional responsibilities came under attack. Constables were accused of heavy-handed tactics in collecting unpopular taxes. The office, in fact, became so burdensome that those elected would sometimes pay a fine rather than serve. Overseers of the poor received more requests for financial assistance than they could satisfy; the needy, in turn, accused the town of insensitivity. Individual entrepreneurs felt thwarted by efforts of town officials to control the marketing of goods, found ways of avoiding local regulations, and sometimes came into open conflict with their elected leaders. The problem was especially serious with respect to the retail sale of liquor. In Portsmouth firewards who ordered the razing of old wooden buildings met with resistance from those who challenged their authority. Communities with large amounts of undistributed common land encountered increasing difficulty in keeping squatters, unauthorized woodcutters, and other intruders off the common property. In some cases town officials won their battles with dissident individuals, in other cases they lost. Regardless of the outcome, the community as a whole suffered some loss of cohesiveness.

Religious conflicts also had a broad disruptive impact on the communities in which they occurred. Sometimes, as in the case of Portsmouth during the second decade of the eighteenth century, competing factions within the same church became so embittered toward each other they went their separate ways and established independent parishes. The same thing happened in Exeter during the Great Awakening. Usually denominational differences triggered the conflict. For thirty years the inhabitants of poor Barrington tried unsuccessfully to agree upon a settled minister. All their efforts, according to one group of witnesses, degenerated into "the greatest disorder and confusion." Baptists, Quakers, and Congregationalists battled over the Newton ministry for more than a decade without resolving their differences. Conflict between Presbyterians and Congregationalists erupted at various times in Londonderry, Hampton, Hampton Falls, Chester, Goffstown, and other communities. Denominational conflict was exacerbated by the unwillingness of many townspeople to accept the principle of religious toleration. As a result, when the provincial government tried to resolve tensions by invoking that principle, the townspeople continued to argue. Wherever religious conflict occurred, it infected other dimensions of town life.

Political discord also broke out in many communities. The competition for control of town offices normally was resolved through elections. Occasionally, however, the election process broke down. Although provincial law gave town suffrage to all adult male inhabitants with £20 or more of taxable property, local voting traditions varied and town moderators who had the legal responsibility for weeding out the unqualified often followed local traditions. In 1737 two different sets of Londonderry town officers were elected, one by a group following the "ancient custom" of allowing all rate payers to vote, the other by a smaller self-defined group citing provincial law as justification for their action. Dunstable had an almost identical problem the following decade. Elections for provincial Assembly representatives proved even more conducive to irregularity, in part because provincial magistrates occasionally tried to fix such elections. Some towns adopted the practice of conducting secret ballots in hotly contested elections, but the technique failed as often as it worked. One moderator was forced to dissolve town meetings when irate citizens confronted him with evidence that the number of ballots exceeded the number of voters. Both political confrontation and manipulation of the election process weakened the sense of common purpose among town inhabitants.

The proprietary townships wrestled with a special kind of political problem. The problem grew out of ambiguities in the relationship between town proprietors and town inhabitants. Theoretically the two groups should have worked in close harmony and in many cases—most commonly where proprietary leaders lived in the township—harmony did prevail. Sometimes, however, it did not. Proprietors hesitant to pump additional money into their investment failed to erect grist mills, build or maintain roads, or fulfill other charter obligations. They also refused to call proprietary meetings in which they might be confronted by angry inhabitants. The inhabitants, for their part, felt cheated, demanded that the proprietors produce, and petitioned the Assembly for redress if their demands were not met. The assemblymen, most of whom themselves owned proprietary rights, gave only token assistance to inhabitants before 1760. After 1760 provincial policy tended to favor inhabitants, absentee proprietors unwilling to cooperate in town development sold out, and the problem of proprietary-inhabitant conflict became less serious. It disappeared altogether only when the proprietary ceased to function as a legal entity.

The rapid pace of geographical expansion, population growth, and economic change in eighteenth century New Hampshire placed the basic institutions of provincial society under pressure. Families, churches, and communities all experienced a degree of disruption and conflict inconsistent with traditional expectations about social order. It would be fruitless to debate whether these strains were more or less intense than they had been earlier in the colonial period, and equally fruitless to debate whether individuals became more or less dependent upon social institutions for their psychological well-being. New Hampshire had never been close to the perfectly ordered model of Christian charity fancied by many of New England's first civil and religious leaders.

The basic direction of social change and collective response to that change, however, is clear. New Hampshire on the eve of the American Revolution provided more social options for its inhabitants than had been the case at the beginning of the century. There was greater flexibility in many households, greater choice in religious life, and greater variety in the kinds of towns they could select as a place of residence. And most individuals, if asked, would have thought change had been for the better. Although they found disruption and conflict painful, they became increasingly skilled at solving new problems, grew accustomed to diversity, and began measuring their success in functional rather than ideal terms. The traditional institutions of family, church and community continued to serve them as well as could be expected.

9

PROVINCIAL POLITICS:
THE WENTWORTH OLIGARCHY

When John Wentworth arrived in New Hampshire during the summer of 1767 to assume the governorship of the province, the selectmen of Londonderry published a welcoming address. They noted the "kind patronage" of Wentworth's grandfather John and his Uncle Benning who had preceded him in office, thought it "a hopeful pressage of much future good" that "an amiable branch, sprung from such ancestors" had "come to fill the chief seat of government," and concluded with a prayer "that the name of Wentworth" be made "hereditary." Although others in the province may have disagreed with the sentiments expressed by the selectmen, no one could deny that the family of the new governor had been the single most dominating force in provincial politics for the past half century. The first John Wentworth gained appointment as lieutenant governor of New Hampshire in 1717, managed the province without significant interference from the titular governor (who served also as governor of Massachusetts), and remained in office until his death in 1730. For the next decade the Wentworths, their relatives, and their associates used appointed and elected office to make life miserable for a chief executive who threatened their power. The Wentworth "clan," a label adopted by its enemies, regained control of the executive in 1741 through the appointment of John's son, Benning, as an independent governor. Within a decade the family had consolidated its authority to such an extent that even its most bitter critics had to admit defeat. The appointment of the second John Wentworth to occupy New Hampshire's highest political office provided fitting recognition of that consolidation.

The Wentworths dominated provincial politics in part because they worked hard, understood the dynamics of colonial government, and had a good deal of luck when they needed it. But more was involved. A complex pattern of personal, social, economic, and constitutional relationships linked the family interests to the interests of others concerned with provincial government. The crown, individual imperial administrators, Assembly representatives and their fellow townsmen, even the inhabitants of unrepresented communities felt, for the most part, satisfied with family rule. To a large extent the Wentworths acquired and retained power by pleasing those whom they served.

Early in the second decade of the eighteenth century provincial politics in New Hampshire was marked by factional competition between two groups of men. The Vaughan and Waldron families led one group; they had gained influence during the 1690s and had remained a powerful force in Council and Assembly affairs despite Governor Joseph Dudley's successful efforts to restrict their leverage. William Vaughan and Richard Waldron lived in Portsmouth and could count on support from town leaders in Dover and Exeter; they also had a past history of cooperation with the powerful Weare family in Hampton. John Wentworth, Samuel Penhallow and Mark Hunking—all councillors appointed after Dudley became governor in 1702—led the opposing faction. Centered in Portsmouth and Newcastle, the group as a whole was much younger in age, included many merchants who competed with the Vaughans and Waldrons for control of overseas trade, and had few political connections with town leaders elsewhere in the province. Local as well as provincial conditions affected relationships between the two factions. They took opposite sides in the bitter religious conflict which split the Portsmouth church after the end of Queen Anne's War.

Developments in England soon accentuated the political competition. The queen's death and the accession of George I prompted a general reassessment of colonial administration. The new king's appointees decided that both Dudley and his unpopular lieutenant governor, John Usher, should be replaced, which meant that new commissions would be drawn up and all Council appointments would have to be reaffirmed. Neither provincial faction possessed sufficient power to influence the gubernatorial appointment—the joint governorship of Massachusetts and New Hampshire went to Elias Burgess, an Englishman with good connections in Whitehall—but the lieutenant governorship and the Council were quite another matter. George

Vaughan, William's son, had been in England for the past decade cultivating friends and became the only serious candidate for Usher's office. He gained Burgess's support, presented testimony gathered in New Hampshire in favor of his appointment, and recommended several political associates for posts on the Council. The Wentworth faction, working through Henry Newman who had been hired by Dudley to represent New Hampshire interests at Whitehall during the war, concentrated on getting its adherents appointed to the Council.

For a while it looked as though neither side would emerge victorious. George Vaughan became the lieutenant governor and sailed immediately for Portsmouth where, in the fall of 1715, he was greeted jubilantly by a population grateful for the demise of his predecessor. But Vaughan must have known he was in for trouble. The Board of Trade, worried that the family interest in lumbering might weaken enforcement of royal white pine policy, had rejected his Council recommendations. Instead it removed his father and another aging member from office, reappointed Wentworth, Hunking, and Penhallow, and accepted the Wentworth group's recommendation that George Jaffrey, Theodore Atkinson, and others be added. Moreover, before Vaughan sailed he learned that Governor Burgess might sell his office to another man preferred by the agents from Massachusetts. Vaughan himself was unpopular with these agents because of his outspoken advocacy of a more efficient system for raising colonial revenue.

The battle lines were quickly drawn. Vaughan, an imperious and ill-tempered man, immediately convened the Council and announced that he intended to run the province. Wentworth and his associates, in turn, responded icily to the lieutenant governor, and when Vaughan made the mistake of trying to ram through a series of tax reforms, they joined with assemblymen in rejecting the proposals. The infuriated Vaughan then dissolved the Assembly, lectured the Council, and wrote to England for help. The Wentworth group began to spread rumors that the province had another Cranfield on its hands.

It took less than two years for the Council to gain complete ascendency. Governor Burgess helped their cause by accepting £1000 and resigning in favor of Samuel Shute. Shute arrived in New Hampshire forewarned that Vaughan's behavior had left the province divided, and made a quick judgment that he could not work with his lieutenant governor. Vaughan's insistence that he, not Shute, controlled the provincial militia confirmed any doubts on that score. By this time a new

Assembly had been elected. Packed with Vaughan supporters, it supported him on the militia issue, complained about a Council drawn entirely from Portsmouth and Newcastle (in the past all towns had been represented) and blamed the Council members for the earlier disputes over taxation. Shute, on the advice of Council, dissolved the new Assembly. He also wrote home asking that Wentworth be made lieutenant governor. In subsequent elections the balance of power shifted once again. Vaughan used the convening of the legislature to precipitate a crisis. Ordered by the now absent Shute not to dissolve the Assembly, he disobeyed his superior and at the same time suspended the councillor he suspected of leading the opposition. "I cannot wonder," Vaughan reportedly informed the entire Council, "at the arrogance and pride of those who do not consider I am a superior match, as being armed with power from my prince, who doth execution at the utterance of the word." Shute had had enough. After learning about the crisis he returned to New Hampshire, suspended Vaughan, ordered the dissolved Assembly to convene, delivered a discourse on the dangers to public order of subordinates who defied authority, and asked the Council to institute libel suits against the representatives who had failed to attend. A few days earlier, though Shute had no way of knowing it, a commission appointing John Wentworth lieutenant governor of New Hampshire had passed the royal seal.

The Council group and its allies in the Assembly moved quickly to consolidate their victory. Wentworth, on Shute's advice, assumed a role of primary leadership even before his commission arrived from overseas. An astute and accommodating man, Wentworth's initial tactic was to make peace. The meddlesome John Usher gave him some unexpected assistance by showing up in Portsmouth and reasserting the validity of the Allen claim. His actions gave Wentworth the opportunity to join with house representatives in condemning the former lieutenant governor. Shortly thereafter Wentworth engineered a compromise settlement to the church dispute in Portsmouth; that too met with approval throughout the province. Probably the most important gesture Wentworth made to his defeated opponents was to have the Council drop its libel suit against the highly respected Nathaniel Weare and meet in Hampton to accept his apologies. Later the Council voted to let George Vaughan's father continue as recorder of deeds even though he no longer was a councillor. Richard Waldron III also was

John Wentworth, lieutenant governor, 1771–1729. Posthumous portrait painted in 1760 by Joseph Blackburn. *Courtesy of the New Hampshire Historical Society.*

retained as clerk of the Council, and his father the judge of probate. George Vaughan's decision to temporarily abandon politics further reduced tension. Wentworth took the oath of office in December, 1717, and the following spring, only six months after the showdown, he told assemblymen how pleased he was "that those coals of contention which were kindled and blowing amongst us are . . . so happily extinguished." In typical fashion he took no personal credit for the change. Instead, he praised the House delegates for their "care" in helping calm the province.

John Wentworth and his circle maintained their dominant position in provincial politics for more than a decade. Two closely related purposes shaped their conduct while in office. One was to utilize the powers of the executive to reward themselves. Governor Shute appointed Penhallow, Hunking, and Jaffrey to the Superior Court, and Wentworth made certain that subsequent judicial appointments went to his supporters. Many high militia appointments went to faction members and their relatives. Political preference usually brought financial gain. Councillors paid no provincial taxes, judges collected fees for their services, and military officers had ample opportunity to benefit economically from their appointment. Equally important, the lieutenant governor and Council, who together granted new townships, made a habit of including themselves as proprietors. The Shute-Wentworth revolution, in short, enabled a group of already prominent men to increase their political power and add to their personal fortunes. They exhibited little restraint in taking full advantage of their opportunity.

The second purpose, a necessary condition for succeeding in the first, was to remain in office. Remaining in office meant pleasing those responsible for their appointments. They had both to court favor in England and to discourage the development of political opposition within New Hampshire. Wentworth and his friends knew full well from personal experience that colonists dissatisfied with royally appointed magistrates could at any time launch a campaign to undermine their standing at home.

The faction employed a number of tactics to cultivate support in England. Wentworth kept home officials fully informed about affairs in New Hampshire; his reports, understandably, tended to emphasize the respect accorded royal government by provincial inhabitants. Henry Newman not only continued to lobby for New Hampshire before the

Board of Trade and other groups responsible for colonial administration but assumed the role of Wentworth's personal agent. He praised the work of the lieutenant governor, helped Wentworth fill Council vacancies with his friends and relatives, and kept Wentworth informed when George Vaughan returned to England in an abortive effort to regain his lost post. Samuel Penhallow travelled overseas, and while in London he visited Whitehall and consulted with a number of colonial administrators. Governor Shute, who left Massachusetts permanently in the early 1720s, undoubtedly informed his superiors of Wentworth's overall effectiveness.

The Wentworth group worked even more assiduously to please those whom they ruled. One problem it had to confront was general resentment toward a Council controlled by Portsmouth merchants. To limit criticism, the lieutenant governor and his allies adopted two basic tactics. They began by conducting a public campaign in defense of the new status quo: it was no surprise, they argued, that seaport residents held most of the seats, for Portsmouth had grown rapidly, almost "all the gentlemen of the province lived there," and the crown always had selected "gentlemen of the best quality and greatest ability to serve the government." They also argued that towns maintained their leverage in provincial affairs through Assembly representation and could not, as the number of incorporated communities increased, expect representation in the Council. The faction also tried to avoid behavior which would expose the Council to accusations of favoritism toward merchant interests. Council members accepted a small impost on imported goods, cooperated with the Assembly in shaping laws to promote agriculture, and when pro-merchant legislation came up for consideration, argued that it would benefit New Hampshire as a whole. The fact that the members of the Vaughan-Waldron faction were also Portsmouth traders helped prevent the issue of seaport Council domination from becoming serious.

The Wentworths adopted similar tactics to allay fears about their appointments and land grant policies. They insisted, with some justification, that Penhallow and the other new judges were better qualified than their predecessors, argued that since the Superior Court met in Portsmouth, seaport inhabitants should be appointed, said that social status and proven managerial skills were necessary for effective military leadership, and pointed out the benefits of having men with adequate capital as town proprietors. The Wentworth group, in addition, shared the rewards of political preference with others. When, for example, the affluent Scottish merchant Archibald MacPhaedris moved to Portsmouth, Wentworth invited him to sit with the Council and eventually obtained a commission for him. MacPhaedris's marriage to one of Wentworth's daughters—the lieutenant governor sired fourteen children in all—cemented the relationship. Wentworth rewarded town leaders with local military and judicial offices, continued to praise all provincial inhabitants who cooperated with the faction, and unabashedly bought support through land grants. At one point the heirs of Samuel Allen received four square miles. Every member of the Assembly was on the list of proprietors for each of the five townships granted in 1727.

The final ingredient of the faction's recipe for gaining internal approval was its handling of governmental responsibilities. Both Wentworth and the Council tried to avoid the kinds of arbitrary conduct that had undermined respect for authority during the administrations of Cranfield, Usher, Allen, and to some extent Vaughan. Instead they focused on providing good government. Good government meant, among other things, clarity in the legal system. The first codification of New Hampshire laws had been printed shortly before Wentworth took the oath of office. The new chief magistrate convinced the legislature to repeal all laws excluded from this first codification and to publish all current enactments; later he obtained a judicial ruling that unprinted laws could not be pleaded in court. Good government also meant fair taxation. New Hampshire's system for apportioning both local and provincial taxes had been the subject of controversy, partly because poll taxes seemed increasingly inequitable in a society where personal fortunes varied so dramatically, partly because local officials used widely varying standards to assess the value of property, and partly because tradition did not include merchants' stock in trade as taxable property. Wentworth and the Council labored long and hard to get approval of a law which compromised differences among inhabitants and provided firm guidelines for assessing estate value.

These and other reforms were possible because the Wentworth group accepted as another principle of good government the idea that elected town representatives in the Assembly should share responsibility for managing provincial affairs. The lieutenant governor, in fact, encouraged the Assembly. He ordered new towns to send representatives, signed a law forcing towns to pay their assemblymen, provided guidance when the House decided to tighten its internal procedures and adopt a dress code, and made it be known the representatives should decide how most local petitions would be handled. Moreover, Wentworth sometimes sided with the House in disputes between it and the Council. The most important issue dividing the two houses was provincial election procedures. Assembly members wanted elections held at least every three years to prevent the legislature from becoming too ingrown. Wentworth agreed to support the idea as long as the property requirements for both voting and candidacy, which previously had not been clearly established, were made sufficiently high to guarantee that only men of substance were elected. The figures agreed upon were £50 of real estate for voters and £300 of property for candidates. Although the councillors initially rejected the proposed "Triannual Act," Wentworth convinced them to change their vote and then lobbied successfully for approval in England.

Finally, good government meant using personal power to promote the territorial and economic interests of New Hampshire as a whole. John Wentworth and his Council not only made the bold decision to seek expanded borders, but generated a strong legal defense of the claims and used their influence in England to combat the counterclaims of Massachusetts. The "clan" joined with assemblymen in passing legislation to promote economic growth. It also tried to create the impression in England that imperial regulations limiting the use of forest resources were being enforced, while making no efforts to enforce the regulations. Given all this, it is not surprising that most provincial inhabitants remained happy with those who occupied the chief offices of "profit and honor" in New Hampshire for the decade following John Wentworth's appointment as lieutenant governor.

In the late 1720s the set of relationships which allowed the Wentworth faction to dominate provincial politics threatened to fall apart. The lieutenant governor and his Council came under serious attack in New Hampshire for the first time since 1718. Imperial officials fired Governor Shute and in 1730—the same year John Wentworth died— appointed a replacement allied with internal enemies of the old oligarchy. The new governor obtained Council commissions for his supporters in New Hampshire, and with their assistance launched a well organized campaign to make certain the Wentworths did not regain their lost influence. In the end, however, the faction prevailed. Led by John Wentworth's son Benning, Theodore Atkinson, Jr., and other Portsmouth traders, a new generation of "clan" members first neutralized the influence of their opponents, then seized power completely. Their victory was complete by the early 1740s.

The Wentworths themselves were partly responsible for the erosion of internal support. Royal instructions made the lieutenant governor and councillors the final Court of Appeals on all judicial cases. The system had never been popular, mainly because of the expenses involved in seeing a case through the Inferior Court of Common Pleas, the Superior Court of Common Pleas, and finally the Council. But before the mid-twenties criticism had been muted by the infrequency of appeals and the even-handed manner in which the Court of Appeals dealt with its responsibilities. All that changed when the court made a series of decisions in favor of faction members who challenged unfavorable decisions in the lower courts. Since many of the cases either directly or indirectly hurt members of the old Vaughan-Waldron faction, the likelihood of political controversy increased.

Developments in England turned likelihood into certainty. The death of King George I in 1727 brought the customary reshuffling of imperial officialdom. Henry Newman, whose interest in New Hampshire had already begun to flag, lost most of his influence at Whitehall. Samuel Shute was removed from the governorship he had held in absentia and was replaced by William Burnet. Wentworth's internal enemies knew a good opportunity when they saw it. Led by Council Clerk Richard Waldron III, and House Speaker Nathaniel Weare, the same man who a decade earlier had been accused of libeling Governor Shute, they apparently contacted friends in Massachusetts and suggested that a new lieutenant governor be appointed. Wentworth began to suspect that he might be in deep trouble when someone, probably Newman, wrote him that agents from the Bay Colony were lobbying against renewal of his commission. Any doubts on that score were removed when he informed the Assembly that "enemies" of New Hampshire sought his removal from office, and the town representatives, angered by the Court of Appeals, made no effort to petition on his behalf.

Open conflict between the Wentworth faction and its opponents broke out early in 1728. The House voted to prohibit Superior Court judges from granting appeals, demanded that appeal cases be heard before juries, and when the Council rejected both actions accused it of assuming "an arbitrary power without foundation or precedent." The House also reopened debate about the composition of the Council, rejected a number of Wentworth's funding requests, considered hiring its own English agent, and refused to join with the Council in greeting Governor Burnet, who had just arrived in New England. Wentworth was furious at the House rebellion. He castigated Speaker Weare, dissolved the Assembly, and ordered new elections. Weare was both returned to office and reelected speaker, at which point Wentworth decided that despite the ambiguity of his instructions on the matter, he would veto Weare's selection. In addition, the lieutenant governor told House members that "designing men . . . who had their own private views at heart more than the good of the people they represented" had been responsible for the disruption. Wentworth then engineered a compromise settlement which involved the election of another speaker, passage of the Triennial Act, and repeal of a controversial tax law. That spring after Wentworth received a commission continuing him in office and Burnet signalled support for his lieutenant, the controversy subsided.

It did not, however, disappear. Resentment against New Hampshire's chief magistrate resurfaced after he fired a House ringleader from his post as provincial sheriff and replaced him with Theodore Atkinson, Jr. The House, in fact, became so infuriated it threatened to send someone to England to request that New Hampshire be reannexed to Massachusetts. More important, Governor Burnet died suddenly in the fall of 1729 and was replaced by Jonathan Belcher, a Massachusetts merchant who as provincial agent in England lobbied intensively for the joint commission. The appointment guaranteed a renewal of hostilities. A kinsman of George Vaughan, Belcher had never forgiven John Wentworth for his behavior more than a decade earlier. Belcher, furthermore, counted as personal friends many of those most opposed to rule by the Wentworth faction. Any doubts about how the new governor and old lieutenant governor would get along disappeared soon after Belcher arrived in Portsmouth. Defying past tradition, Governor Belcher refused to give his subordinate a portion of the salary voted by the Assembly. Wentworth, who had become seriously ill, mustered enough energy to announce he could take care of himself and took solace in the fact that the embarrassed assemblymen decided to award him a separate payment. He died soon thereafter.

For the next decade the remaining members of the Wentworth group and their opponents fought tooth and nail for control of provincial politics. In some instances the opposition prevailed. Belcher convinced three existing Council members (Henry Sherburne, Richard Wibird, and Shadrach Walton) to support his anti-Wentworth campaign, and obtained commissions for five other supporters including Richard Waldron III, and the deposed Sheriff Benjamin Gambling. Belcher failed in his efforts to have Sherburne made lieutenant governor. The post went instead to David Dunbar, an English placeman appointed because he promised vigorous enforcement of timber cutting regulation. Belcher compensated for his defeat by making frequent visits to New Hampshire and assuming direct personal responsibility for most executive matters, and Waldron, whom Belcher appointed provincial secretary, kept him fully informed. Control of the Council allowed the Waldron-Belcher faction to appoint their associates to vacant civil and military offices, and to create vacancies by dismissing their political enemies. It also allowed them to reward themselves and their friends with generous land grants. Six different Sherburnes, Gambling, a member of the Vaughan family, and a number of other cooperative provincial officeholders were among the proprietors of Kingswood, a huge unincorporated territory along the shores of Lake Winnipesauke patented in 1737.

Belcher and the Council majority also enjoyed occasional success in their attempts to gain support among assemblymen. Their major strength lay with representatives from Exeter, where the powerful Gilman family dominated town politics, and from Dover, the town Richard Waldron's grandfather had once ruled with an iron hand. Belcher courted voters in these towns and in the town of Hampton early in his administration by signing a bill which permitted provincial courts to hold sessions in all four of New Hampshire's original townships. The gesture worked: the Assembly accepted Belcher's recommendation to negotiate directly with Massachusetts concerning disputed boundaries and passed a resolution thanking the king for Belcher's appointment. The Governor and Council worked long and

Richard Waldron III, a major political opponent of the Wentworth oligarchy until his death in 1753. Artist unknown. *Courtesy of the Society for the Preservation of New England Antiquities.*

hard to gain House acceptance of their financial program—the central issues were repayment of outstanding debt and the emission of currency—and late in the 1730s won a partial victory. House members, in addition, cooperated with the Council on a number of matters involving local and personal petitions to the provincial government.

But in far more important ways, the Wentworth faction bested the governor and his allies. They gained their initial leverage through the Assembly. Soon after he assumed office Belcher was forced by the recently passed Triennial Act to call new elections. The Wentworth group campaigned heavily and successfully at the local level. When the new Assembly met early in 1731 it quickly became apparent that the balance of power had shifted. Three Piscataqua representatives, Atkinson, John Rindge, and Joshua Pierce, convinced the House to withhold support for Belcher's proposed boundary commission and when the dynamics of the resulting dispute dictated compromise, Atkinson and Pierce were chosen by the House to represent it in negotiations with Massachusetts. After the negotiations floundered, the House, despite the opposition of Belcher and the Council, hired Rindge as its own agent to prosecute the "boundary matter" in England. Rindge left New Hampshire carrying among his papers a private petition accusing Governor Belcher of favoritism toward Massachusetts and other sins. Rindge, Atkinson, Pierce, Councillor George Jaffrey, House Speaker Andrew Wiggin, John and Benning Wentworth (both sons of the lieutenant governor), and eight others had signed the document.

The House remained under faction influence the rest of the decade. On ten separate occasions Belcher dissolved the group and called for new elections, but he never succeeded in obtaining a cooperative majority. Benning Wentworth won the seat vacated by Rindge, became even more assiduous than his predecessor in making life difficult for the governor, and continued to work behind the scenes after Rindge returned from England and resumed his old position. When Rindge retired another Wentworth brother took his place. Paul Wentworth, Benning's cousin, served as one of Dover's representatives for six years before moving elsewhere. Each time the Assembly convened the same ritual occurred. Belcher formally announced what he expected the House to accomplish, the House refused to accept his program and voted one of their own, the Council refused to approve the House legislation, and an angered Belcher dissolved the Assembly and called for new elections. Compromise on financial matters provided the only significant variation in this pattern.

The Wentworth faction gained additional influence through cooperation with Lieutenant Governor Dunbar. Dunbar arrived in New Hampshire shortly after the first showdown between Belcher and the Assembly and let it be known that as the lieutenant governor he would assume full executive authority unless the governor were physically within the province. Belcher, who had had a previous confrontation with his subordinate, made it just as clear that Dunbar would not. He refused to let Dunbar take a seat on the Council, rejected Dunbar's advice on civil appointments, and encouraged Dunbar to leave for England. The governor, moreover, made no attempt to hide his personal animosity toward Dunbar: at one point he described him as a "lump of malice and perfidy and everything else that is vile." He answered one Dunbar inquiry with a note that ended: "Your letters in general are really so rude and unmannerly as I really think beneath even so little a man as you are."

Dunbar, quite understandably, became a close ally of the Wentworths. In 1732 the Board of Trade accepted his recommendation that Atkinson, Pierce, and Benning Wentworth be made Council members; the three men, as soon as they felt the House could get along without them, took their oaths of office and tried to moderate the behavior of the pro-Belcher majority. Dunbar also campaigned for Belcher's removal by reporting home that unless a change were made it would be impossible for him to enforce imperial white pine regulations. The complaint carried weight because Dunbar was the Surveyor General of the King's Woods as well as provincial lieutenant governor. Finally, Dunbar used his authority as surveyor general to embarrass Belcher. His one serious effort to arrest those guilty of illegal lumbering occurred in Exeter, led to violence, and forced the governor to take a public stand against effective enforcement. The Wentworths made no effort to defend Dunbar's conduct as the surveyor general, but they did support him in his other disputes with Belcher and for a time considered him the most likely person to replace their unpopular chief magistrate.

Control of the Assembly and cooperation with Dunbar enabled the Wentworths to neutralize Belcher's power in New Hampshire. It did not, however, give them the same degree of control they had exercised during the 1720s. In order to regain what had been lost, the faction members knew they had to court favor in England. Aggressiveness and good luck enabled them to succeed. While in England Rindge hired John Thomlinson to replace Newman as House agent in the boundary dispute with Massachusetts; Thomlinson, who already had developed commercial contacts with Atkinson and other Piscataqua merchants, agreed at the same time to seek Belcher's removal. The choice of Thomlinson proved most fortunate. Thomlinson's main political connection was with the Duke of Newcastle and by the late 1730s Newcastle had replaced Robert Walpole as the single most powerful politician in England. The Wentworths gained additional leverage by joining forces with William Shirley, an ambitious lawyer who wanted the Bay Colony governorship and had little interest in New Hampshire affairs. Dunbar's decision to return home further strengthened support in England.

The "interest" of the Wentworths at Whitehall became increasingly evident as time passed. The Council appointments of 1732 (for which Thomlinson probably deserved as much credit as Dunbar) provided the first indication that things had changed. Three years later the Privy Council reprimanded Belcher by rescinding the law which permitted provincial courts to hold sessions outside Portsmouth. The imperial government, at Thomlinson's urging, appointed its own commission to make recommendations on the long standing boundary dispute; that too indicated Belcher was in trouble. In 1738 and again in 1739 the Board of Trade rejected Belcher nominees for the Council; instead they appointed Rindge and another "clan" member. When Belcher learned about the appointments, which left the Council split six to six on factional lines, even he had to admit defeat. The most he could do was to write home blaming "malcontents" for his impending demise.

Complete restoration of Wentworth influence came as the result of Thomlinson's maneuvering. As events unfolded, the indefatigable agent sensed bigger game than he and his New Hampshire friends had thought possible earlier in the decade. Why not, he decided, recommend a dramatic solution to the problems of governance which had disrupted northern New England for the past half century. His proposal had three major components: the boundaries between Massachusetts and New Hampshire should be drawn to make New Hampshire as large as possible; New Hampshire should have an independent governor; and to promote the mast trade and encourage effective enforcement of white pine policy, the independent governor of New Hampshire should also be appointed Surveyor General of the King's Woods. Exactly when Thomlinson concocted his scheme is not clear, but it is clear that the Wentworths liked the idea. Their only worry was that the departed Dunbar might become governor. Thomlinson took care of that too. Since Benning Wentworth had just lost an expensive cargo of timber in Portugal, mainly because of diplomatic conflict between rulers of that nation and England, Thomlinson suggested that Wentworth be compensated for his loss by appointment as an independent governor. He then convinced Dunbar to sell the surveyorship, obtained Shirley's approval for the plan, and aided by Wentworth's creditors in England sold the package to Newcastle and other imperial officials. When news of his success reached Portsmouth, the "clan" held a private celebration of such proportions that provincial inhabitants still gossiped about it years later.

The faction completely dominated provincial politics for the next quarter century. Benning Wentworth successfully repulsed the one serious effort to remove him from office and remained governor until 1767. His tenure, in fact, was the longest of any colonial governor in British North America. Family members gained increasing leverage in the Council: when Wentworth retired the group included his brother Mark, three brothers-in-law, and four other men who were nephews or cousins. The Wentworths, furthermore, managed to convince most voters and their elected representatives that what Richard Waldron liked to label "family government" served New Hampshire well. One brief period excepted, the assemblymen cooperated fully with their governor and councillors in the management of provincial affairs. The last fifteen years of Benning Wentworth's long administration were as free from internal controversy as the first decade of his father's service as lieutenant governor.

The new generation of family members ruled much as the old generation had. They too took full personal advantage of political preference. The governor appointed relatives and associates to most important provincial offices: Atkinson, for example, became in addition to a council member the Chief Justice of the Superior Court, provincial secretary, and a militia colonel; and Benning Wentworth, Jr., became a military officer while still in his teens, as did his younger brother

Benning Wentworth, governor 1741–1767. Portrait by Joseph Blackburn painted in 1760. *Courtesy of the New Hampshire Historical Society.*

and a cousin. The Governor and Council together rewarded virtually every male member of their kinship group with land grants. Benning Wentworth required that the proprietors of each new township outside the Masonian Patent set aside a plot of five to eight hundred acres for their royal governor, and that the list of proprietors include a few of his close friends. In addition, many "clan" members, though not the governor himself, were part owners of the Masonian Patent and thus controlled distribution of undeveloped land within sixty miles of the seacoast. The Masonians purchased the old title from Thomlinson soon after Wentworth became governor.

The family utilized its position for one further self-interested purpose. Late in the 1730s Thomlinson used his influence in England to obtain large masting contracts from the Admiralty. Mark Wentworth served as Thomlinson's primary overseas agent for procuring the masts, while his brother as surveyor general allowed those who supplied Mark with good quality masts to cut other timber in violation of imperial regulations. The arrangement worked to everybody's advantage. Lumbermen throughout the province appreciated the governor's lack of aggressiveness in attempting to enforce white pine policy—in twenty-five years not a single violation was successfully prosecuted—Mark Wentworth accumulated an immense personal fortune, and Benning Wentworth not only received occasional gifts from lumbermen and millowners, but probably took kickbacks from his brother. When a potential competitor for the masting business arrived at Portsmouth early in the 1760s he reported that the naval stores industry was "in the hands of a few associated gentlemen of very large fortunes," who had the surveyor general "entirely at their devotion" and opposed any interference in their affairs. The disappointed entrepreneur also noted that it cost the Wentworths only a small fraction of the eventual sales price to purchase masts for overseas shipment.

At the same time the Wentworth group adopted an effective strategy for preventing the same kind of political coup it had engineered. The strategy, like the one adopted while John Wentworth held office, involved calculated courtship of officials in England. Thomlinson played the key intermediary role in that courtship. Both Atkinson and the governor wrote him at frequent intervals about affairs in New Hampshire, asked for his advice if uncertain how to please imperial officials, and in general followed his directions as closely as possible.

Thomlinson, in turn, did everything in his power to assure preservation of the status quo. He developed relationships with officials in Parliament, the Privy Council, the Board of Trade, the Admiralty, the Treasury, the Naval Board, and the Board of Ordinance, and hired a highly respected solicitor to represent New Hampshire in several legal disputes. Thomlinson used his friendship with Newcastle, whose general influence in colonial affairs remained strong until the 1760s, to gain leverage not obtainable elsewhere. According to one knowledgeable observer of English politics, Thomlinson and his business partner carried more "personal weight and interest with the ministry" during the 1750s than any other "two merchants in London."

Governor Wentworth helped Thomlinson by presenting a picture of complete loyalty and administrative competence to his English superiors. He named townships after important civil and military leaders like Admiral Boscawen, the Duke of Grafton, and the Earl of Strafford. He promoted the interests of the Anglican Church—many family members including the governor, had converted to Anglicanism in the 1730s and with Thomlinson's help established the first congregation in the province—by recommending the creation of an American bishopric, and insisting that town proprietors set aside a lot for both the Society for the Propagation of the Gospel and the first settled Anglican minister. The governor, to protect himself against accusations of ineffectiveness as surveyor general, wrote periodic reports emphasizing the few efforts he made to enforce existing policy; he also reported that no illegal commerce existed in New Hampshire even though the Piscataqua was notorious for smuggling. In all his official correspondence Wentworth gave the impression that his devotion to the royal prerogative and to his gubernatorial instructions was absolute, and that primarily through his stubborn loyalty to the crown New Hampshire had become a productive and peaceful part of the British empire. No wonder he remained in office twenty-five years.

Internally, the governor and his associates pursued a number of policies designed to gain acceptance of their authority. To begin with, they tried to make peace with their factional opponents. Ellis Huske, a councillor who had given Belcher strong support, was kept as Chief Justice of the Superior Court until shortly before his death. Huske, Henry Sherburne and his brother John not only remained on the Council, but continued to play an important role in shaping legislative decisions. Previous critics of the "clan" fared almost as well in the distribution of local offices and land grants as did those they had criticized. It is impossible to measure the general effectiveness of these gestures, but they worked in at least one specific case. When Richard Waldron rejected the Wentworth's peace offering and organized a campaign to rid New Hampshire of family government, Henry Sherburne refused to cooperate.

The family also shared the rewards of political preference with community leaders not deeply involved in factional politics. Wentworth distributed justice of the peace commissions so lavishly that one wag described his administration as

> the happy silver age
> When magistrates, profoundly sage
> O'erspread the land; and made, it seems
> Justice run down the streets in streams.

The last two wars with the French and Indians gave Wentworth ample excuse to make military appointments even more lavishly than he did judicial appointments. The chief magistrate, his Council, and the Masonian proprietors gave just about every socially prominent and politically influential inhabitant generous land grants: at one point the governor bought Assembly cooperation by allocating an entire township to its members. The fact that the Wentworths had been partly responsible for the boundary settlement and later conducted a successful legal defense against individual Massachusetts claimants to land in the disputed territory further contributed to acquiescence in family rule. Weak enforcement of lumbering and customs regulations had a similar effect.

Finally, the Wentworths courted public acceptance of their authority by cooperating as fully as conditions permitted with elected representatives in the Assembly. Much of the time cooperation came naturally. Benning Wentworth held office during a period when New Hampshire was constantly threatened with attack. When he asked for appropriations to support the military, the House usually complied with his requests. As individuals they benefitted from supply contracts and as representatives of the people they sought protection of the frontiers. Moreover, the only way to finance war was to issue paper money backed by further taxes. Since provincial inhabitants found business easier to conduct with paper money than without, they encouraged their chief magistrate to permit emissions and applauded his successful efforts to gain royal approval for the resulting legislation. Governor Wentworth and the Assembly joined forces in resisting the efforts of New York to gain jurisdiction over land in what is now the state of Vermont. Wentworth also adopted a general policy that matters of local interest should be handled by the legislature and at times let it be known he would accept whatever the House recommended. The Council accepted this arrangement for settling local disputes.

Occasionally, however, the cooperation did not come naturally: Governor Wentworth always thought he deserved a larger salary than the House provided; the merchant dominated Council disagreed with House members who wanted a larger tax on stock in trade; and the Assembly continued to push for judicial reform which would have compromised family influence in the courts. When trouble arose, the Wentworths worked hard to prevent animosities from getting out of hand. Sometimes they bribed assemblymen with appointments and land grands, sometimes they compromised, sometimes they agreed to have the dispute arbitrated in England, and sometimes they stuck to their guns. Whatever the tactic, they treated Assembly spokesmen with respect and tried to avoid conduct which would expose them to accusations of arbitrariness. After mid-century the governor established the practice of inviting assemblymen to his house for drinks at the close of each legislative session. Few House members refused the invitation.

The one time relationships between the Wentworth oligarchy and the Assembly broke down completely, the oligarchy won a complete victory. The struggle began in 1744 after the House, led by former allies of Governor Belcher, refused to authorize military expenditures which Wentworth had been instructed by home officials to provide. The governor blamed the controversy on his factional opponents, dissolved the Assembly, called for new elections, invited several previously unrepresented towns to send delegates, and helped organize successful election campaigns in the older towns for men who would support him in the controversy. The first phase of the battle ended in a stand off. The new Assembly voted the supplies, but refused to seat delegates from the towns which before 1744 had not been extended the privilege

Wentworth-Coolidge House, colonial residence of Governor Benning Wentworth. The Council Chambers of the provincial government were located in
the building. *Courtesy of the New Hampshire Historical Society.*

of representation. The assemblymen insisted that they, not the governor, had the constitutional responsibility for making such decisions. Wentworth didn't press the issue, instead, he asked Thomlinson to obtain a specific royal instruction granting him the right the house members claimed.

The second phase of the struggle took place between 1748 and 1752. Richard Waldron, whom Wentworth had suspended from the Council and removed from his civil and military offices, took advantage of impending Assembly elections to seek Wentworth's removal from office. Waldron gained election from Hampton and the Assembly refused once again to seat delegates from towns issued election precepts without its approval. The House then chose Waldron as its speaker, and when Wentworth vetoed the selection, readied a formal petition complaining of the governor's conduct. Meanwhile Waldron, with help from Belcher and several other Massachusetts politicians, had contacted potential allies in England and tried to convince the influential William Pepperrell of Kittery to seek the governorship of New Hampshire. But the scheme failed. Thomlinson obtained formal instructions from the Board of Trade which backed Wentworth, Pepperrell wrote Waldron that he was not qualified to fill "the breach made in your state affairs," and Wentworth, as soon as he sensed victory, once again called new elections. This time the Assembly seated the controversial delegates and elected a compromise speaker. The possibility of further disputes was further reduced when failing health forced Waldron to resign from the Assembly; he died in 1753. Soon thereafter his political associate, John Sherburne, confessed that the House would make "no complaints at the Governor, do what he will." For the next fifteen years, the Wentworth oligarchy experienced little difficulty maintaining harmonious relations with elected assemblymen.

John Wentworth, his descendants, and their associates erected the single most enduring and powerful political machine in all of colonial America. For more than a half century they controlled the dynamics of provincial government in their native New Hampshire. They protected themselves at home, turned back factional threats from the one major group within the province with sufficient wealth and influence to challenge their authority, and managed at the same time to provide what most imperial officials and local residents considered good government. While they ruled, New Hampshire grew in size and population, prospered economically, and matured socially. Much of the change stemmed directly from the policies they implemented while in office. They encouraged new migration, stubbornly fought for the expanded borders and independence from Massachusetts, helped as individuals to develop the mast trade and as provincial magistrates to permit full exploitation of forest resources, and were partly responsible for New Hampshire's religious diversity. Eighteenth century New Hampshire, in short, was deeply influenced by the Wentworths.

Family government, however, did not last much longer. The Wentworths's political leverage began to decline even before Benning Wentworth stepped down as governor; it disappeared completely in the mid-1770s. Both the Wentworth oligarchy and the system of government they understood and manipulated so well fell victim to the American Revolution.

10

THE COMING OF REVOLUTION

Viewed from many perspectives, the decade following 1765 was much like the previous half century. Population continued to grow; by the start of the last quarter of the eighteenth century New Hampshire had nearly 75,000 inhabitants. More townships were settled, more churches established, more meeting houses constructed, and more acreage cleared for farming. Although the exportation of forest products began to level off and the mast trade actually declined in importance, overseas commerce remained the cornerstone of New Hampshire's still prospering economy. John Wentworth replaced his uncle Benning as governor; he and the other members of the family-run Council enjoyed what John Adams once labeled "the pomps and vanities and ceremonies of that little world Portsmouth," and until 1774 the internal politics of New Hampshire remained relatively harmonious and stable.

But from one fundamental perspective dramatic changes occurred. Developments in England, in New Hampshire itself, and in other parts of America gradually undermined both the effectiveness of the Wentworths and the authority of the imperial government they represented. The family was in serious political trouble by 1773. The following year New Hampshire citizens for the first time joined fully in protests against what they increasingly considered the arbitrary and unjustified acts of a Parliament and ministry determined to subvert traditional liberties. In the spring of 1775 royal government in New Hampshire collapsed completely; John Wentworth felt so personally threatened he fled from the province. Even before he left, local leaders formed a provincial congress to coordinate the resistance movement. The congress members assumed general authority for management of provincial affairs after Wentworth's departure, and in January 1776 framed a constitution to legitimize their assumption of power. The Declaration of Independence, which the vast majority of provincial inhabitants supported, terminated formal allegiance to the king. New Hampshire's existence as a British colony had come to an abrupt conclusion.

The coming of revolution to New Hampshire involved two separate but mutually reinforcing processes: the collapse of the family dominated royal government, and the organization of a resistance movement whose leaders eventually formed a new provincial government managed by elected, not appointed, officials. The former began well before the latter. In the early 1760s the Wentworth oligarchy lost much of its influence in England. The central problem was the simple fact that after the accession of George III, Newcastle and his supporters fell from power and their replacements had little stake in continued Wentworth rule. Both English and American opponents of the status quo found members of the new imperial administration, Charles Townshend and George Grenville especially, responsive to complaints about New Hampshire's royal magistrates. At the same time the aging John Thomlinson retired from politics. His son, who replaced him as provincial agent, proved ineffective; both Thomlinsons died soon after mid-decade.

These developments soon disrupted the political calm which Benning Wentworth had enjoyed since the early 1750s. Soon after Townshend became president of the Board of Trade, the group held formal hearings on the long standing land dispute with New York, recommended the Connecticut River be declared New Hampshire's western boundary, and gained Privy Council approval of the recommendation. Wentworth complained, but could do nothing to have the decision reversed. Even worse, the boundary hearings blossomed into a full scale investigation of royal government in New Hampshire. The Board of Trade accused Wentworth of "negligence, misconduct and disobedience," then recommended his dismissal. John Huske, the son of former councillor and Belcher-supporter Ellis Huske, reported gleefully from England that the governor's removal was a foregone conclusion and that most of the Council "no doubt" would lose their commissions once a different chief magistrate was selected. The family sent Benning Wentworth's nephew John overseas to shore up its crumbling political fortunes. The young man's first report corroborated the rumors which had already begun to circulate in Portsmouth. "It is notorious," he

John Wentworth, governor 1767–1775. Copy by U. D. Tenney from a pastel drawn by John Singleton Copley in 1769. *Courtesy of Dartmouth College.*

wrote dejectedly, "that we are scarcely known and not considered but in the most diminutive way, and as a province...have no rights or interests."

Only good luck saved the family. While in England John Wentworth successfully courted the patronage of his distant kinsman the Marquis of Rockingham, who had emerged as leader of the old Newcastle faction in English politics. The connection proved invaluable. In July 1765, as a result of the Stamp Act crisis, Rockingham replaced Grenville as head of the ministry. He and Lord Dartmouth, the new president of the Board of Trade, decided after a brief deliberation that Benning Wentworth should be allowed to resign from his offices, that John Wentworth should be appointed as a replacement, and that several family members should be appointed to vacancies in the Council. Before leaving England the governor-designate convinced Thomlinson's influential partner in trade, Barlow Trecothick, to accept the responsibility of becoming agent for both the province of New Hampshire and for the future political interests of the family.

Unhappily for the Wentworths, Rockingham remained in power only thirteen months. Following his eclipse, the influence of the family declined again. Trecothick found it impossible to shape Whitehall policy affecting royal government in New Hampshire and became so frustrated that he lost interest in his job. Wentworth tried to locate an effective replacement, but could not get Assembly approval for Paul Wentworth, the man he considered most qualified for the position. The governor's continuing courtship of Rockingham—he wrote the Marquis regularly, sent gifts (including a moose), and named his first child "Charles-Mary" after the nobleman and his wife—accomplished little, for Rockingham never regained the ministry. Dartmouth proved more interested in saving his own skin than in helping the Wentworths. Despite the governor's decision to name a college for him, Dartmouth disassociated himself from the family's political affairs.

The dangers of dependence on men out of power became increasingly evident as time passed. In the early 1770s Peter Livius, a councillor appointed without family approval, organized a scheme to oust John Wentworth. Livius travelled to England, drew up a lengthy list of complaints about favoritism, misuse of public revenues and other matters, presented the list to the Board of Trade, and succeeded in having the Board—with Dartmouth's apparent cooperation—recommend dismissal. Rockingham and Paul Wentworth mustered enough support in the Privy Council to save the governor, but not enough to thwart Livius completely. Livius was given a mandamus to replace Atkinson as the Chief Justice of New Hampshire's Superior Court; his friend, Woodbury Langdon, was promised a Council commission. Soon thereafter George Boyd, an affluent Portsmouth shipbuilder outside the family circle, travelled to London. After meeting Lord North (the leader of the ministry) and what he described as "several other great people" Boyd gained the distinct impression that Wentworth had lost all support. "I am sure [my interest] at this time is more than his is now or ever was this side of the water," he wrote another political opponent of the governor, and proved the point by purchasing a Council commission. It is quite possible that the revolution, which destroyed the Wentworth oligarchy, rescued it from a less honorable demise.

In New Hampshire itself Wentworth experienced a different set of problems. Both his grandfather and his uncle had been able to construct a political system which prevented the development of effective internal opposition to family rule. As governor John Wentworth did his best to preserve that system. Much of his behavior, for example the judicious distribution of offices and land grants, aped techniques employed in the past. Wentworth also courted popularity by helping to establish a county court system, by chartering Dartmouth college whose graduates were expected to fill many vacant congregational pulpits in New Hampshire, and by adopting a much more affable personal manner than his predecessor. But he failed. By 1774, complaints about Wentworth and the family compact circulated in all parts of the province, and the effectiveness of New Hampshire's royal officials had been seriously eroded.

The loss of support stemmed in part from changes in England. Mark Wentworth, the governor's father, lost the mast agency to others with better imperial connections; as a result the family no longer controlled the distribution of subcontracts to woodsmen in the interior. The boundary decision reduced by two-thirds the land available for granting at a time when demand increased rapidly. Trecothick and Rockingham's ineffectiveness meant that those seeking royal commissions found it useful to disassociate themselves from the oligarchy.

Equally important, the new colonial administrators in Whitehall insisted that royal officials everywhere in America, including New

Hampshire, follow their instructions closely. One of Benning Wentworth's great strengths had been to ignore orders from England when obedience would have jeopardized his local position; if trouble arose, Thomlinson took care of things. John Wentworth had much less room in which to maneuver. Pressed by his superiors to enforce white pine regulations, he did so and came under attack from lumbermen and woodsmen throughout the province. The one time Wentworth flagrantly disobeyed his formal instructions—he signed an Assembly bill contrary to a recently passed act of Parliament—the new secretary of state sent him a stiff warning. "Good God," the governor complained in private correspondence, must a colonial magistrate act as "verbatim instructed," and so alienate his subjects that "his windows are demolished" before he can hope to be supported? He paid closer attention to orders after that, but his obedience undermined his popularity in New Hampshire.

Economic developments within New Hampshire also weakened the governor's political hand. For the previous half century the province had been so dependent on the mast trade, lumbering, and shipbuilding that resistance to rulers who permitted the exploitation of forest resources would have been foolish. The naval stores industry went into a gradual decline after the war with France ended. In the mid-1760s overseas demand for lumber and ships fell, merchants who had benefitted from military supply contracts had to rearrange their business affairs, and everyone suffered from imperial regulations which prevented the legislature from emitting further paper currency. Dissatisfaction with the ruling oligarchy spread easily among the economically distressed. Livius, for example, blamed his commercial reverses on the "clan." And those who managed to augment their personal fortunes despite the changed economic conditions did so without assistance from the Wentworths. George Boyd sold his ships to men Wentworth did not know. Woodbury Langdon traded through Lane, Fraser and Sons, not through Trecothick. It was not accidental that Livius, Boyd, Langdon, and their friends led the opposition to family government in the years before the revolution.

Demographic change had a parallel, though different impact on the effectiveness of family and royal government. The surge of population into the Connecticut and upper Merrimack river valleys in the fifteen years before revolution weakened the bonds between provincial inhabitants as a whole and their rulers. The new settlers traded through Newburyport, Salem, Boston, and Hartford, not through Portsmouth, and chafed under a government dominated by royal appointees and a seaboard merchant aristocracy. Wentworth's attempts to dilute sectional tension created as many problems as they solved. The Assembly refused to finance his program for building east-west roads in the province. The division into counties met with public approval, but many of the men Wentworth appointed to county judicial offices did not. One western inhabitant worried that the new system might introduce an unwanted "swarm of pettifoggers, who like the Egyptian locusts" destroyed "all before them." Piscataqua residents, including many of his relatives on the Council, wanted the courts to remain in Portsmouth. Peter Livius argued that "the province has so increased ... it is now of great importance to dissolve a family combination which has already been productive of so much injustice." For others the concern was more abstract. "Laws and regulations which prove very effectual for small communities," wrote a worried *Gazette* correspondent, "by no means answer the same good ends when they ... become more extensive." He urged provincial officials to initiate a far-reaching program of legal reform.

John Wentworth's task as royal governor, then, was much more difficult than that of his uncle and grandfather. Changing political conditions in England and postwar economic adjustments in New Hampshire reduced the leverage he could bring to bear on men potentially dissatisfied with family rule. The expansion of settlement produced sectional attitudes which further divided his subjects and provided fertile ground for political opposition. Yet, despite the seriousness of these developments, to Wentworth himself they were of secondary importance. While he governed New Hampshire a more fundamental challenge to his rule emerged.

That challenge was directed at the governor because he and his relatives represented a system of imperial authority which the colonists increasingly distrusted. Criticism first appeared after Parliament in 1765 enacted a stamp tax to increase colonial revenues. Many New Hampshire residents joined eagerly in the subsequent protest. A group of Portsmouth leaders formed a local "Sons of Liberty" organization, pressured the town to petition for repeal, supported demonstrations, forced

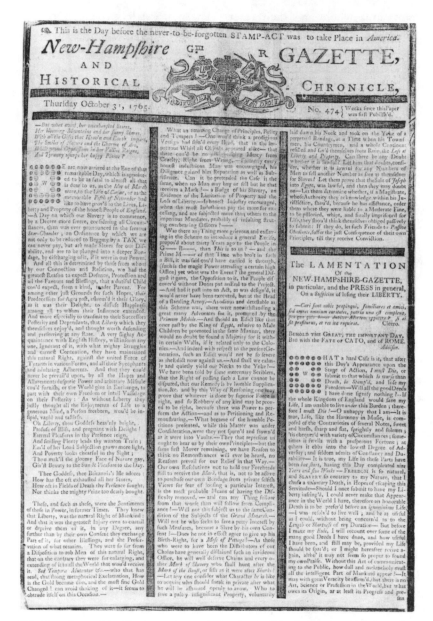

The New Hampshire Gazette published the day before the Stamp Act went into effect. *Courtesy of the New Hampshire Historical Society.*

the stamp collector George Meserve to resign his commission, and began publishing a newspaper to counteract the influence of what they considered the much too conservative *Gazette.* The ruling oligarchy tried hard to avoid association with parliamentary policy—Benning Wentworth refused to enforce the Stamp Act and John Wentworth cooperated closely with Rockingham in the successful campaign for repeal—but the resistance movement occasionally spilled over into suggestions that New Hampshire's appointed magistrates were insufficiently "warm" in their opposition. One radical accused the *Gazette* publisher of dependence on men in power; several others complained about the governor's and Council's refusal to support sending provincial representatives to the Stamp Act Congress, which met in Philadelphia to coordinate intercolonial opposition to the unpopular legislation.

Criticism of New Hampshire's royal officials increased after John Wentworth decided not to oppose the Townshend duties, new taxes passed in 1767 to replace the revenue lost by repeal of the Stamp Act. Wentworth's decision was not a whimsical one—he was in no position to alienate his superiors, he probably thought the taxes just, and many Portsmouth residents agreed with his position—but it cost him dearly. Woodbury Langdon, George Boyd, and a number of other unhappy merchants sponsored a movement to have the Assembly petition for repeal; Wentworth's opposition to the plan seemed to them arbitrary and unnecessary. Many residents outside Portsmouth also thought the colony should adopt a non-importation policy. Samuel Langdon, the highly respected minister of Portsmouth's north parish, claimed that "the independent part of the province" [he meant those not under the influence of the Wentworths] was "as patriotic...as any part of the continent." Subsequent events suggest he may have been correct. After the Boston massacre a number of communities adopted non-importation resolutions and the Assembly finally petitioned the crown. Controversy subsided only because Parliament eventually repealed the legislation imposing new taxes.

Meanwhile other complaints about royal officials in New Hampshire had arisen. The Stamp and Townshend Acts were part of a much broader effort to increase the efficiency of the colonial revenue system. The effort involved the tightening of customs regulations, replacement of ineffective customs officials with men willing to enforce the regulations, and if necessary the stationing of royal troops in the colonies to facilitate enforcement. Although the Wentworths opposed most of these reforms—the governor once described the conduct of new customs officials as "absurd, inflamatory, and contumacious"—they could not avoid involvements in the resulting controversies. In the late 1760s the imperial government sent a Board of Customs Commissioners to oversee collections in America. The Board appointed a new collector for the Piscataqua who immediately began confiscating ships and cargos, most of them owned by political opponents of the Wentworths. The victims, understandably, suspected collusion on the part of their Governor and Council. No British regulars were stationed in New Hampshire, but they marched up occasionally from Massachusetts and every time they appeared trouble arose. On one occasion a local magistrate appointed by Wentworth helped capture two army deserters and delivered them to military officers passing through Londonderry. He, and by implication the governor, were publicly condemned by irate citizens who rescued the deserters.

Accumulated specific grievances against imperial authorities and provincial officials soon spilled over into a general reassessment of the entire governmental system. Ironically, John Wentworth himself was one of the most perceptive critics of the status quo. As early as 1765 he began to complain that officials responsible for American policy knew little about actual conditions in the colonies and made their decisions more for political reasons than anything else. His frustrations as governor sharpened his attack. How, he asked at one point, could order be maintained when the home government censured him for cooperating with the Assembly? Wentworth also thought existing constitutional arrangements should be altered. "It is rather to be wondered that there are not more riots," he wrote an English friend in 1768, "when we consider the natural imbecility" of an administration "where every civil official from the Governor to the constable are dependent on the people for annual support." Such dependence destroyed the "respect and confidence necessary to subordination." Wentworth's concrete recommendations for dissipating crisis reflected his personal situation. Make royal officials "more independent," he advised. "Entrust them to dispense the benefits to the friends of government, hear and consider candidly their advice and information, leave them more discretionary power."

Other critics framed the problem in different terms. Wentworth's logic rested on two assumptions: that Parliament had the right to legislate for the colonies, and that Americans would accept both taxation and reform as long as they were judiciously managed. Unfortunately for him and for royal government as a whole, few provincial inhabitants still accepted these assumptions. Between passage of the Stamp Act and repeal of the Townshend duties public and private discussion of constitutional matters altered the way in which the colonists thought about imperial authority. Dover's Congregational minister, Jeremy Belknap, wrote later in his *History of New Hampshire* that "political inquiries were encouraged, and the eyes of the people were opened." Inquiry gradually crystalized into a set of beliefs and fears so dangerous in their implications that thoughtful men began to suspect a revolution in the making.

Attention focused initially on the nature and limits of parliamentary authority. Samuel Langdon summarized emerging opinion in a letter to the Boston Sons of Liberty. "We claim a right to be governed by our own laws, and to grant our own monies to the King." Parliament, he argued, should only "make the most effectual provision for the general welfare and prosperity of the whole empire, and preserve a proper balance betwixt the national interest and that of the colonies." The Stamp Act, Townshend duties, and new customs regulations all violated these principles and thus were illegal. Soon the king's advisors in the ministry came under attack. They were accused of burdening the colonists with officers "whose life depends upon drawing the veins of the body politic" and of subverting Parliament. English officials, in short, seemed engaged in a deliberate plot to prevent the inhabitants of New Hampshire and other colonies from enjoying their just and traditional rights as Englishmen. The only way to prevent the plot from succeeding was to resist all manifestations of arbitrary authority and to maintain constant vigilance. The home government simply could not be trusted.

For that matter, neither could royally appointed provincial officials. The behavior of the Wentworths was increasingly subject to close scrutiny. "Our situation is really deplorable," complained Langdon, "His Excellency and his Council are appointed by the Crown and we wish their sole motives did not seem to be an implicit adherence to what they apprehend may soothe the present ministry." Criticism of judicial appointments and the Court of Appeals resurfaced. To some, especially among the Congregational clergy, the dancing, gambling, and other diversionary activities which the oligarchy so cherished seemed symptomatic of a general moral decline in the English-speaking world. These critics linked the actions of the home government to a general decadence which enabled a designing ministry to buy off Parliament and they suggested a similar process had taken place in New Hampshire. The Anglicanism of the Wentworths accentuated these fears. A number of dissenting clergymen and their parishioners thought it quite possible the Wentworths would support their minister, the Reverend Arthur Browne, in his efforts to have a separate bishopric for North America established. If that happened, then Congregationalists and other dissenters might become the victims of religious oppression.

The gradual erosion of respect for the executive branches of government led many of these same critics to examine the role of the Assembly in provincial politics. The examination produced both complaints and demands for reform. House members were accused of representing private interests, not the interests of the people as a whole, and of loyalty to a suspect administration; their moderate response to the Stamp Act and Townshend duties seemed in retrospect inexcusable. Soon writers throughout New Hampshire urged the Assembly to assume the same rights exercised by the General Court in Massachusetts. One correspondent to the *Gazette* asked that a House journal be printed and that public galleries be constructed. Townsmen began giving their elected representatives written instructions. So widespread was the furor that "Americanus" could write, with obvious approval: "The people being now better informed of the nature of government, can be a better judge of their own importance in supporting the dignity of their part of the legislature."

Political debate subsided in the months following repeal of the Townshend duties, but the damage had been done. John Wentworth was not fooled. "I fear the present calm does not proceed from content," he warned Rockingham in the summer of 1771, "alienation takes deeper root in these quieter times than when much evaporated in passion." New Hampshirites and other Americans had begun to pass judgment on the entire system of provincial and imperial government.

The beliefs and anxieties on which they based their conclusions provided a continuing threat to the authority of all royal officials.

Loss of influence in England, changing economic conditions and patterns of settlement in New Hampshire, the civil disorder and constitutional debate set off by colonial reform all made it impossible for the Wentworths to exercise the tight control over provincial political affairs which had been so pronounced in earlier years. The Assembly proved increasingly reluctant to accept the recommendations of the chief executive and after 1773 became almost totally defiant. For the first time since Governor Belcher's administration the Council became a source of trouble. The towns not only elected uncooperative House representatives, but assumed responsibility for organizing local resistance to imperial policy. Individuals and groups of citizens defied constituted authority. Gradually the effectiveness of royal government in New Hampshire weakened; in the spring of 1775 it collapsed entirely.

The initial difficulties developed when the House, in 1768, received a letter from the Massachusetts General Court recommending that the colonies unite to protest the Townshend duties. A majority of the representatives wanted to respond affirmatively to the letter, but were discouraged from doing so by Wentworth and Speaker Peter Gilman, whom the governor had recently promised a Council appointment. That summer, after receiving a copy of the Virginia Resolves, the Assembly approved a petition demanding redress of grievances and ordered Gilman to forward it to Trecothick. Wentworth convinced Gilman not to send the petition and informed key assemblymen that if the petition were sent, the proposed division into counties certainly would be disallowed in England. But the scheme failed. In 1770 the House again ordered the speaker to forward the petition. Although this time Gilman obeyed, he lost his seat in elections held the following year. The speaker who replaced Gilman (another John Wentworth, though not a close relative of the governor) advocated provincial cooperation with other colonies.

Meanwhile the traditional harmony of Council proceedings had been disrupted. In 1765 Peter Livius, who had political connections with Charles Townshend, obtained a Council commission without either the knowledge or approval of the Wentworths. He moved to Portsmouth, tried unsuccessfully to enter the mast trade, became friends with factional opponents of the oligarchy, and when Benning Wentworth tried to buy him off by appointing him to the Inferior Court of Common Pleas, made a number of judicial decisions against New Hampshire's ruling elite. In the Council itself Livius exhibited the same hostility. The only member not related to the governor, he consistently complained about the Council's appointments, executive policies, legislative recommendations, and above all the family bias reflected in almost everything the councillors did. Not surprisingly, it was the Council's action on a matter of immense importance to the Wentworth family that gave rise to Livius's most vigorous protest.

Benning Wentworth had married his housekeeper Martha Hilton in 1760. The family regretted the indiscretion but kept quiet hoping that the aging magistrate would at least have sense enough to leave most of his fortune to his kinsmen. He left everything, however, to his widow and when the will was opened in 1770 John Wentworth took action. He sued the estate for money owed the crown by his predecessor and asked the Council for an opinion concerning the legality of land grants which the deceased governor had bestowed upon himself. After brief deliberation the Council declared the grants illegal and announced that the land belonged to the crown. The whole affair so infuriated Livius he entered a detailed objection, retired from the Council, drafted a petition to the Board of Trade in which he accused the governor of abusing his power, gathered depositions (most of them in interior communities) to support his claims, and spent the next two years of his life trying to dislodge the Wentworths. Fortunately for the political harmony of the Council, his efforts carried him back to England.

Livius left in 1772. The next year conflict shifted back to the Assembly. In May Speaker John Wentworth received letters from Virginia and Rhode Island asking New Hampshire to appoint a standing Committee of Correspondence to communicate with other colonies in matters of general interest. The governor tried his best to prevent acquiescence, but the latest provincial elections had altered the House membership sufficiently to guarantee his pleading would fall on deaf ears. The House members appointed the committee, and when Wentworth prorogued them to forestall further mischief, they returned to their respective communities where they informed voters about the increasingly distasteful conduct of the once popular chief magistrate.

The Tea Act, passed by Parliament that fall, precipitated still more protest. In Boston irate colonists unceremoniously dumped a quantity of East India Company tea into the sea and promised to repeat the procedure should anyone attempt to import more of the commodity. New Hampshire mobilized in sympathy with its neighbors to the south. In mid-December the Portsmouth town meeting approved radical resolutions which stated in unequivocal terms the constitutional case against the new taxes and regulations. Any parliamentary effort to tax the colonists was "unjust, arbitrary and inconsistent with the fundamental principles of the British Constitution," and violated the natural right of Englishmen "to have the power of disposing of their own property, either by themselves or their representatives." If the logic of the Tea Act were carried to an extreme the colonial Assemblies, which did have the right to tax, would be stripped of their powers. Dover, Newcastle, Exeter, Hampton, and dozens of other towns passed similar resolutions in the next few weeks. Many towns formed committees to prevent consumption of the "noxious herb" and organized boycotts against merchants who tried to sell their remaining stock.

The success of these measures and the intensity of feeling expressed by opponents of the Tea Act soon forced New Hampshire's more conservative inhabitants to speak out. No disagreement arose about the impropriety of the tax—even Wentworth publicly criticized the ministry—but the methods adopted to oppose it seemed to many unwise. Six of the thirteen men chosen to draw up the Portsmouth resolves, including Atkinson and Jaffrey, refused to sign them. Correspondents to the *Gazette* warned about the possibility of ministerial reprisal and accused local tea merchants of employing political rhetoric to protect their personal economic fortunes. Some inhabitants of western New Hampshire, already angry at eastern control of governmental office, shared these suspicions. Agitation against the Tea Act, claimed the town of Hinsdale, had been organized "because the intended method of sale by the East India Company would probably hurt the private interest of many persons who deal largely in tea."

Encouraged by what seemed a growing reaction against protest, Wentworth decided in January 1774 to risk reconvening the Assembly. His hopes for legislative assistance were soon dashed. When he asked for laws to combat the "infectious and pestilential disorders being spread among the inhabitants," the House ignored his request. Later, after the backlog of local petitions and other noncontroversial business had been transacted, the representatives voted to write other colonial Assemblies expressing New Hampshire's complete agreement with organized procedures of resistance. Wentworth immediately adjourned the group, then dissolved it, and with foreboding called for the new elections required by law.

The spring elections of 1774 provided a fresh opportunity for inhabitants to assess provincial politics, just as the Tea Act had stimulated a new critique of Parliament and the ministry. Much of the discussion focused on the problems of representation. Citizens accused the governor of sending new election precepts only to those communities where likely candidates for election were his friends. They complained about the fact that only a third of New Hampshire's incorporated towns sent members to the Assembly: "there is no drawing a line of representation," wrote one infuriated resident, "every freeholder in the most distant parts of the province has an equal right thereto." Another writer suggested that election of delegates "who will withstand oppression to its face" might lead to redress of such grievances as favoritism in land grants and the presence of a biased Court of Appeals.

Wentworth could hardly have been pleased by the election results. Several of his supporters lost their seats and were replaced by known radicals. The Portsmouth representatives showed up at the first session with formal instructions bound to keep the House in turmoil. The session itself confirmed the governor's worst fears. He took, as he later explained to Dartmouth, "great pains to prevail on them not to enter into any extra-provincial measures" but failed completely. After the delegates twice voted to continue the Committee of Correspondence Wentworth adjourned them, spent several agonizing days conferring with Council members on what to do, and on June 8 dissolved the Assembly for entering on matters "inconsistent with His Majesty's service and the good of this province."

Tension increased rapidly during the summer of 1774. A tea consignment arrived in Portsmouth, and only Wentworth's unwillingness to protect the shipment and the promise of the consignee to return the tea unopened prevented the outbreak of violence. Parliament's decision to close the port of Boston stimulated a new wave of protests and gave inhabitants the chance to send voluntary contributions to victims of the home government's latest oppression. The Portsmouth Committee of Correspondence passed a nonimportation covenant, sent copies to local officials in every provincial town, and urged all patriotic citizens to affix their signatures. In July the provincial committee, which had continued to meet despite Wentworth's dissolution of the Assembly, asked each town to elect representatives to a general congress which would coordinate resistance in New Hampshire. When the delegates convened they selected two members, John Sullivan of Durham and Nathaniel Folsom of Exeter, to attend the proposed Continental Congress. Few provincial inhabitants resisted these activities, and those who did often were coerced into silence. Governor Wentworth sat by helplessly, lamented his "small influence," and wrote a series of increasingly pessimistic letters to England.

In October an incident occurred which intensified antagonism to royal authority. General Gage, unable to hire carpenters in Massachusetts to construct barracks for his troops, asked Wentworth for help. Torn between what he considered his official duty and the knowledge that compliance would further jeopardize his already crumbling authority, the governor compromised: he hired the artificers but tried to conceal his conduct by selecting men who lived near his country estate at Wolfboro and by not telling them what they would be doing in Boston. The maneuver backfired. His actions became a matter of public knowledge, one radical group in Portsmouth branded him "an enemy . . . to the community," and citizens elsewhere in the province were so infuriated they committed, according to Wentworth, "several reprehensible violences" against royal officials.

Two months after the carpenter fiasco an even more dramatic episode occurred. Paul Revere arrived in Portsmouth bearing a message from Boston that the ministry had banned further export of military stores to the colonies and that British troops were on their way to take possession of Castle William and Mary, the fort at Newcastle which protected both Portsmouth and Kittery. On December 14 a crowd 400 strong assaulted the fort, took as much powder as they could carry, and sent it in small boats to nearby communities; there was a repeat performance the next day. Wentworth could do nothing to stop these proceedings. He tried to muster the militia, but no one obeyed; the Council members and local magistrates he asked to join him in con-

Province of N E W - H A M P S H I R E

A PROCLAMATION,
BY THE GOVERNOR.

WHEREAS several Bodies of Men did, in the Day Time of the 14th, and in the Night of the 15th of this Instant December, in the most daring and rebellious Manner invest, attack, and forcibly enter into His Majesty's Castle William and Mary in this Province, and overpowering and confining the Captain and Garrison, did, besides committing many treasonable Insults and Outrages, break open the Magazine of said Castle and plunder it of above One hundred Barrels of Gunpowder, with upwards of sixty Stand of small Arms, and did also force from the Ramparts of said Castle and carry off sixteen Pieces of Cannon, and other military Stores, in open Hostility and direct Oppugnation of His Majesty's Government, and in the most atrocious Contempt of his Crown and Dignity ;----

I Do, by Advice and Consent of His Majesty's Council, issue this Proclamation, ordering and requiring, in his Majesty's Name, all Magistrates and other Officers, whether Civil or Military, as they regard their Duty to the KING and the Tenor of the Oaths they have solemnly taken and subscribed, to exert themselves in detecting and securing in some of his Majesty's Goals in this province the said Offenders, in Order to their being brought to condign punishment ; And from Motives of Duty to the King and Regard to the Welfare of the good People of this Province : I do in the most earnest and solemn Manner, exhort and injoin you, his Majesty's liege Subjects of this Government, to beware of suffering yourselves to be seduced by the false Arts or Menaces of abandoned Men, to abet, protect, or screen from Justice any of the said high handed Offenders, or to withhold or secrete his Majesty's Munition forcibly taken from his Castle ; but that each and every of you will use your utmost Endeavours to detect and discover the Perpetrators of these Crimes to the civil Magistrate, and assist in securing and bringing them to Justice, and in recovering the King's Munition ; This Injunction it is my bounden Duty to lay strictly upon you, and to require your Obedience thereto, as you value individually your Faith and Allegiance to his Majesty, as you wish to preserve that Reputation to the Province in general ; and as you would avert the dreadful but most certain Consequences of a contrary Conduct to yourselves and Posterity.

GIVEN at the Council-Chamber in Portsmouth, the 26th Day of December, in the 15th Year of the Reign of our Sovereign Lord GEORGE the Third, by the Grace of GOD, of Great-Britain, France and Ireland, KING, Defender of the Faith, &c. and in the Year of our Lord CHRIST, 1774.

By His EXCELLENCY's Command,
with Advice of Council.

J. WENTWORTH.

Theodore Atkinson, Sec^{ry}.

GOD SAVE THE KING.

Governor's Proclamation issued the day after the first attack on Castle William and Mary. *Courtesy of the New Hampshire Historical Society.*

fronting the mob refused to get involved; the crew of his personal barge would not row him out to the fort. Only the arrival of two men-of-war from Boston prevented additional trouble.

The authority of royal officials throughout New Hampshire deteriorated rapidly after the looting of Castle William. Wentworth became so frightened he asked Gage to station troops in Portsmouth and helped found an association of local residents—most of them public officials or members of the family oligarchy—who vowed to protect each other "from mobs, riots or any unlawful attacks whatsoever." Angry residents prevented the courts from convening in Hillsborough and Cheshire counties. In towns throughout the province, royal magistrates were subjected to personal harassment. Many responded by resigning their commissions, others simply sat tight and let locally appointed committees maintain order, and several left the countryside for Portsmouth or Boston. The militia fell completely under the control of resistance leaders. John Sullivan, whose commission Wentworth withdrew, urged his fellow officers to resign en masse and organized weekly drills in Durham and neighboring towns. When a captain in Newton refused to muster his troops, they elected new officers, began to train, and publicized their efforts as an example for others to follow. The importance of these changes became apparent in April 1775, after fighting erupted at Lexington and Concord. Hundreds of angry New Hampshire militiamen flooded southward to aid their stricken fellow colonists.

John Wentworth's last desperate effort to restore some semblance of constitutional order precipitated the final collapse of royal government. Sometime in March the governor decided to convene the Assembly and concocted an elaborate plan to gain its support: he added three small Connecticut valley towns where personal friends supposedly dominated local politics to the list of those eligible for representation, timed the elections to coincide with the expected arrival of British troops, and prepared to arrest any successful candidates who had instigated or participated in the attack on Castle William. But the plan, like almost everything else Wentworth tried in his last hectic weeks as New Hampshire's royal governor, failed miserably. The governor was roundly condemned for attempting to pack the Assembly. Gage sent no troops. The new House contained so many radicals Wentworth postponed the first session until early May. This too caused trouble. A *Gazette* correspondent described the adjournment as the latest in a series of arbitrary measures which had "deprived the people from any share in their own government for near twelve months" and reduced them "to the sad necessity of being governed by the Crown, or its immediate servants, or of being reduced to a state of anarchy." Such conduct, he concluded, had helped destroy the "much deluded" chief magistrate's popularity and power.

The Assembly session itself dashed Wentworth's last hope of moderating lawlessness. In an emotional introductory speech he reminded the assemblymen that the "strongest ties of kinship, religion, duty, and interest" bound them to the parent state and pleaded with them to consider measures which would "lead to a restoration of the public tranquility." But the delegates could not be moved. They first appointed a committee to report on the many petitions complaining about representatives returned in an "unconstitutional manner," then asked for an adjournment to consult their constituents. Wentworth hesitated, for he knew that many of the representatives planned to attend an illegal congress of town delegates. But when it became evident the House would break up anyway, he granted their request. The delegates gathered again in June, by an overwhelming majority refused to seat the representatives from the three Connecticut valley towns, told the governor they were "entirely at a loss" to know what measures might re-establish the "much needed reconciliation," and when Wentworth's friend John Fenton—one of the men excluded by the vote on representation—tried to defend the governor and imperial officials, shouted him down. Wentworth immediately announced a second adjournment, this time without being asked.

That evening Fenton visited the governor's house. As the men dined a crowd demanding Fenton's arrest gathered outside. Fenton at first refused to appear, but after the mob brought up a cannon and started beating on the house with clubs he surrendered. That night Wentworth, his wife, and their five month old child moved to Castle William where they would be protected by the guns of His Majesty's ship *Scarborough*. The flight completed the disintegration of family and royal government. Atkinson tried to keep up appearances in Portsmouth, but possessed no effective authority; Wentworth himself could do nothing but issue orders through Atkinson and hope that Gage would send troops. When the *Scarborough* left for Boston late that summer Wentworth and his family were aboard. In September he hired a sloop, sailed to the Isles of Shoals, and buffetted by a set of powerful and conflicting emotions formally prorogued the Assembly. New Hampshire's last royal governor never again returned to his native province.

In some localities the collapse of royal government threatened further social and political chaos. Men who gathered to silence suspected Tories often, as one revolutionist put it, exceeded "the bounds of reason." Individuals took revenge on personal enemies by accusing them of disloyalty, and local officials found their authority weakened and their right to perform normal civil functions challenged. These disruptions, however, were limited in scope and of short duration. Even before Governor Wentworth fled, concerned citizens had constructed a network of local organizations to guarantee the maintenance of peace and good order. Leaders in the old Assembly assumed responsibility for forming a new institution made up of town delegates—labeled the "Provincial Congress"—to act for the province as a whole. The movement toward setting up a revolutionary government accelerated during the spring and summer of 1775. The Congress handled more and more matters while the towns authorized individuals and groups to exercise power previously wielded by royally appointed officials. In January 1776 the Congress declared itself the new House of Representatives and adopted a written constitution to legitimize its authority. All in all it was a remarkably smooth transition. By the time the Continental Congress formally declared independence from the crown, the people of New Hampshire had formed an effective and stable system of state authority.

Royal government, even at the peak of the Wentworths's power, was never deeply rooted at the town level. Appointed local officials—justices of the peace, militia officers, and after 1771 county magistrates—derived their authority as much from their social and economic status as from their commissions, and most matters of political importance were decided in town meetings. Officials elected at these gatherings collected taxes, enforced or chose not to enforce provincial laws, and in general saw to the maintenance of civil order. As a result, when imperial authority began to collapse, most local authority remained intact. Many appointed magistrates continued to enforce the law although their commissions had become worthless. Locally elected officials did the same. In Hillsborough County, for example, the grand jury instructed a constable who had been criticized for invoking the authority of the crown to break up a fight to keep the peace but avoid mentioning the king's name. The Provincial Congress recommended soon after Wentworth's flight "that with regard to all those who have been in the usual reasonable manner chosen into any office in towns, they should as formerly be considered as the proper officers," and instructed all local officials to "proceed in the usual manner" in fulfilling their traditional responsibilities.

Local institutions served the citizens of New Hampshire well during the revolutionary crisis. The militia, which more than any other town based colonial organization was under the ruling oligarchy's influence, not only survived the disintegration of royal government but proved an effective instrument for resisting imperial innovation. Many officers resigned their commissions and asked the rank and file to elect replacements. Unless past behavior made them suspect, they usually gained through election what they had voluntarily relinquished. Local militia groups played an important role in distributing the guns and powder taken in the attacks on Castle William. Entire regiments hurried down to Massachusetts in the dead of night when messengers brought news of the fighting at Lexington and Concord. After that the Provincial Congress used local militia units to build a reasonably effective military organization for all of New Hampshire.

The revolutionists found their primary civil institution equally useful in the political crisis. Town meetings were convened frequently, in some communities every few weeks. The meetings passed resolves against the Tea Act, provided aid to the victims of the Boston Port Bill, voted funds and supplies to the militia, helped enforce recommendations of the Provincial and Continental Congresses, and in general were instrumental in articulating the logic which justified resistance to imperial legislation. They also responded readily when asked to elect representatives to the emerging state government. One device employed with regularity was the appointment of special committees to make certain essential activities took place. Such committees had been used earlier in the colonial period, but not since the days of Edward Cranfield to openly defy royal authority. Committees of Correspondence were organized in many towns to resist the Tea Act and assure compliance with the non-importation agreement recommended by the Continental Congress. After royal government collapsed in the spring of 1775 almost every community appointed a Committee of Safety (sometimes called the Committee of Ways and Means) charged with responsibility for doing whatever seemed necessary to protect the colonists and maintain good order. The committee in Portsmouth, where large numbers of unemployed seamen made the problem of disorder most serious, arranged for nightly patrols, dealt with refugees seeking asylum, and provided a forum in which potentially explosive personal disputes could be moderated. Committees elsewhere adopted similar tactics.

The stability and continuity of local government made possible the creation of political organizations which assumed authority to act for more than the individual community. Some of these formed at the county level. Before the revolution the Court of General Sessions, attended by specially selected justices of the peace, conducted much of the important county business. These courts provided a ready instrument for inter-community action once royal government began to weaken. In November 1774, court members in Hillsborough County helped organize a meeting where local representatives gathered to discuss the critical state of affairs. Although the first session accomplished little, the second—whose members Governor Wentworth accused of "high treason"—took a number of actions: it passed a resolution condemning "licentious attacks" on persons and property, recommended disciplined military training for all communities, attempted to strengthen the county judicial system, and eventually formed a county Committee of Safety to punish ordinary criminals as well as suspected Tories. A congress of town delegates in Cheshire County also met and passed several resolutions. The county organizations, however, served only short term purposes. By the fall of 1775 their main functions had been taken over by the new Provincial Congress.

The Committee of Correspondence appointed by the House of Representatives in 1774 provided the initial stimulus to the formation of New Hampshire's revolutionary government. When Wentworth dissolved the Assembly in an attempt to keep the committee from meeting, its members refused to disperse. Instead they issued a summons for the representatives to reconvene. That night, after the governor repeated his order to disband, the group met at a local tavern and issued invitations for each town in the province to elect members for a general congress to meet at Exeter. Eighty-five delegates, mostly from the seaboard area, responded to the call. In a hurried session they not only chose Sullivan and Folsom to attend the Continental Congress, but appointed a treasurer to receive the £200 contributed by towns to defray their expenses, formed a committee to instruct them, and in a final gesture of defiance recommended that all communities in New Hampshire send aid to Boston.

The Committee of Correspondence called a second Provincial Congress for January 1775. After appointing Sullivan and John Langdon— the two leaders of the attacks on Castle William—to the Continental Congress, the delegates debated whether or not they should assume some degree of general responsibility for governing the province. Meshech Weare, the man whom Benning Wentworth had accepted as the compromise House speaker back in 1752, urged caution, but the logic of more radical members prevailed. The Congress selected its own Committee of Correspondence, issued a set of recommendations emphasizing the necessity of obedience to locally elected officials, pointedly avoided any statement which would have bolstered royal authority, and urged all citizens to arm and train themselves. Governor Wentworth labeled the recommendations an attempt to assume "uncontrolled dictatorial power" by a group of "unwise men" who pandered to popular fears. His decision to convene what became New Hampshire's last colonial Assembly was the direct result of the second Provincial Congress.

The Congress continued to accumulate power. After the fighting in Massachusetts it met for the third time and appointed Folsom commander-in-chief of all New Hampshire troops who remained in the Bay Colony to guard against further encroachment by British regulars. Its leaders controlled the proceedings of the Assembly which met in May. All five members of the congressional Committee of Correspondence gained election to the House and the same man (the other John Wentworth) who chaired the first three Congresses was chosen speaker. "The voice of the convention," Belknap noted later, "was regarded by the House as the voice of their constituents." Meanwhile the fourth Congress convened and began taking full control of provincial affairs. The delegates—by now virtually all sizable communities in New Hampshire had sent representatives—voted to raise 2000 troops, appropriated over £10,000 to support them, created committees of safety and supply to handle the details, and issued instructions for the arrest and incarceration of suspected Tories. The colonial records and public money still in the possession of Treasurer George Jaffrey were seized and moved from Portsmouth to Exeter. The Congress created a post office system. When it adjourned on July 8, President Meshech Weare reported that New Hampshire was "wholly governed by this Congress and the committees of the respective towns." Wentworth told Dartmouth the same thing a few days later.

The last step in the transition from royal to revolutionary government involved regularizing the ground rules for representation in the Congress and legitimizing the authority that the Congress exercised in fact. The problems of representation were serious ones. By the 1770s most colonists resented the exclusion of more than half the provincial towns and nearly half its voters from participation in Assembly elections. As a result most towns had responded to the general invitation to send delegates to the Congresses. The fourth Congress included 153 members from 113 communities. If the existing arrangement continued, the number of delegates, already too large, might grow still larger. Furthermore, many citizens had begun to complain about the colonial laws which since 1728 had limited voting for assemblymen to those worth £50 and candidates for office to men possessing at least £300 of property. Why, they asked, should only the prosperous take part in elections? Defenders of the status quo argued that the function of government was to protect property, that those with property had a greater stake in provincial affairs, and that only the wealthy had the time, education, and proven ability to be trusted with power. Finally, there was disagreement over how many representatives the larger towns should have. Inland inhabitants feared that if representation were proportional to population, seaboard communities would retain the same control over provincial government they had exercised under the imperial system.

All these issues were compromised. Late in December the fourth Provincial Congress decided to terminate its existence and call for new elections. The fifth Congress would have eighty-nine members. The property qualification for candidates was reduced to £200 and voting privileges were extended to "every legal inhabitant paying taxes." Small towns would be grouped in "classes" containing approximately 100 voters, each class to have one delegate. Most other towns had a single representative, but five were given two delegates and Portsmouth three.

The net effect of the new arrangement was to broaden the suffrage and to minimize the likelihood that provincial affairs would be controlled by a merchant elite. Towns within ten miles of Portsmouth had provided two-thirds of the membership in the last colonial Assembly. They sent only one-fourth the members of the fifth Provincial Congress.

The need to legitimize authority grew out of New Hampshire's status as a royal colony. Unlike Massachusetts, it had no charter to fall back on once legally constituted government collapsed. The initial position of most revolutionary leaders was to maintain the fiction that they had organized only to resist British tyranny and would not consider "taking up government" unless instructed to do so by the Continental Congress. Wentworth's flight and the battle of Bunker Hill made them more aggressive. In July 1775, Weare asked the Continental group for guidance; a few months later the New Hampshire delegates in Philadelphia engineered a congressional resolution authorizing the provincial convention to assume full civil authority. It was anticipation of this resolution which led the revolutionary leaders to compromise their differences on representation, issue new election precepts, and disband. The precepts asked voter permission for the fifth Provincial Congress to resolve itself into a House of Representatives.

The members, who convened in mid-December, did just that. They also debated at length about the structure of the new government and decided to accept the advice of Weare, Langdon, Sullivan, Josiah Bartlett (a Kingston physician who had replaced Sullivan in the Continental Congress when Sullivan accepted appointment as a general in the continental army) to appoint a Council which would share governmental authority within the traditional bicameral framework. The first Council would be drawn from the House delegates; after that councillors would be elected by the counties. A committee charged with specific responsibility for drafting "a new constitution" consistent with this and other votes by the representatives presented its recommendations on January 5th 1776. Despite the opposition of several delegates who had become anxious about the whole affair, the House adopted the proposed constitution by a better than two to one majority.

The constitution was fully operative long before the Declaration of Independence. The House chose twelve of its members to become councillors and ordered elections to fill the resulting vacancies. Both branches of the legislature then adopted rules to govern their internal

Colony of New-Hampſhire.

By the COUNCIL and ASSEMBLY,

A PROCLAMATION.

WHEREAS the CONGRESS of this Colony have, agreeable to a Recommendation from the Honorable CONTINENTAL CONGRESS, reſolved on, and form'd themſelves upon a PLAN of GOVERNMENT by a COUNCIL and Houſe of REPRESENTATIVES ; which Plan has been publiſhed, and diſperſed through the Colony, and is to be in Force during the preſent Diſpute with Great-Britain, unleſs otherwiſe advis'd by the Continental Congreſs :---conformable to which ſaid Plan of Government, the Council and Aſſembly have choſen, and appointed the proper Officers for the Adminiſtration of Juſtice, in the ſeveral Counties, who are to be ſworn to the faithful diſcharge of their ſeveral Truſts ;--It is therefore expected, that no Perſon or Perſons, claim, or exerciſe any civil Authority, but ſuch as are, or may be appointed as aforeſaid, on the Penalty of being deemed inimical to their Country.

Provided nevertheleſs, and this PROCLAMATION is intended not to interfere with the Power of the neceſſary Committees of Inſpection, or Safety, choſen in the ſeveral Towns through the Colony, by Virtue, and in Conſequence of, any Recommendation or Reſolves of the Continental Congreſs,---Whereof all Perſons concerned, are to take due Notice, and govern themſelves accordingly.

And at the ſame Time it is earneſtly recommended, that in this diſtreſſing Day of public Calamity, when our Enemies are watching all Opportunities to enſnare and divide us, every one would ſtrive to prevent, and if poſſible, to quell all Appearance of party Spirit, to cultivate and promote Peace, Union and good Order, and by all Means in their Power, to diſcourage Profaneſs, Immorality, and Injuſtice.

By Order of the Council and Aſſembly at Exeter, the 19th Day of March, Anno Domini 1776.

M. WEARE, Preſident of the Council.

E. THOMPSON, Secretary.

GOD SAVE THE PEOPLE.

PORTSMOUTH, Printed by DANIEL FOWLE.

Broadside printed for the revolutionary government soon after the Constitution of 1776 went into effect. *Courtesy of the New Hampshire Historical Society.*

proceedings. A joint committee was established to recommend revisions in the legal code; for the present, laws passed by the colonial legislatures, with a few obvious exceptions, were to remain in force. Before adjourning, the Council and House members began filling the local, county, and provincial offices left vacant by the collapse of royal government. They also passed a tax bill, made the necessary military appropriations, and created a Committee of Safety to handle executive affairs while they recessed. The legislators, in short, assumed full responsibility for the conduct of provincial affairs. Later they voted to have the word "colony" replaced by the word "state" in all official documents. Nobody opposed the change in wording.

EPILOGUE

As far as the inhabitants of New Hampshire were concerned the colonial period came to an end with the Declaration of Independence. Officials in England, however, did not acknowledge independence until the formal signing of the Treaty of Paris in September 1783. Events of immense importance both to the revolutionists themselves and to future state residents took place in the intervening seven years.

The war itself had relatively little direct impact on New Hampshire. No fighting took place within state borders. New Hampshiremen who joined the Continental Army and state militia regiments occasionally saw active duty, but the percentage of adult males who left their homes for any length of time remained much smaller than in each of the colonial wars. After 1776 the total never exceeded one-tenth of those eligible for service. The only section of the state hurt economically by the struggle for independence was the Piscataqua, which suffered a sharp decline in maritime trade. The rest of New Hampshire experienced a moderate prosperity. Population continued to increase and by the mid-1780s reached 95,000. Agricultural products were in heavy demand, real estate values increased, and plentiful paper money facilitated the exchange of commodities. Many state inhabitants were significantly richer at the end of the war than at its start.

New Hampshirites, of course, were vitally interested in the outcome of the fighting, but they were just as concerned about another matter. The ultimate purpose of the war was political. The revolutionists declared independence because they had become convinced that continued existence within the framework of imperial authority threatened their political rights. Severance of imperial ties would give them the opportunity to form a government less susceptible to corruption and better geared to the protection of popular liberties. Although the constitution adopted in January 1776 provided a step in the right direction, it would last only for the duration of the military conflict. Furthermore, the leaders of the resistance movement had been so preoccupied with criticism of colonial officials, Parliament, the ministry, and ultimately King George III—half the constitution itself was a cataloging of past imperial sins—they had not articulated a systematic philosophy to guide them in the future. Once in power they began to think more concretely about the long term political purposes of the revolution.

Experience during the colonial period conditioned their thought. Weare, Bartlett, Langdon, and others who assumed provincial authority in the revolutionary crisis shared a deep faith in the institutions of local government and the capacity of town officials to manage most affairs honestly and efficiently. They also believed that elected magistrates could be trusted more than appointed magistrates. Past experience at the local level, the uneven record of colonial governors, councillors, and judges, and the frequent success of the colonial Assembly in protecting the public against imperial tyranny all lent credence to the belief. In addition, the revolutionists continued to think in terms of divided authority. No individual or group of individuals, even though elected, should be left unchecked. Town officials should be restrained by the state, representatives should share power with councillors, and any executive authority in the central government should be subject to limitation by the legislature as a whole. New Hampshire's new leaders had no intention of abandoning the colonial traditions of localism, the election of public officials, mixed government, and bicameralism.

The revolutionists, however, did abandon other colonial traditions. Contemporary British constitutional assumptions placed ultimate political sovereignty in King and Parliament. Since the authority of both had been totally rejected, some new way of defining the source of governmental power had to be determined. In New Hampshire and elsewhere in America debate over the precise nature of political sovereignty continued for more than a decade, but the central conclusion of that debate became clear almost immediately. Sovereignty lay in the "people," not in any governmental institution or set of institutions. Rulers gained their authority through the voters, were responsible to the public, and could be removed from office if the people or their elected representatives chose to remove them. As early as March 1776 the Council and Assembly of the state adopted a policy of concluding its proclamations with the phrase "God save the People"—a pointed change from the colonial practice of using "God save the King"—and in subsequent years the state government was gradually reformed so that more and more officials were elected directly by the people. Property qualifications for both officeholding and voting were eventually eliminated altogether.

Commitment to the sovereignty of the people, in turn, necessitated a changed attitude toward the origin and limits of government. Great Britain had no written constitution. The term "constitution" meant to Englishmen the entire body of traditions, parliamentary enactments, royal directives, and judicial decisions which constituted the law of the land. Moreover New Hampshire, unlike the other New England colonies, had no charter. The commissions and instructions of the various governors were the only written documents defining the limits of provincial authority. When royal government collapsed the leaders of the rebellion felt obliged to justify their assumption of authority. They did so by adopting the constitution of 1776, but soon came under attack—mostly from inhabitants in the Connecticut River valley—for not having submitted the constitution to the people for approval. The arguments of the critics were so widely accepted that as early as 1777 plans were made to call a full convention of popularly elected representatives to recommend a new constitution. The document finally approved by state voters six years later defined the structure of state government, the limits of its authority, and the ground rules for making future constitutional amendments. A written constitution had become the vehicle through which a sovereign people protected themselves from usurpation of power by civil authorities. Without a written and popularly sanctioned constitution, there could be no legitimate government.

Finally, the revolutionists began to view the various elements of their political ideology as an integrated commitment to what classical scholars had labeled "republicanism." The formal definition of the term, government in which political power emanated from the people ruling through elected representatives, fit with what they had established in the constitution of 1776 and what they had found satisfactory in their colonial experience. Republicanism was supposed to work best in small units where the people could check closely on those in power. What could be more "republican" than a system based on local autonomy operating in an area as restricted as New Hampshire? One further convergence of contemporary belief with traditional assumptions cemented the association. Republics could succeed only if the people practiced frugality, industry, and temperance, and if their elected representatives resisted the temptation to use public power for personal gain. "Virtue," explained one patriot clergyman in August 1776, "is the basis of a republic," and without it "we shall soon become corrupt... anarchy and confusion will take place and we shall be in a worse state than if we had remained as we were." And "virtue" was precisely what the revolutionists felt they possessed and the now departed imperial officials lacked.

The experiment in republicanism worked well enough to convince the inhabitants of New Hampshire that their faith had not been misplaced. Towns continued to manage their internal affairs effectively. Most elected officials at both the local and state levels avoided behavior which might expose them to public accusations of corruption. The Council and Assembly kept a close check on each other and together managed the war effort successfully. They also prevented political dissent in two sections of the state, the Piscataqua and Grafton County, from seriously disrupting the affairs of New Hampshire as a whole. Commitment to the sovereignty of the people helped sustain public support for the revolution even though the fighting dragged on much longer than anyone expected. Few men ever questioned the wisdom of written constitutions. Indeed, one main reason it took seven years to adopt a new constitution was widespread approval of the temporary document. And those who pushed with eventual success for reform did so in part by arguing that their proposals were entirely consistent with the principles of republicanism. The past and the present had been permanently fused.

Vestiges of the colonial and revolutionary periods abound in present day New Hampshire. The structure of government has retained many eighteenth century qualities. Towns, which are still frequently called "Little Republics," have probably more autonomy than anywhere else in the United States. State executive authority is shared by a governor and council, both linear descendants from the days of royal government.

There are more than 400 House delegates largely because towns in New Hampshire have refused to give up their right to direct representation. Consistent with traditions of the past, the delegates receive almost no pay for their services. In general the inhabitants of the state have a deep distrust of central government. That too originated in the pre-national experience.

Place names in the state also reflect the past. Many mountains, lakes, and rivers bear Algonkian labels. Towns like Weare, Jaffrey, Atkinson, Gilmanton, Sullivan, and Langdon bear the names of important early families and individuals. Grafton, Cheshire, Hillsboro, Strafford and Rockingham counties as well as several towns provide a continuous reminder of John Wentworth's efforts to please his imperial benefactors. Patterns of migration to New Hampshire can roughly be traced through close scrutiny of a state map. Piscataqua towns bear English names, New Ipswich and New Boston were settled first from Massachusetts, the Scotch-Irish founded Londonderry, Peterboro, and Dublin, and the migrants from Connecticut gave their frontier communities familiar names taken from the towns they left. Laconia reflects the abortive attempt of John Mason and others to exploit natural resources in the interior.

Other linkages can be found. State boundaries in all but the northern tip of the state were drawn in colonial times, and most towns have the geographical outlines defined in their original charters. Parts of New Hampshire retain enough of the "yankee" traditions associated with New England as a whole to attract both tourists and permanent residents who for a variety of reasons find association with those traditions attractive. The current economic boom in the state is closely related to widespread public nostalgia for what people imagine to have been the simpler times of the past. Entrepreneurs call their developments "Colonial Gardens" or "Heritage Village," construct houses modeled on the homes of the eighteenth century, sell buildings actually constructed in colonial times for fantastic prices, and advertise the beauties of life in a small town.

All this has stirred renewed interest in the early history of the state. Local historical societies are thriving. Professional historians, tourists, and genealogists visit the New Hampshire Historical Society at Concord in increasing numbers. The state government has launched a serious effort to make archival material more available to interested citizens.

Historical restorations like Strawbery Banke in Portsmouth and Fort Number Four in Charlestown have blossomed. *Colonial New Hampshire: A History* is my best effort both to educate and entertain those who find themselves caught up in the movement to understand the origins of the Granite State.

BIBLIOGRAPHY

To the best of my knowledge no systematic bibliography of colonial New Hampshire has previously been published. I therefore have made this bibliographical essay more than a listing. It is an attempt to inform potential students of early state history about existing bibliographic aids, about the major collections of primary material, and about both primary documents and secondary works used in writing individual chapters of *Colonial New Hampshire: A History*. The organization of this essay necessitated some repetition of references: I have used a shortened form of citation when a work has been mentioned previously. The bibliography is not exhaustive. Anyone wishing further information should feel free to write me directly in care of the History Department, Dartmouth College, Hanover, New Hampshire 03755.

BIBLIOGRAPHIES

John D. Haskell, Jr. and T. D. Seymour Bassett, eds., *New Hampshire: A Bibliography of Its History* (Boston, 1979), published by the Committee for a New England Bibliography, is the first attempt at a comprehensive listing of publications on New Hampshire state history. For books and articles dealing primarily with the state, its towns, and its counties, the volume is nearly exhaustive and supplants all the more limited bibliographies conveniently listed in the New Hampshire section of T. D. Seymour Bassett, "A List of New England Bibliographies," *New England Quarterly*, XLIV (1971), 178–200. Students of the colonial period, however, should be aware of the self-imposed limitations which guided the editors of the bibliography: most manuscripts, printed primary sources, biographies, genealogical works, and publications which deal only partially with New Hampshire are not included. A great deal of important information about early New Hampshire history is available only in these unlisted works. For the period before the mid-eighteenth century the footnotes and bibliography in David E. Van Deventer, *The Emergence of Provincial New Hampshire, 1623–1741* (Baltimore, 1976) should be consulted. The same parts of Jere Daniell, *Experiment in Republicanism: New Hampshire Politics and the American Revolution, 1741–1794* (Cambridge, 1970) are useful for the late colonial period. The bibliographical essay in Charles Clark, *The Eastern Frontier: The Settlement of Northern New England, 1610–1763* (New York, 1970) covers the entire pre-revolutionary period. Sometime in the not too distant future the Committee for a New England Bibliography expects to publish a volume listing works on New England in general, which will also be of help to students of colonial New Hampshire.

The Haskell and Bassett volume does not include unpublished theses and dissertations. These are listed in William Copely, "Doctoral Dissertations in New Hampshire History," *Historical New Hampshire,* XXXI (1976), 44–51, and two articles by Richard S. Sliwoski, "Additional Doctoral Dissertations in New Hampshire History" and "History from the Masters: Theses on New Hampshire History from New Hampshire Colleges and Universities," *Historical New Hampshire,* XXXIII (1978), 334–345 and XXXV (1980), 66–74 respectively.

COLLECTIONS OF PRIMARY SOURCE MATERIAL

Manuscripts relevant to New Hampshire's colonial history are concentrated in three locations. The British Public Record Office has reams of material, the bulk of it in the Colonial Office Papers, Class 5, vols. 924–969. Charles M. Andrews, *Guide to the Materials for American History to 1783 in the Public Record Office of Great Britain* (2 vols., Washington, 1912–1914; New York, 1965) remains the standard guide and identifies New Hampshire items not in the Class 5 series. Transcripts and microfilms of some Public Record Office manuscripts are available in the Library of Congress, Baker Library at Dartmouth College, and the New Hampshire Historical Society in Concord.

The New Hampshire Historical Society is the second major repository. In addition to Public Record Office transcripts, it houses a variety of personal, family, and institutional papers too numerous to list completely. Of special importance are the Jonathan Belcher correspondence, the letter books of George Boyd and Peter Livius, the Rindge, Vaughan, Waldron, and Wentworth family papers, the Society for the Propagation of the Gospel papers, various church records and a collection of Inventories of the Polls and Estates in New Hampshire from the period 1727–1773. Some of the colonial material in the archives of the Society is still in the process of being catalogued.

The New Hampshire State Archives, also in Concord, houses even more manuscript material from the colonial period. Systematic cataloguing of this material has begun only recently and will take years to complete. The collections include land deeds, records of the Masonian Proprietors, the treasury accounts of the provincial government, miscellaneous papers and records gathered by executive and legislative officials in the colonial period, an index of court cases, a copy of the letter book of Governor John Wentworth, and the Meshech Weare Papers. Much of the manuscript material in the state archives has been published, especially official government records; but much has not. For a partial listing of archival holdings see Frank C. Mevers and Harriet S. Lacy, "Early Historical Records (c. 1620–c. 1817) at the New Hampshire State Archives," *Historical New Hampshire,* XXXI (1976), 108–119.

Repositories containing lesser amounts of New Hampshire material include the Massachusetts Historical Society, the New Hampshire State Library, the Portsmouth (N.H.) Athenaeum, Baker Library at Dartmouth College, and the Library of Congress. For specific collection items, see the bibliographies in Van Deventer, *Emergence* and Daniell, *Experiment.* The only available listing of manuscripts in local New Hampshire archives is the now outdated WPA survey *Guide to Depositories of Manuscript Collections in the United States: New Hampshire* (Manchester, 1940).

By far the single most important collection of printed primary material is Nathaniel Bouton, et. al., eds., *Documents and Records Relating to the Province of New Hampshire* (cited hereafter as *NHPP*), 40 vols. (Concord and Manchester, 1867–1941). The titles of this series vary. The volumes are grouped in general as follows: vols. I–VII, XVIII, and XIX—Provincial Papers, 1623–1776; vols. VIII, X, and XVIII–XXII—State Papers, 1776–1793; vols. XIV–XVII and XXX—Revolutionary Papers; vols. IX, XI–XIII and XXIV–XXIX—Town Papers; vols. XXXI–XL—Probate Records. Volume XXIII is a list of New Hampshire documents in the Public Record Office, London. For a more detailed description of volume contents see R. Stuart Wallace, "The State Papers? A Descriptive Guide," *Historical New Hampshire,* XXXI (1976), 119–128. Most of the documents published in this series are from the manuscript collections at the New Hampshire State Archives. Unfortunately, the series is poorly edited, inadequately indexed, and frequently lacking in logical organization.

Several other general collections of primary documents exist. The first three volumes of Albert S. Batchellor and Henry H. Metcalf, eds., *Laws of New Hampshire,* 8 vols. (Manchester and elsewhere, 1904–1920) cover the colonial period. W. M. Sainsbury, et. al., eds. *Calendar of States Papers, Colonial Series, America and West Indies, 1661–1738,* 44 vols. (London, 1880–1969) includes material essential to the understanding of New Hampshire's early political history, as does John S. Jennes, comp., *Transcripts of Original Documents in the English Archives Relating to the Early History of New Hampshire* (New York,

1876). Both the *Collections of the New Hampshire Historical Society* (cited hereafter as *Collections NHHS*), 15 vols. (Concord, 1834–1939) and John Farmer and Jacob B. Moore, eds., *Collections, Topographical, Historical and Biographical Relating Principally to New Hampshire*, 3 vols. (Concord, 1822–1824) contain a variety of primary documents. The basic collections of Massachusetts official records for the colonial period is Nathaniel B. Shurtleff, ed., *Records of the Governor and Company of the Massachusetts Bay*, 5 vols. (Boston, 1853–1854).

TOPICAL BIBLIOGRAPHY:
PRIMARY AND SECONDARY

A.   GENERAL

Over the years a number of authors have written books which at the time of their publication covered the entire history of the state. Jeremy Belknap, *History of New Hampshire*, 3 vols. (Philadelphia and Boston, 1784–1792) remains, despite its age, the most useful of these for students of the colonial period. George Barstow, *History of New Hampshire* (Concord, 1842) and Edward D. Sanborn, *History of New Hampshire* (Manchester, 1875) provide an unsatisfactory mixture of legend and fact. Pre-revolutionary New Hampshire is treated more accurately in John N. McClintock, *History of New Hampshire* (Boston, 1888), though McClintock adds little to Belknap. Edward S. Stackpole, *History of New Hampshire*, 4 vols. (New York, 1917) was published for the American Historical Society; the colonial chapters reflect the author's familiarity with the large body of primary documents not available to previous historians. The most recent general histories are J. Duane Squires, *The Granite State of the United States: A History of New Hampshire from 1623 to the Present*, 4 vols. (New York, 1956), Squire's much shorter *The Story of New Hampshire* (Princeton, 1964), and Elizabeth F. and Elting E. Morison, *New Hampshire: A Bicentennial History* (New York, 1976).

Several books deal largely or exclusively with colonial New Hampshire. The most important are Van Deventer, *Emergence* and Clark, *Eastern Frontier*. Van Deventer is definitive on economic matters and contains a wealth of statistical information bearing on social and political developments; Clark gives New Hampshire and Maine equal attention, focuses on the details of everyday life, and is especially perceptive on the social and religious history of the eighteenth century. Three other works, Sybil Noyes, et. al., eds., *Genealogical Dictionary of Maine and New Hampshire*, 2 vols. (Portland, 1928–1929); William G. Saltonstall, *Ports of the Piscataqua* (Cambridge,

1941); and Elizabeth C. Nordbeck "The New England Diaspora: A Study of the Religious Culture of Maine and New Hampshire, 1613–1763" (unpublished Ph.D. dissertation, Harvard University, 1978) emphasize interprovincial linkages. Topical volumes exclusively on New Hampshire are numerous. Albert S. Batchellor, *Outline of the Development of Probate Law and Probate Jurisdiction in New Hampshire, 1623–1675* (Concord, 1907) and Elwin L. Page, *Judicial Beginnings in New Hampshire, 1623–1700* (Concord, 1959) discuss the early history of the court system. Charles H. Bell, *Bench and Bar of New Hampshire* (Cambridge, 1894) contains biographical sketches of many colonial jurists. The entire colonial political system is the subject of William H. Fry, *New Hampshire as a Royal Province,* Columbia University Studies in History, Economics, and Public Law, XXIX (New York, 1908). The colonial sections of Robert F. Lawrence, *The New Hampshire Churches* (Claremont, 1856) and Charles B. Kinney, *Church and State: The Struggle for Separation in New Hampshire, 1630–1800* (New York, 1955) cover religious developments. Maurice H. Robinson, *A History of Taxation in New Hampshire,* Publications of the American Economic Association, 3rd ser., vol. III (New York, 1903) summarizes the subject well.

Many books treat New Hampshire in the context of colonial New England or colonial America as a whole. Volumes I found especially useful include the following: for military history, Douglas Leach, *The Northern Colonial Frontier, 1607–1763* (New York, 1966) and the same author's *Arms for Empire: A Military History of the British Colonies in North America, 1607–1763* (New York, 1973). For regional economic developments, Percy W. Bidwell and John Falconer, *History of Agriculture in the Northern United States, 1620–1860* (Washington, D.C., 1925); Howard S. Russell, *A Long Deep Furrow: Three Centuries of Farming in New England* (Hanover, 1976); Raymond McFarland, *A History of the New England Fisheries* (New York, 1911); and William B. Weeden, *Economic and Social History of New England, 1620–1789* (Boston, 1891). Lois K. Mathews (Rosenberry), *The Expansion of New England* (Boston, 1909) traces the growth of settlement in colonial New Hampshire. Biographies of many important New Hampshire citizens appear in Clifford S. Shipton, *Sibley's Harvard Graduates: Biographical Sketches of Those Who Attended Harvard College . . .,* vols. in progress (Boston, 1873–   ). The development of the naval stores industry and imperial policies affecting that development are covered in Robert G. Albion, *Forests and Sea Power: The Timber Problem of the Royal Navy, 1652–1862* (Cambridge, 1926) and Joseph J. Malone, *Pine Trees and Politics: The Naval Stores and Forest Policy in Colonial New England* (Seattle, 1964). For provincial history as a whole, Charles M. Andrews, *Colonial Period of American History,* 4 vols. (New Haven, 1934–1938) should be consulted.

B.   CHAPTER BIBLIOGRAPHIES

1. *The Algonkians*

Very little professional writing on New Hampshire's Native American population has been published. Gordon Day, "The Western Abenaki" in Bruce Trigger, ed., *Handbook of North American Indians,* XV (Washington, 1979), 148–159, focuses on tribal identification. The two most widely read volumes on cultural contact in New England—Alden T. Vaughan, *The New England Frontier: Puritans and Indians, 1620–1675* (Boston, 1965) and Francis Jennings, *Invasion of America: Indians, Colonialism, and the Cant of Conquest* (New York, 1975)—make occasional references to New Hampshire. Gordon Day, "Indian Occupation of Vermont," *Vermont History,* XXXIII (1965), 365–374; Ronald O. MacFarlane, "The Massachusetts Bay Truck-Houses in Diplomacy with the Indians," *New England Quarterly,* XI (1938), 48–65; and George H. Evans, *Pigwacket* (Conway, 1939) all contain information about natives who lived in what eventually became New Hampshire. The first chapter of Nathaniel Bouton, *History of Concord* (Concord, 1856) includes biographies of Passaconaway and other Pennacook sachems.

Three additional kinds of sources exist. Contemporary comments by Englishmen on natives and native culture appear in a number of primary documents. Among the most revealing are Christopher Levett, *A Voyage into New England* (London, 1628), reprinted in Charles H. Levermore, *Forerunners and Competitors of the Pilgrims and Puritans,* II (Brooklyn, 1913), 609–642; Thomas Shepherd, *The Clear Sunshine of the Gospel...* (London, 1648 and New York, 1865); John Eliot, *A Brief Narrative...* (Boston, 1896); John Winthrop, *Winthrop's Journal,* edited by James K. Hosmer, (*Original Narratives in Early American History,* J. Franklin Jameson, ed.), 2 vols. (New York, 1908).

Several pamphlets and articles about native culture written by well intentioned amateurs contain a mixture of fact, legend, and fiction. The following list is by no means complete: Edward Ballard, "Character of the Pennacooks," *Collections NHHS,* VIII (1866), 428–445; Charles E. Beals, Jr., *Passaconaway in the White Mountains* (Boston, 1916); Ronald W. Gallup, *Algonquian New Hampshire...* (n.p., 1970); Mary A. Proctor, *The Indians of the Winnipesauke and Pemigewasset Valleys* (Franklin, 1930); Eva A. Speare, *Indians of New Hampshire* (Little, 1965); and Edgar H. Wilcomb, *Ancient Aquadoctan...* (Worcester, 1923). All these publications should be used with caution.

Finally, students of New Hampshire's native population should consult the increasingly sophisticated literature about Algonkian speaking natives in general. Particularly helpful are Alfred G. Bailey, *The Conflict of European and Eastern Algonkian Cultures, 1504–1700,* 2nd ed. (Toronto, 1969); T. J. C.

Brasser, "The Coastal Algonkians: People of the First Frontiers," in Eleanor B. Leacock and Nancy Lurie, eds., *North American Indians in Historical Perspective* (New York, 1971), 64–91; Cornelius J. Jaenen, *Friend and Foe: Aspects of French-Amerindian Cultural Contact in the Sixteenth and Seventeenth Centuries* (New York, 1976); Nancy O. Lurie, "Indian Cultural Adjustment to European Civilization," in James M. Smith, ed., *Seventeenth Century America: Essays on Colonial History* (Chapel Hill, 1959), 33–60; Calvin Martin, "The European Impact on the Culture of a Northeastern Algonkian Tribe: An Ecological Interpretation," *William and Mary Quarterly*, XXXI (1974), 3–26; and Neal Salisbury, "Red Puritans: The 'Praying Indians' of Massachusetts Bay and John Eliot," *William and Mary Quarterly*, XXXI (1974), 27–54.

2. Adventurers, Planters, Émigrés

Most of the general histories of New Hampshire describe the origins of settlement in some detail. Works placing settlement in a broader context include Ralph Davis, *The Rise of the Atlantic Economies* (Ithaca, 1973); J. H. Parry, *The Age of Reconnaissance, 1420–1620* (New York, 1963), David B. Quinn, *England and the Discovery of America, 1481–1620* (New York, 1974); Samuel E. Morison, *The European Discovery of America: The Northern Voyages* (Boston, 1971); and Charles K. Bolton, *The Real Founders of New England* (Boston, 1929). The narrative of Martin Pring's voyage is published in Henry S. Burrage, *Early English and French Voyages . . .* (New York, 1906), 343–352.

Several books and articles cover the role of specific individuals in the founding of the various plantations. Of special importance is John W. Dean, ed., *Capt. John Mason*, Publications of the Prince Society, XVII (Boston, 1887). Dean worked from information gathered earlier by Charles W. Tuttle who before his death had written a set of papers concerning New Hampshire. These papers were later edited by Albert H. Hoyt and published under the title *Capt. Francis Champernowne . . . and other Historical Papers* (Boston, 1889). Richard A. Preston, *Gorges of Plymouth Fort: A Life of Sir Ferdinando Gorges* (Toronto, 1953); Charles E. Banks, "Edward Godfrey, His Life Letters and Public Services, 1584–1664," *Collections of the Maine Historical Society*, IX (1887), 295–384; Charles H. Pope, *The Pioneers of Maine and New Hampshire, 1623–1660* (Boston, 1908); Charles H. Bell, *John Wheelwright, His Writings . . .*, Publications of the Prince Society, IX (Boston, 1876) and John N. Brown, "Memoir of Hansard Knollys, M.A.," *Collections NHHS*, V (1937), 175–179 all provide accurate biographical information.

Other works helpful to students of early settlement in New Hampshire are John S. Jenness, *Notes on the First Planting of New Hampshire and on the Piscataqua*

Patents (Portsmouth, 1878) and the same author's *The Isles of Shoals* (Boston, 1901); Richard A. Preston, "The Laconia Company of 1629: An English Attempt to Intercept the Fur Trade," *Canadian Historical Review*, XXXI (1950), 125–144; and two more general studies, Bernard Bailyn, *The New England Merchants in the Seventeenth Century* (Cambridge, 1955) and Emery Battis, *Saints and Sectaries* (Chapel Hill, 1962). The last of these deals with the Antinomian controversy which helped shape the founding of Exeter. The several local histories cited in the next section of the bibliography all contain important detail about the years before 1640.

3. *Community Development, 1640–1680*

Local histories provide the richest source of specific information about community development before 1680. The best study of Portsmouth is Gary T. Lord, "The Politics and Social Structure of 17th Century Portsmouth" (unpub. Ph.D. dissertation, University of Virginia, 1976). John Albee, *New Castle, Historic and Picturesque* (Boston, 1884); Timothy Alden, Jr., *An Account of the Several Religious Societies in Portsmouth* (Boston, 1808); Ralph May, *Early Portsmouth History* (Boston, 1926); Nathaniel Adams, *Annals of Portsmouth* (Portsmouth, 1825); and Charles W. Brewster, *Rambles about Portsmouth*, 2 vols. (Portsmouth, 1859–1869) should also be consulted, although Adams and Brewster can't always be trusted. For Exeter, see Charles H. Bell, *History of the Town of Exeter, New Hampshire* (Exeter, 1888), and to a lesser extent his *John Wheelwright*. Alonzo H. Quint, *Historical Memoranda of Ancient Dover* (Dover, 1900); John Scales, *History of Dover, New Hampshire* (Manchester, 1923); and George Wadleigh, *Notable Events in the History of Dover, New Hampshire* (Dover, 1913) discusses the early history of that community. The standard work on Hampton is Joseph Dow, *History of the Town of Hampton, New Hampshire*, 2 vols. (Salem, 1893). John Demos, "Witchcraft and Local Culture in Hampton, New Hampshire," in Richard Bushman, et. al., eds., *Uprooted Americans: Essays to Honor Oscar Handlin*, 9–42 provides a fasinating supplement to Dow.

Much of Chapter 3 of the present work is based on a close reading of the primary material in *NHPP*, I, and Frank W. Hackett, ed., *1645–1656 Portsmouth Records* (Portsmouth, 1886). Dean, *Capt. John Mason*, describes the confusion created by Joseph Mason's visit to Portsmouth. Samuel Maverick's *A Briefe Description of New England* (Boston, 1885) was written in 1660 and contains comments on the Piscataqua settlements then. Jenness, *Notes on the First Planting* makes sense of the various patent controversies. For relations between Massachusetts and the four towns see Robert E. Wall, *Massachusetts Bay: The Crucial Decade, 1640–1650* (New Haven, 1972) and more generally

Charles F. Carroll, *The Timber Economy of Puritan New England* (Providence, 1973). A convenient summary of the literature on New England towns on a whole is John Waters, "From Democracy to Demography: Recent Historiography on the New England Town," in Alden T. Vaughan and George A. Billias, eds., *Perspectives on Early American History: Essays in Honor of Richard B. Morris* (New York, 1973). Bruce C. Daniels, *Town and County: Essays on the Structure of Local Government in the American Colonies* (Middletown, 1978) should also be consulted. The best discussion of the role played by ministers in community development is David D. Hall, *The Faithful Shepherd: A History of the New England Ministry in the Seventeenth Century* (Chapel Hill, 1972).

4. *The Royal Colony of New Hampshire*

No detailed secondary account of how New Hampshire became a royal colony has previously been published. Some details of the process are described in Percy L. Kaye, "English Colonial Administration under Lord Clarenden, 1660–1667," *Johns Hopkins University, Studies in Historical and Political Science,* XXIII (1905); Bailyn, *New England Merchants;* Malone, *Pine Trees;* Dean, *Capt. John Mason;* Carroll, *Timber Economy;* and the state histories written by Belknap and Stackpole. For the role of Randolph and Blathwayt see Michael G. Hall, *Edward Randolph and the American Colonies, 1676–1703* (Chapel Hill, 1960); Gertrude A. Jacobsen, *William Blathwayt, A Late Seventeenth Century English Administrator* (New Haven, 1932); and Stephen S. Webb, "William Blathwayt, Imperial Fixer," *William and Mary Quarterly,* XXV (1968), 3–21 and XXVI (1969), 373–415. The most complete narrative appears in Peter R. Barry, "The New Hampshire Merchant Interest, 1609–1725" (unpublished Ph.D. dissertation, University of Wisconsin, 1971).

Both Barry and I have relied almost entirely on primary material. The vast majority of the relevant documents are located in *NHPP,* I, and Jenness, *Transcripts.* See also Robert N. Toppan and Thomas S. Goodrick, eds., *Memoirs of Edward Randolph: Including His Letters and Official Papers from the New England,* Publications of the Prince Society, 7 vols. (Boston, 1898–1909) and W. L. Grant and James Munro, eds., *Acts of the Privy Council, Colonial Series,* 6 vols. (London, 1908–1912), I and II.

5. *Twelve Years of Turmoil*

All the works listed for Chapter 4 were used in writing Chapter 5. Additional primary material may be found in the following: *NHPP,* II; Batchellor and Metcalf, *Laws,* I; *Collections NHHS,* I; Sainsbury, *Calendar,* XII. Useful secondary works are Tuttle, *Champernowne,* Theodore B. Lewis, "Royal Government in New Hampshire and the Revocation of the Charter of Massachusetts Bay Colony, 1679–1683," *Historical New Hampshire,* XXV (1970), 3–45; Franklin B. Sanborn, "Churchmen on the Piscataqua: Edward Gove and his Confiscated Estate," *Proceedings of the Massachusetts Historical Society,* XLV (1911–1912), 211–243 and 628–640; and the same author's *Edward Gove and Walter Barefoote, 1653–1691, The So-Called Rebellion of 1683* (Pamphlet, no place of publication, no date). Three general studies, David S. Lovejoy, *The Glorious Revolution in America* (New York, 1972); Viola Barnes, *The Dominion of New England: A Study in British Colonial Policy* (New Haven, 1923); and Thomas C. Barrow, *Trade and Empire: The British Customs Service in Colonial America, 1660–1775* (Cambridge, 1967) help place the New Hampshire events in a broader context.

6. *Testing Time: War and Politics in*
"Little New Hampshire"

The basic primary material for the years 1692–1715 is in *NHPP,* II and III, and Sainsbury, *Calendar,* XIII–XVII. See also the journal of John Pike in *Collections NHHS,* III, 40–67; Cotton Mather, *Decennium Luctuosum,* in C. H. Lincoln, ed., *Narratives of the Indian Wars, 1675–1699 (Original Narratives of Early American History,* J. Franklin Jameson, ed.) (New York, 1913), 179–300; Samuel Penhallow, *The History of the Wars of New England with the Eastern Indians* (Boston, 1726), republished in *Collections NHHS,* I, 14–133; and appendix 1 in Belknap, *History,* III, 252.

Many of the secondary works listed for chapters 4 and 5 touch upon economic and political events in turn of the century New Hampshire. In addition, the following should be consulted. For the wars, consult Leach, *Arms for Empire,* and the superb monograph by Kenneth Morrison, "People of the Dawn: The Abenaki and their Relations with New England and New France, 1600–1721" (unpublished Ph.D. dissertation, University of Maine, 1975). Kathryn Whitford, "Hannah Dustin: The Judgment of History," *Essex Institute Historical Collections,* XVIII (1972), 304–325 summarizes the literature of that regionally famous woman. William Letwin, *Sir Joshua Child, Merchant Economist* (Boston, 1959); Philip A. Muth, "The Ashurts: Friends of New England" (unpublished Ph.D. dissertation, Boston University, 1967); John H. Plumb, *Origins of Political Stability, England 1675–1725* (Boston, 1967); and Ian K. Steele, *Politics of Colonial Policy: The Board of Trade in Colonial Administration, 1696–1720* (Oxford, 1968) all help with the English political background. On New Hampshire specifically see Philip S. Haffenden,

New England in the English Nation, 1689–1713 (Oxford, 1974); George F. Hodgdon, *Reminiscences and Genealogical Record of the Vaughan Family of New Hampshire* (Rochester, 1918); Everett Kimball, *The Public Life of Joseph Dudley,* Harvard Historical Studies, XV (New York, 1911); and Paul W. Farrell, "The Administration of Governor Joseph Dudley in New Hampshire" (unpublished MA thesis, University of New Hampshire, 1966) and Otis G. Hammond, "The Masonian Title and Its Relations to New Hampshire and Massachusetts," *Proceedings of the American Antiquarian Society,* XXVI (1916), 245–263. Appendix H of James Savage, ed., *The History of New England from 1630 to 1649 by John Winthrop, Esq.,* 2 vols. (Boston, 1853), I, discusses the forged Wheelwright deed.

7. *Patterns of Growth, 1715–1765*

The documents relating to the boundary controversy with Massachusetts are in *NHPP,* IV, XVIII, and XIX. For a secondary account see Jonathan Smith, "The Massachusetts and New Hampshire Boundary Controversy, 1693–1740," *Proceedings of the Massachusetts Historical Society,* XLIII (1909–1910), 77–88. Primary material on the wars after 1715 is scattered throughout *NHPP.* Leach, *Northern Frontier* places the wars in an imperial and regional context. John R. Cunco, *Robert Rogers of the Rangers* (New York, 1959); Elizabeth K. Folsom, *Colonial Garrisons of New Hampshire* (Exeter, 1937); and the various histories of New Hampshire towns in the upper Merrimack and Connecticut River valleys cover local details.

Estimates of New Hampshire's population at the beginning of the eighteenth century vary considerably: for a recent educated guess see Terry L. Anderson and Robert P. Thomas, "White Population, Labor Force, and Extensive Growth of the New England Economy in the Seventeenth Century," *Journal of Economic History,* XXXIII (1973), 634–667. Robert V. Wells, *The Population of the British Colonies in America before 1778* (Princeton, 1975) analyzes the census of 1767 fully and provides a convenient summary of recent demographic literature. The Scotch-Irish migration is discussed in Ian C. C. Graham, *Colonists from Scotland* (Ithaca, 1956); James G. Leyburn, *The Scotch-Irish: A Social History* (Chapel Hill, 1962); Edward L. Parker, *The History of Londonderry* (Boston, 1851); and Gordon Woodbury, "The Scotch Irish and Irish Presbyterian Settlers of New Hampshire," *Proceedings of the New Hampshire Historical Society,* IV (1899–1905), 143–162. No one has studied the black population of colonial New Hampshire systematically: Isaac W. Hammond, "Slavery in New Hampshire," *Magazine of American History,* XXI (1889), 63–65, includes some useful detail, as does Lorenzo Greene, *The Negro in*

Colonial New England (New York, 1942). The epidemic which temporarily reduced population growth is fully described in Ernest Caulfield, *A True History of the Terrible Epidemic Vulgarly Called the Throat Distemper . . .* (New Haven, 1939).

The best general description of town founding in eighteenth century northern New England is Chapter XII of Clark, *Eastern Frontier.* I have relied heavily on information in local histories which are far too numerous to list. No careful study of how the original four towns were subdivided has been made, although students interested in the process should read Kenneth A. Lockridge, *A New England Town: The First Hundred Years* (New York, 1970). The relationship between conflicting Massachusetts and New Hampshire land grants is discussed in George Anderson, "Land Grants Made in New Hampshire by Governor Benning Wentworth to Boston Men," *Publications of the Colonial Society of Massachusetts, XXV: Transactions* (1922–1924), 33–38; George M. Bodge, *Soldiers in King Philip's War* (Leominster, 1896); and Joseph B. Walker, "The Controversy Between the Proprietors of Bow and Those of Penny Cook, 1729–1789," *Proceedings of the New Hampshire Historical Society,* III (1895–1899), 261–292. Hammond, "The Masonian Title," is the best published work on the operation of the proprietorship. The classic study of speculative proprietorships in New England as a whole—Roy V. Akagi, *Town Proprietors of the New England Colonies* (Philadelphia, 1924)—vastly exaggerates conflict between proprietors and settlers. Samuel E. Morison, *Proprietors of Peterborough, New Hampshire* (Peterborough, 1930) and John F. Looney, "Benning Wentworth's Land Grant Policy: A Reappraisal," *Historical New Hampshire,* XIII (1968), 3–13 both provide more judicious assessments of the dynamics of town founding. My conclusions stem largely from scattered reading in town records both published and unpublished.

Van Deventer, *Emergence,* describes economic developments fully. Additional works on commerce include Saltonstall, *Ports*; Byron Fairchild, *Messrs. William Pepperrell: Merchants at Piscataqua* (Ithaca, 1954); and Samuel J. McKinley, "Economic History of Portsmouth" (unpublished Ph.D. dissertation, Harvard University, 1931). For economic life in inland settlements see Clark, *Eastern Frontier*; William H. Brown, *Colonel John Goffe* (Manchester, 1950); *Diary of Matthew Patten of Bedford, New Hampshire* (Concord, 1903); Joseph B. Walker, *Chronicles of an Old New England Farm—The Farm of the First Minister* (Concord, 1906); and Charles L. Hansen, ed., *A Journal for the Years 1739–1803 by Samuel Lane of Stratham, New Hampshire* (Concord, 1937). Belknap, *History,* III, contains useful observations on agricultural life. A perceptive, broader work is George R. Taylor, "American Growth Before 1840: An Exploratory Essay," *Journal of Economic History,* XXIV (1964), 428–444.

Studies in the material culture of New Hampshire provide the best evidence of how prosperous the province had become by the 1760s. Most of the literature focuses on the Portsmouth area. Of the various publications by Strawbery Banke, Inc., *Architecture Near the Piscataqua* (Portsmouth, 1964) and the *Official Guidebook and Map* should be consulted. See also John M. Howell, *Architectural Heritage of the Piscataqua* (New York, 1937); Mary C. Rogers, *Glimpses of an Old Social Capital* (Boston, 1923); James L. Garvin, "Portsmouth and the Piscatqua: Social History and Material Culture," *Historical New Hampshire*, XXVI (1971), 3–48; and Elizabeth A. Rhodes, "The Furnishings of Portsmouth Houses, 1750–1775," *Historical New Hampshire*, XXVIII (1973), 1–20. For colonial buildings outside the Piscataqua, John M. Howells, *The Architectural Heritage of the Merrimack* (New York, 1941), and Bryant Tolles with Carolyn K. Tolles, *New Hampshire Architecture: An Illustrated Guide* (Hanover, 1979) are the most convenient sources. Louis Pichierri, *Music in New Hampshire, 1623–1800* (New York, 1960) contains information on cultural life as a whole. Van Deventer, *Emergence,* contains statistical tables about the distribution of wealth in mid-century New Hampshire, as does Alice H. Jones, *American Colonial Wealth: Documents and Methods,* 3 vols. (New York, 1977). See also Bruce C. Daniels, "Defining Economic Classes in Colonial New Hampshire," *Historical New Hampshire,* XXVIII (1973), 53–62.

8. *Social Institutions: Family, Church, and Community in a Changing World*

The secondary literature on family life in eighteenth century New Hampshire is thin. Students of the subject should consult the relevant parts of Clark, *Eastern Frontier.* For the formal education of children see Eugene A. Bishop, *The Development of a State School System: New Hampshire* (New York, 1930) and William V. M. Robertson, "Town Sponsored Education in New Hampshire during the Colonial Period: A Study in Early Public Education in America" (unpublished MA thesis, University of New Hampshire, 1953). For the most part, I have relied on information scattered throughout the primary documents, town histories, and biographies mentioned elsewhere in this bibliographical essay. Studies which helped shape my conclusions about New Hampshire include Bernard Bailyn, *Education in the Forming of American Society* (Chapel Hill, 1960); George F. Dow, *Everyday Life in the Massachusetts Bay Colony* (Boston, 1935); Stephen Foster, *Their Solitary Way: The Puritan Social Ethic in the First Century of Settlement in New England* (New Haven, 1971); Philip J. Greven, *Four Generations: Population, Land and Family in Colonial Andover, Massachusetts* (Ithaca, 1970); and Edmund S. Morgan, *The Puritan Family:*

Religion and Domestic Relations in Seventeenth Century New England (New York, 1961).

The literature on church history is much richer. Virtually all town histories contain accounts of church founding and biographical detail on individual ministers. The many individual biographies of New Hampshire clergymen in Shipton, *Sibley's Harvard Graduates* are indispensible; for full treatment of a single minister see Joseph B. Walker, "Life of Reverend Timothy Walker," 2 vols. (typescript, *NHHS*). Henry A. Hazen, *The Congregational and Presbyterian Ministry and Churches of New Hampshire* (Boston, 1875); Frederick L. Weis, *The Native Ministry of New Hampshire* (Concord, 1906); and the same author's *The Colonial Clergy and the Colonial Churches of New England* (Lancaster, 1936) include a wealth of information. Chapter 4 of Daniel Calhoun, *Professional Lives in America* (Cambridge, 1965) compares the lives of colonial New Hampshire clergymen to clergymen after the revolution. The relationship between government and religion is discussed fully in Kinney, *Church and State*. Arthur J. Worrall, *Quakers in the Colonial Northeast* (Hanover, 1980) includes information on Quaker organizations in New Hampshire. Three regional studies—Edwin S. Gautstad, *The Great Awakening in New England* (New York, 1957); C. C. Goen, *Revivalism and Separatism in New England, 1740–1800* (New Haven, 1962); and Elizabeth Nordbeck, "Almost Awakened: The Great Revival in New Hampshire and Maine, 1727–1748," *Historical New Hampshire*, XXXV (1980), 23–58—and Alan Heimert's monumental general study, *Religion and the American Mind From the Great Awakening to the Revolution* (Cambridge, 1966) deal with religious developments affecting eighteenth century New Hampshire. J. William T. Youngs, *God's Messengers: Religious Leadership in Colonial New England, 1700–1750* (Baltimore, 1976) should also be read.

Primary material on church life is scattered. The diaries of Timothy Walker were edited by Joseph B. Walker and published in *Collections, NHHS*, IX (1889). The Nicholas Gilman Diary is in the manuscript collection at the New Hampshire Historical Society. For George Whitefield, see his *The First Two Parts of his Life, with his Journals* (London, 1756) and Ernest E. Ells, "An Unpublished Journal of George Whitefield," *Church History*, VII (1938), 297–346. Additional documents from the period of the Great Awakening are John and Woodbridge Odlin, *An Account of the Remonstrance of the Church in Exeter...* (Boston, 1748); "Account of the Revival of Religion at Portsmouth in New Hampshire," *Church History*, I (1932), 383–394; and "A Record of the Transactions of the Annual Convocation of Ministers in New Hampshire...," *Collections NHHS*, IX (1889). Relatively few New Hampshire clergymen published sermons. Most of those which were published are identified in the footnotes to the biographies in Shipton, *Sibley's Harvard Graduates*.

By far the best generalized discussion of town life in the late colonial period is Michael Zuckerman, *Peaceable Kingdoms: New England Towns in the Eighteenth Century* (New York, 1970). Darrett B. Rutman, "People in Process: The New Hampshire Towns in the Eighteenth Century," *Journal of Urban History,* I (1975), 268–291 presents a model of population change which serves as a useful supplement to Zuckerman, and has the advantage of focusing specifically on New Hampshire. My conclusions about community life in the eighteenth century are drawn from selective reading in town histories and examination of the relevant documents in *NHPP,* XI–XIII and XXVII–XIX especially, and Batchellor, *Laws,* II and III.

9. *Provincial Politics: The Wentworth Oligarchy*

Chapter 9 is based largely on the documents published in *NHPP,* vols. III–V and XVIII. Other primary material useful in understanding provincial politics may be found in Sainsbury, *Calendar,* vols. XXX–XLIX; *Collections NHHS,* I; and Robert M. Howard, ed., *Records and Letters of the Family of the Longs of Longville, Jamaica, and Hampton Lodge,* Surrey, 2 vols. (London, 1925).

The best institutional study of royal government in the province is Fry, *New Hampshire.* For the English background to colonial developments see Leonard W. Cowie, *Henry Newman: An American in London, 1708–1743* (London, 1956) and two broader studies, James A. Henretta, *"Salutary Neglect:" Colonial Administration under the Duke of Newcastle* (Princeton, 1972) and John H. Plumb, *Sir Robert Walpole: The Making of a Statesman,* 2 vols. (London, 1956–1960). Biographical information on colonial political leaders may be found in John Wentworth, *The Wentworth Genealogy...,* 3 vols. (Boston, 1878) and Shipton, *Sibley's Harvard Graduates.* The concluding section of Barry, "Merchant Interest," has a solid account of John Wentworth's accession to the lieutenant governorship. For politics in the thirties, Malone, *Pine Trees,* and John A. Schutz, "Succession Politics in Massachusetts, 1730–1741," *William and Mary Quarterly,* 3rd ser., XV (1958), 508–520 should be consulted. The literature on Benning Wentworth is extensive. The most thorough study is John F. Looney, "The King's Representative: Benning Wentworth, Colonial Governor, 1741–1767" (unpublished Ph.D. dissertation, Lehigh University, 1961). The treatment here follows closely the article I published first as "Politics in New Hampshire under Benning Wentworth, 1741–1767," *William and Mary Quarterly,* 3rd ser. XVIII (1966), 76–105 and subsequently in a slightly altered form as Chapter 1 of *Experiment.* Detailed references for the last third of Chapter 9 may be found in the footnotes to these works. See also James K. Martin, "A Model for the Coming American Revolution: The

Birth and Death of the Wentworth Oligarchy in New Hampshire, 1741–1776," *Journal of Social History,* IV (1970), 41–60.

10. *The Coming of Revolution*

Chapter 10 is a shorter version of chapters 2 through 4 of Daniell, *Experiment,* the footnotes of which identify both the published and manuscript primary material relevant to the coming of revolution to New Hampshire.

Secondary literature on the coming of the revolution is abundant. Volumes dealing with the English background to events in New Hampshire include J. Steven Watson, *The Reign of George III, 1760–1815* (Oxford, 1960); Louis B. Namier, *England in the Age of the American Revolution* (London, 1930); Paul Langford, *The First Rockingham Administration, 1765–1766* (Oxford, 1973); Charles R. Ritcheson, *British Politics and the American Revolution* (Norman, 1954); Bernard Donoughue, *British Politics and the American Revolution: The Path to War, 1773–1775* (New York, 1965); and Charles M. Andrews, *The Colonial Background of the American Revolution* (New Haven, 1924). For the activities of New Hampshire colonial agents in England, Michael G. Kammen, *Rope of Sand: The Colonial Agents, British Politics, and the American Revolution* (Ithaca, 1968); Theodore D. Jervey, "Barlow Trecothick," *South Carolina Historical and Genealogical Magazine,* XXXII (1931), 157–169; and D. H. Watson "Barlow Trecothick" *Bulletin of the British Association for American Studies,* I (1960), 36–49 and II (1961), 29–39 should be consulted. Among the most stimulating general works concentrating on developments in the colonies are Randolph G. Adams, *Political Ideas of the American Revolution* (Durham, 1922); Bernard Bailyn, *The Ideological Origins of the American Revolution* (Cambridge, 1967); and Merrill Jensen, *The Founding of a Nation: A History of the American Revolution, 1763–1776* (New York, 1968).

Events in New Hampshire can be traced in part through biographical studies. The most thorough treatments of John Wentworth are Lawrence S. Mayo, *John Wentworth, Governor of New Hampshire, 1767–1775* (Cambridge, 1921) and Paul W. Wilderson, "Protagonist of Prudence: A Biography of John Wentworth, the King's Last Governor of New Hampshire" (unpublished Ph.D. dissertation, University of New Hampshire, 1977). The chapter on Wentworth in Wilbur C. Abbott, *Conflicts with Oblivion* (Cambridge, 1935) and the sketch by Clifford Shipton in *Sibley's Harvard Graduates,* XIII, 650–681 are also perceptive. The appropriate parts of Charles T. Adams, *Matthew Thornton of New Hampshire* (Philadelphia, 1903); Lawrence S. Mayo, *John Langdon of New Hampshire* (Concord, 1937); and Charles P. Whittemore, *A General of the Revolution, John Sullivan of New Hampshire* (New York, 1961) describe protest movements in the province, as do portions of two manuscript biographies, Elwin L. Page, "Rider for Freedom: Josiah Bartlett," a copy of which is in the New Hampshire Historical Society, and Avery J. Butters, "New Hampshire History and the Public Career of Meshech Weare, 1713–1786" (unpublished Ph.D. dissertation, Fordham University, 1961). Among the numerous brief biographies of public figures in the coming of revolution are Charles W. Akers, "New Hamsphire's 'Honorary' Lieutenant Governor: John Temple and the American Revolution," *Historical New Hampshire,* XXX (1975), 79–100; Charles R. Corning, *John Fenton* (Concord, 1886); George B. Kirsch, "Jeremy Belknap and the Coming of the Revolution," *Historical New Hampshire,* XXIX (1975), 151–172; and Lawrence S. Mayo, "Peter Livius, the Trouble Maker," *Granite Monthly,* LV (1923), 83–90.

Several publications discuss specific episodes related to the fall of the Wentworths and the coming of revolution. Both Allan R. Raymond, "Benning Wentworth's Claims in the New Hampshire-New York Boundary Controversy," *Vermont History,* XLIII (1975), 20–32 and John W. Durel, "Dividing the Province of New Hampshire into Counties," *Historical New Hampshire* XXXII (1977), 28–42 describe attempts by royal governors to deal with problems of westward expansion. Jere R. Daniell, "Reason and Ridicule: The Tea Act Resolutions in New Hampshire," *Historical New Hampshire,* XX (1965), 23–28; Elwin L. Page, "The King's Powder, 1774," *New England Quarterly,* XVIII (1945), 83–92; and the several essays in *Historical New Hampshire,* XXIV (1974) treat various aspects of the protest movement. The last ditch efforts to protect Governor Wentworth and his loyalist friends are described in Kenneth Scott, "Tory Associators of Portsmouth," *William and Mary Quarterly,* 3rd ser., XVII (1960), 507–515. Edward D. Boyleston, *The Hillsborough County Congresses* (Amherst, 1884); Karen E. Andresen, "A Return to Legitimacy: New Hampshire's Constitution of 1776," *Historical New Hampshire,* XXXI (1976), 155–164; and two works by Joseph B. Walker, "The New Hampshire Covenant of 1774," *Granite Monthly,* XXXV (1903), 188–197 and *New Hampshire's Five Provincial Congresses, July 21, 1774–January 5, 1776* (Concord, 1905) treat the growth of revolutionary authority.

Epilogue

Richard F. Upton, *Revolutionary New Hampshire* (Hanover, 1936) provides a full discussion of developments through the signing of the Treaty of Paris in 1783. John K. Gemmill, "The Problems of Power: New Hampshire," XXII (1967), 27–38 focuses on political events during the same period, while

Daniell, *Experiment,* extends the political narrative through the mid-1790s. General works helpful for placing post-independence constitutional change in a national context include Willi P. Adams, *The First American Constitutions: Republican Ideology and the Making of the State Constitutions in the Revolutionary Era* (Chapel Hill, 1980); Allan Nevins, *The American States during and after the Revolution, 1775–1789* (New York, 1924); Gordon S. Wood, *Creation of the American Republic* (Chapel Hill, 1969); and two studies by Jackson T. Main, "Government by the People: The American Revolution and the Democratization of the Legislatures," *William and Mary Quarterly,* 3rd ser., XXIII (1966), 391–407 and *The Upper Houses in Revolutionary America, 1763–1788* (Madison, 1968). Fred M. Colby, *Manual of the Constitution of the State of New Hampshire* (Concord, 1912) describes some nineteenth century changes in the structure of New Hampshire's government. The origin of many New Hampshire place names is traced in Elmer M. Hunt, *New Hampshire Town Names and Whence They Came* (Peterborough, 1971).

INDEX